Dear Reader:

The book you are about to read is the latest bestseller from the St. Martin's True Crime Library, the imprint the *New York Times* calls "the leader in true crime!" Each month, we offer you a fascinating account of the latest, most sensational crime that has captured the national attention. St. Martin's is the publisher of perennial bestselling true crime author Jack Olsen, whose SALT OF THE EARTH is the true story of one woman's triumph over life-shattering violence; Joseph Wambaugh called it "powerful and absorbing." Fannie Weinstein and Melinda Wilson tell the story of a beautiful honors student who was lured into the dark world of sex for hire in THE COED CALL GIRL MURDER. St. Martin's is also proud to publish two-time Edgar Award–winning author Carlton Stowers, whose TO THE LAST BREATH recounts a two-year-old-girl's mysterious death, and the dogged investigation that led loved ones to the most unlikely murderer: her own father. In the book you now hold, DEATH OF A DOCTOR, True Crime Library veteran Carlton Smith details what happens when a clandestine affair goes horribly wrong . . .

St. Martin's True Crime Library gives you the stories *behind* the headlines. Our authors take you right to the scene of the crime and into the minds of the most notorious murderers to show you what really makes them tick. St. Martin's True Crime Library paperbacks are better than the most terrifying thriller, because it's all true! The next time you want a crackling good read, make sure it's got the St. Martin's True Crime Library logo on the spine—you'll be up all night!

Charles E. Spicer, Jr.
Executive Editor, St. Martin's True Crime Library

"The guy next to me is not involved," he said. "I'm the guy you want."

That was the first inkling anyone had that the man Sica and his partners had ordered into the dirt at gunpoint was anything but the hardened carjacker they might have been expecting.

There, lying face-down with his hands cuffed behind his back, 39-year-old Doctor Kevin Paul Anderson, one of Pasadena's most beloved pediatricians—a man who had zealously tended the health of thousands of small children, who had sat with them and their worried parents through illnesses as mundane as chicken pox and as tragic as leukemia. So loved was Kevin Anderson that even after he would confess to murder, legions of mothers and fathers would willingly swear that as far as they were concerned, there had to be some horrible mistake—the Dr. Anderson they knew was just about the kindest, gentlest, most self-effacing, least aggressive person they had ever known.

And even when he was lying handcuffed on the ground, newly embarked into a previously unimagined existence as a criminal, Dr. Kevin Anderson couldn't stop himself from trying to help others, in this case the Good Samaritan who had stopped to help him with his truck:

"The guy next to me is not involved," he said again. "He was just helping me out. I'm the one you're looking for, unfortunately."

St. Martin's Paperbacks True Crime Library Titles by Carlton Smith

Blood Money
Death of a Little Princess
Seeds of Evil
Dying for Daddy
Death in Texas
Murder at Yosemite
Bitter Medicine
Hunting Evil
Shadows of Evil
Death of a Doctor

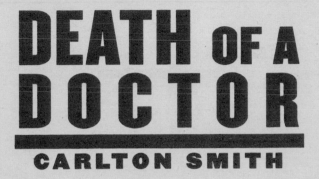

DEATH OF A DOCTOR

CARLTON SMITH

St. Martin's Paperbacks

DEATH OF A DOCTOR

Copyright © 2002 by Carlton Smith.

Cover photograph credits: Stethoscope courtesy Getty, eyes courtesy Photodisk.

ISBN: 0-312-97794-8

Printed in the United States of America

St. Martin's Paperbacks edition / February 2002

St. Martin's Paperbacks are published by St. Martin's Press, 175 Fifth Avenue, New York, N.Y. 10010.

10 9 8 7 6 5 4 3 2 1

For Eric Denner

The Mountain

1

It had been one of those days for Jay La Riviere. First, with his own car in the shop for repairs, La Riviere had needed to rent a car for his trip. And then, wouldn't you know it, just when he was ready to go home, he'd locked the keys inside the rental. What to do?

By the time he was able to get inside to get the keys, nearly an hour and a half had gone by. As a result, La Riviere began his trip back across the San Gabriel Mountains in the twilight. The delay was a minor irritation to La Riviere, but for others it would soon come to represent the work of Fate's mysterious hand.

A twenty-by-fifty—mile swatch of wilderness, a 650,000-acre tangle of mile-high peaks and dead-end canyons, the San Gabriels loomed over the Los Angeles Basin like the guardian angel for which they were named. Two main roads split the all-but-impenetrable terrain, Angeles Forest Highway, which crossed the mountains south from Palmdale to the crest of the range, and Angeles Crest Highway, which began in the south at La Canada—Flintridge, wound up to the top of the escarpment and then meandered east along the ridge line some forty miles into San Bernardino County. One other road, Big Tujunga Canyon Road, came up into the middle of the mountains from the San Fernando Valley on the west, and ended just before Angeles Forest Highway merged into Angeles Crest.

Traveling south from Palmdale into the darkness, La Riviere pushed his rented Pontiac Grand Am along smartly. The road was curvy, but La Riviere enjoyed the challenge of holding the sleek machine under control, even in the darkness. The narrow blacktop first followed a canyon up into the brush-covered higher elevations, then surmounted a low ridge and began running downhill for some distance.

As the terrain changed, the brush gave way to large ever-green trees, mostly on the north, back side of the mountains, barely visible now except in the sweep of La Riviere's high beams as the Grand Am negotiated the curves.

After some miles, the road began to climb again, this time ascending the back side of 5,600-foot Josephine Peak. About a third of the way up, La Riviere flashed past the junction with Big Tujunga Canyon Road. Still the road climbed, and eventually it turned all the way around Josephine Peak to the front side of the mountain. At the head of Clear Creek Valley, Angeles Forest Highway at last joined Angeles Crest Highway, and here the road ran fairly level for some distance before beginning its winding descent down into the Los Angeles basin. There was a Forest Service station at the junction, but it appeared to be closed.

Just after entering this straight and level stretch at the crest of the San Gabriels' front line, La Riviere came to a turnout he knew to be favored by lovers and other rubber-neckers for its spectacular view of the sprawling lights of the Los Angeles Basin below. As La Riviere flew past, he saw two vehicles in the turnout, bumper-to-bumper; and just as La Riviere saw them, the forward-most of them, a white sport utility vehicle, plunged over the side of the mountain. The time was just before 8 P.M. on Veterans Day, Thursday, November 11, 1999.

La Riviere was a fourth-grade teacher for the Los Angeles Unified School District. A hiker, mountain climber, skier and mountain-bike racer, La Riviere was in excellent physical condition. Moreover, he'd been regularly driving the Angeles Crest Highway for more than a decade, often to visit friends in the Palmdale area.

From his mountain-biking experience, La Riviere was well aware that there was no off-road trail over the side of the turnout he had just passed—at least, there hadn't been before, to his knowledge. La Riviere was pretty sure he knew what was going on: someone was committing an insurance fraud by tipping the white car over the cliff. La Riviere slowed down at the next turnout, made a U-turn and drove back to the place where he'd seen the two vehicles end-to-end.

Only one vehicle remained, a black Toyota 4Runner truck. The Toyota had its lights off. La Riviere couldn't see anyone inside. He swung his own car around so that the lights shone on the Toyota. He still couldn't see anyone. La Riviere continued trying to make sense of what he had seen. Had a second vehicle really gone over the side? Had he just imagined it? Idly, he wondered whether the people in the Toyota were making out, and whether some irate lover would take offense at his lights. How would he explain himself?

"I thought what I did was pretty bold," La Riviere said later.

Suddenly, the black Toyota began to move. It rolled onto the blacktop of the highway, its own lights still off. Then, as La Riviere watched, it shot back up the highway toward Palmdale. Some distance up the road, the Toyota's taillights went on.

La Riviere got out of his car and went to the downhill side of the turnout. One thing was sure: there weren't any off-road trails here. The turnout overlooked a steep ravine, more nearly a cliff, that ran down hundreds of feet before disappearing in the darkness. La Riviere could see the twinkling lights of the city of Pasadena far below.

La Riviere yelled into the gloom, but got no response. He tried to peer over the side. He thought he saw something at the bottom of the ravine, but couldn't quite make it out. He smelled the strong odor of spilled gasoline.

La Riviere went back to the blacktop of the highway. He could still see the lights of the Toyota receding in the distance, and those of another vehicle not far behind.

La Riviere went back to his rented Pontiac. *Should I go after him, or should I just go home?* he thought.

It could be dangerous. If the driver of the Toyota had just committed an insurance fraud by dumping the white

Mercedes over the cliff, and if the driver of the following car was an accomplice, La Riviere realized he could find himself in trouble. He decided to go after the Toyota, at least to get close enough to see the license plate. Then, he decided, he'd find a place to report the plate number.

La Riviere was confident he could catch the receding Toyota. After all, he was familiar with the mountain highway, and he was driving a car which took the curves quite well, while the Toyota was hardly built for racing. La Riviere started off in pursuit. Ahead of him in the darkness, La Riviere saw the Toyota's taillights race past the junction that led east along the crest of the mountains toward Mt. Wilson, where all the Los Angeles–area television antennas were located. Instead the Toyota took the Angeles Forest Highway toward Palmdale, the same road that La Riviere had just come over. La Riviere sped up as the caravan of three vehicles raced on into the night—now past the front side of Josephine Peak, again around the side of the mountain and down the back side. La Riviere guessed that the Toyota's driver was unfamiliar with the road, but still he was surprised at how easily he was catching up.

"Every time I go around the corner," he said later, "I would see him get closer and closer . . . And then as I got fairly close, the . . . lights disappeared."

La Riviere's Grand Am shot past another turnout along the mountain side of the highway. Out of the corner of his eye in the darkness, La Riviere saw both the Toyota and the other car stopped in the turnout. He slowed down as he approached another turnout some distance farther down the highway toward Palmdale.

La Riviere didn't want the two drivers to think he was suspicious of them. He made still another U-turn and started back. He slowly approached the turnout, this time from the opposite direction. La Riviere stopped and called out across the two traffic lanes.

"Need any help?" he asked.

A tall man was bending down, looking underneath the Toyota, which La Riviere could see was "high-centered" on a dirt berm on the far side of the turnout. It appeared to have gone off the highway at high speed and been unable to stop before lurching over the berm. The Toyota's wheels straddled the earthen barrier.

The man beside the Toyota straightened and glanced in La Riviere's direction. La Riviere couldn't see his full face. The man was wearing jeans and a dark jacket. He told La Riviere that he didn't need any help, that he would simply put the Toyota into four-wheel drive and back it over the berm. La Riviere waved acknowledgment, then steered the Grand Am into the turnout, shining his headlights on the Toyota's license plate. He jotted the Toyota's plate number on a used envelope and left, heading toward Los Angeles once more.

At the intersection where the Angeles Crest Highway joined Angeles Forest, La Riviere stopped at the Forest Service station to tell officials there what he had seen. He bypassed the darkened main building and made his way to an outbuilding some distance from the station, where he could see lights. He knocked. An older man wearing a robe came to the door. La Riviere had the impression that he had interrupted dinner.

La Riviere quickly described what he had seen to the older man, a civilian volunteer for the Forest Service named John McGough. McGough was slightly taken aback by La Riviere's excitement. "He seemed, frankly, a little bit flighty," McGough said later. Still, McGough took down the information about the car over the side, and La Riviere's theory that someone was trying to pull an insurance fraud. McGough and others at the Ranger Station were familiar with the location La Riviere was describing. Over the years a number of vehicles had gone over the edge at the same place, for various reasons.

La Riviere thought McGough was taking his story much too casually. He gave McGough the license number he'd taken and suggested that if the cops hurried, they might still be able to catch the driver farther up the road to Palmdale. McGough asked La Riviere to write down his own particulars, such as his name, address and telephone number, and a short account of what he'd seen. La Riviere thought McGough didn't quite believe him, or understand the urgency of the situation.

"They told me they would take care of it," La Riviere said later, "and they went back eating. I walked out, kind of stunned that they didn't jump or anything."

La Riviere went back to the rented Pontiac. He drove back to the turnout where he'd seen—or thought he'd seen—the white SUV go over the side. He parked and got out, went back to the edge of the cliff and looked over. It was too dark to make anything out. La Riviere returned to his car and detached the halogen light from his mountainbike, which he had in the rear. He played it over the bottom of the ravine far below. There in the light from his lamp La Riviere could see the wreckage of the white car he was sure he'd seen go over.

He decided to go down and see for himself. Picking his way through the chaparral on the side of the steep hill, using his hands and feet, La Riviere laboriously climbed part way down the side. At one point he saw a semi-path chopped out of the brush, and made his way over to that. About 400 feet down, in his estimation, he came to the wreckage of the crashed white SUV, which La Riviere now realized was a late model Mercedes. The odor of gasoline was still very strong. The wreckage seemed to be teetering on something; La Riviere had the idea that it might slide farther down the hill if its equilibrium was altered. The front of the car was facing uphill, and its sunroof was open. It seemed likely that the car had flipped completely end-over-end at least once, as well as rolled over from side-to-side, to end up the way it had.

La Riviere looked inside the car. He saw the registration lying on the front seat. He also noticed what appeared to be a bottle of medicine, a stethoscope, and a white lab coat in the car. La Riviere looked at the medicine, and saw that the name on the bottle was the same as on the car registration—Gupta.

He now proceeded to examine the area around the car. It all seemed a bit spooky. "I was hearing some bushes moving around," he said later. "It was really dark down there. I was by myself. I thought the vehicle wasn't settled because of the way it was moving. But then I heard some other bushes, like someone was around."

He began climbing back up the ravine. As he did so, he saw headlights appear in the turnout above. La Riviere wondered whether it was the driver of the Toyota returning to the scene of the crime. He decided to turn off his light, just in case. After the light went out, La Riviere heard voices shouting down at him. He realized the new arrivals were probably from the ranger station, and he called out to let them know where he was. The voices asked if he'd seen any bodies. La Riviere shouted back that he hadn't.

After some minutes, La Riviere made it back up to the top of the hill, where he was met by two Forest Service firefighters, Tony Martinez and Doug Bennick. La Riviere need not have worried; as it happened, McGough had alerted the Forest Service firemen just after he had driven away.

Martinez was a fifteen-year veteran of the Forest Service. He'd spent the past six years at the Clear Creek Ranger Station, the place where La Riviere had stopped to give his report to McGough. The station was less than a mile from the turnout, which Martinez knew was called George's Gap. The Gap was the short stretch of the Angeles Crest Highway that was almost flat, and because it was at the very top of the front rank of mountains, it was possible to see a long distance into the Los Angeles basin, as well as down into Clear Creek Valley on the other side of the road, and Josephine Peak, farther to the north.

After climbing back to the head of the ravine, La Riviere puffed out his tale to Martinez and Bennick: how he'd been passing the turnout, how he'd seen the white SUV go over the side. How he'd then chased the Toyota 4Runner toward Palmdale, and how it had run off the road, where, La Riviere explained again, it probably still was, if only people would get a move on to nab the driver.

Martinez seemed phlegmatic in the face of La Riviere's excitement. This was at least the fifth time in the six years he'd been at the Clear Creek station that someone had used George's Gap to dispose of a car. They were almost always stolen and stripped before going over the side. He told Bennick, who, at 23, was both younger and more agile than Martinez was, to fetch a light from the Forest Service utility truck, and to go down and check it out.

Bennick got the light from the truck, but it wasn't as powerful as La Riviere's. La Riviere loaned the fireman his light instead, and Bennick started working his way down the steep slope into the ravine, mostly sliding on the seat of his pants. Martinez continued to talk to La Riviere. Bennick was about halfway down the steep ravine when Martinez and La Riviere heard him shouting.

"I got a body here!" Bennick screamed.

Martinez shouted back, asking Bennick if the body was still alive, and Bennick shouted that it wasn't. For some reason La Riviere now decided to go see for himself. He made his way back down the slope, leaving Martinez on top trying to get in touch with his dispatcher over his hand-held portable radio. When La Riviere got down to where Bennick was, he saw a pair of bare legs sticking out from beneath a bush. La Riviere realized the victim was a woman. Her feet were bare, and her dress had been flipped up around her waist. She appeared to be lying on a bumper that had been torn from the wreck. La Riviere came closer, and asked Bennick whether he was sure the person was dead. Bennick said he'd already checked for vital signs, and hadn't found any. Then Bennick checked again, just to be sure. He told La Riviere to stay back from the body. She was still warm to the touch, but she was definitely dead, Bennick said.

La Riviere then worked his way farther down the ravine to the wreck, where he had seen the medicine and the car registration earlier. Bennick followed him. La Riviere took the registration form from the seat of the car as Bennick watched. Bennick was becoming concerned about possible interference with what was beginning to look like the scene of a crime. He and La Riviere, who was still holding onto the car registration, then began climbing back up the ravine.

When they got back to the top, Martinez took the registration from La Riviere. The paperwork indicated that the wrecked vehicle was a 1999 Mercedes sport utility vehicle registered to Vijay and Deepti Gupta, with a Glendale, California, address.

Suddenly this no longer seemed at all routine to Martinez. This was not just a case of another stolen car: based on La Riviere's description of seeing the Toyota shoving the white SUV over the side, and the presence of the dead woman under wreckage that had obviously come off the vehicle, Martinez was pretty sure he had a possible case of murder on his hands. He radioed the information back to the dispatcher, and within a few minutes, elements of the Los Angeles County Sheriff's Department began to move.

At about 8:15 P.M. that night, Sheriff's Deputy David Willard, assigned to the Sheriff's Department substation at La Crescenta, down in the valley below the Los Angeles side of the mountains, was sent to meet Martinez, Bennick and La Riviere at the George's Gap turnout, which was also known to the sheriff's department and the state Department of Transportation as the turnout at Mile Marker 33.

Willard was not initially clear on what the call was really about. There seemed to be two things going on at the same time—in one, a car was over the side of the Angeles Crest Highway, and there was a dead body, possibly a homicide, if the dispatcher had the story straight; and in the other, there was another car, possibly a Toyota, also off the side, some distance away, but that somehow seemed to be connected to the first wreck.

Willard arrived at Mile Marker 33 about 8:30 P.M. Martinez, Bennick and La Riviere were waiting for him. Willard tried to assemble the information they had, but La

Riviere's presence as both a witness with information about two different locations and events, and as a participant in going to the wreckage apparently confused him. He began peppering La Riviere with questions, which irritated the teacher.

"They were asking me questions that I thought were not to the point," La Riviere said later. If they wanted to catch the guy, La Riviere told them, they probably still could: the man driving the Toyota was high-centered farther down the road. What Toyota? Willard asked. La Riviere explained all over again.

Willard now understood what the message regarding the Toyota had been about. Just after 8:30 P.M., Willard called the dispatcher to alert other deputies to check the Angeles Forest Highway for the Toyota. Because La Riviere had seen the Toyota stranded on Angeles Forest Highway, well past the junction with Angeles Crest Highway, that meant that even if the Toyota's driver had freed his truck from the dirt berm, there were only two ways out. Either the Toyota had to go all the way to Palmdale, where deputies would have ample time to intercept him when he emerged from the mountains, or the Toyota would have to take the only other viable paved road out, Big Tujunga Canyon Road.

This message in turn was picked up at the Crescenta Valley Sheriff's Substation by three deputies who were just booking a suspect into the station's holding cells when the call came in. Detective Gary Sica and his two partners were normally assigned to the department's fugitive detail, which specialized in tracking down people who had proven skilled at not being caught. It was often a dangerous task. Sica and his partners jumped into a car and raced for the road into Big Tujunga Canyon. Sica reasoned that if the guy in the Toyota did get free of the berm and didn't try for Palmdale, he had to come down Big Tujunga Canyon Road and right into the waiting arms of Sica and his partners.

The three detectives raced up the canyon toward the place where Big Tujunga Canyon Road joined Angeles Forest Highway. Just before 9 P.M., as their unmarked car came around the last curve on its way uphill to the junction, Sica and the others saw a dark Toyota 4Runner stuck on a dirt berm off to the side of the road about 100 yards to the right. Skidding to a stop in the turnout, Sica and his two partners pulled their guns and ordered two men standing near the Toyota to get face-down on the ground without delay.

Even as Sica and his partners were ordering the two men into the dirt, other sheriff's deputies were arriving. One, Michael Brandriff, had originally been detailed to go to Mile Marker 33 to join Deputy Willard, but was redirected to the place where the Toyota was believed to be; Sica had beaten Brandriff to the collar.

Brandriff approached the two men lying in the dirt of the turnout. Both men were African-American, one elderly, the other about 40. Brandriff began putting plastic bags over the suspects' cuffed hands to preserve any evidence, in case of gunshot residue or other manifestations of a violent encounter. The younger of the two men now spoke up.

"The guy next to me is not involved," he said. "I'm the guy you want."

That was the first inkling anyone had that the man Sica and his partners had ordered into the dirt at gunpoint was anything but the hardened carjacker they might have been expecting.

There, lying face-down with his hands cuffed behind his back, was 39-year-old Doctor Kevin Paul Anderson, one of Pasadena's most beloved pediatricians—a man who had zealously tended the health of thousands of small children, who had sat with them and their worried parents through illnesses as mundane as chicken pox and as tragic as leukemia. So loved was Kevin Anderson that even after he would confess to murder, legions of mothers and fathers would willingly swear that as far as they were concerned, there had to be some horrible mistake—the Dr. Anderson they knew was just about the kindest, gentlest, most self-effacing, least aggressive person they had ever known.

And even when he was lying handcuffed on the ground, newly embarked into a previously unimagined existence as a criminal, Dr. Kevin Anderson couldn't stop himself from trying to help others, in this case the Good Samaritan who had stopped to help him with his truck:

"The guy next to me is not involved," he said again. "He was just helping me out. I'm the one you're looking for, unfortunately."

Karma

2

Karma is a word that has crept into the popular American idiom only in the past generation, linguistic seepage from the Beat poets by way of the Vietnam era. From what was once a specific meaning, the word, like many imports to our conversation, has come to mean something rather more general. Nowadays, people often use the word casually, without awareness of its ancient and powerful provenance. Someone might say, "It's bad karma," or "You must have good karma, man," with the same sort of sense one has when talking about luck.

True, there is a second shade of meaning that accompanies the popular use of the word, and that touches slightly on the notion of fate—the nebulous awareness that something more than just blind luck might be involved. Beyond this general sense, more atmospheric than anything else, most do not care to think further. As Americans, we don't like the idea of fate, at least as some sort of force that exists beyond our influence or control. It smacks too much of a negation of free will, and if there is any concept that is venerated in our society, it is the idea that each of us can be masters of our own destiny—the pursuit of happiness, as our Founders put it.

But if karma is an alien concept that has gradually taken casual root in our popular culture, it nevertheless has some intriguing resonance with traditional Western religious ideas as well as recent discoveries in quantum physics. While no one living can prove that karma exists—at least in the same way that scientists can measure such things as light or heat—the mysterious nature of time and gravity, along with the dual nature of light as both a particle and a wave, suggests to some that there may indeed be some validity to the idea that our pasts create our future.

At its heart and in its origin, the theory of karma is one of moral accountability. At the most basic level, according to the theory, every living thing has a karmic account—a sum of all thoughts and actions, for good and ill. As one's life proceeds, these thoughts and actions adhere to the soul in much the same way that dust binds to a piece of cloth. Throughout life, the constant accretion of thoughts and actions on the soul directly influences the outcome of events. Put into the simplest terms, as one sows, so does one reap. In that sense, the concept of karma is in harmony with the ethical notions encompassed by Judaism, Christianity and Islam.

Although the notion of karma is usually associated with Eastern religious beliefs, chiefly Hinduism and Buddhism, there is no dispute that the idea predates those beliefs by a thousand years or more. No one, in fact, knows who first formulated the concept, although Indian religious scholars have speculated that it first arose as a simple ethical system among primitive agricultural societies in prehistoric times.[1] What is also clear is that in its origins, the notion of karma was more than mere philosophy; instead, as it was first conceived, karma actually had a physical basis, in that the soul was believed to be composed of a viscous material that attracted thoughts and actions much as a cloth charged with static electricity attracts dust motes; this in turn accounts for at least some of its resonance with the principles of particle physics. Under the theory of karma, eventually, the soul becomes so clogged with karma that it begins to sink, unless something is done to release the accumulated bits of action.

It is at this point that the notion of karma veers sharply away from parallels with physics, however. As a science, of course, physics is conceived as morally neutral: the question of good and evil is simply a non-starter when one is

---

[1]See, for example, *Jain Philosophy, Historical Outline*, Narendra Nath Bhattacharyya, Munshiram Manoharlal Publishers Pvt. Ltd., New Delhi, 1976.

seeking to measure physical phenomena, at least by all known means of scientific measurement. But karma recognizes action as either "good" or "bad." "Good" action—or righteous behavior, in religious terms—is said to have the effect of releasing karma, in effect clearing the sticky soul from its dusty burden and releasing it to ascend to higher, more developed awareness. "Bad" or unrighteous acts or thoughts have the opposite effect—that is, they tend to blot out the light of the soul, and cause the soul to sink into the depths of depravity and despair.

Up to this point, moreover, the so-called Law of Karma has much in common with the Western religious tradition of atonement and good works as the path to God's blessings. After all, sin is sin, whether it takes place in Portland, Paris, Phnom Penh or Peking. Bad actions are recognized wherever they take place: envy, greed, lying and murder are universally condemned, no matter what the language or culture, while acting righteously is seen as liberating the spirit.

But where Western religion views human existence as a one-shot experience, culminating (for Christians, at least) in a final judgment with the prospect of eternal paradise (or damnation), the Eastern religious tradition encompasses no such limits. Both Hinduism and Buddhism hold as a central tenet the concept of the transmigration of souls, and the engine of this transmigration—from the lowliest insect to the highest prince—is, in this system, the Law of Karma.

"Every being of this vast universe is guided by its own Karma," opines a leading Indian religious scholar, Narenda Nath Bhattacharyya.[2] "The heavenly bodies, and even the gods, are not exceptions. Owing to the inclinations generated by its past Karma, a [soul] comes to inhabit different bodies successively. Trees, plants and animals come into existence owning to the Karma or actions of their previous lives. The same holds good in the case of human beings. Every event of the life of an individual is due to the Karma

---

[2]Bhattacharyya, *Jain Philosophy, Historical Outline*, op. cit., p. 146.

of his previous life. Birth and death, pleasure and pain, disease and suffering, everything is dependent on this peculiar concept of Karma . . ."

Once one accepts this concept, even provisionally, it can readily be seen that karma is both individual as well as communal: in other words, it is one person's karma to be affected by the karma of another. In this way, the past, present and future of every living thing is influenced by the past, present and future of every other living thing. In this sense, we are all subjects of karma, as well as its instruments, whether the event is love, work, pleasure or even murder.

It is doubtful that any of this esoterica about past lives, karmic law, transmigrations of souls, or even sin and redemption was streaming through the mind of Dr. Kevin Paul Anderson on that Thursday evening as the men from the Los Angeles County Sheriff's Department "hooked him up," as the parlance had it. There, lying in the dirt with his hands immobilized behind his back, Anderson was only aware that his respectability was rushing away from him at light speed, and he was hard-pressed to explain, even to himself, how it had all come about. It was only later—much later—that he came to see the entire train of events as somehow beyond his control from the very start, almost as if it was . . . karma.

But at the moment of this shattering turn of fortune, Dr. Anderson was very nearly beyond coherency. After he was placed in the rear seat of Brandriff's patrol car, another deputy, dog handler Steve Wilkinson, wanted to make sure there weren't any other suspects.

No, Anderson said softly, he was the only one involved. And then Anderson began trying to explain himself, in a disjointed discourse that didn't make much sense to the deputy.

"He was rambling on about how he had had a business relationship with this woman," Wilkinson said later, "and that he'd had a falling out with her and her husband, and

that . . . they had met to look at the stars through a telescope. He went on to say that . . . she threatened to sue him
regarding some type of business dealing. That's all he
would say. That's all he said, and that he snapped."

3

Kevin Paul Anderson was born on the 27th of January, 1959, the son of another Pasadena-area doctor, Howard Whigham, and his wife Ruth. The Whigham marriage came apart in the early 1960s, and sometime later Ruth Whigham married William Anderson, who adopted Kevin when he was about eight years old.

Kevin was the oldest of four boys, two of them sons of William and Ruth Anderson. According to Kevin's childhood acquaintances, Kevin and his younger brother had virtually no contact with Dr. Whigham while they were growing up. The Anderson family lived in a middle-to upper-middle-class neighborhood in Altadena, the unincorporated area of Los Angeles County high on the slopes of the San Gabriel Mountains just north of Pasadena.

In their subsequent recollections of Kevin and his childhood, Anderson's friends most frequently remarked on two facets of Kevin's upbringing: first, that Kevin was inordinately bright, and second, that the Anderson household was renowned throughout the neighborhood for its strict discipline.

William Anderson owned his own auto repair business, according to Kevin's childhood friends, and later taught auto repair at Pasadena City College. Most remembered Mr. Anderson as being very demanding of Kevin and the other three boys. No one, however, recalls that William Anderson was ever physically abusive—just strict.

"I just knew he laid down the law," recalled one childhood friend. "There were a lot of restrictions. Kevin couldn't sleep over at anyone's house." The friend had a sense that Kevin's activities were closely monitored. There were chores around the house for which Kevin was responsible, and woe betide him if he failed to perform them.

Many of Kevin's friends came to believe that Mr. Anderson had a temper, and that he wasn't averse to displaying it. As a result, Kevin grew up with an extraordinary degree of self-control, as well as a strong penchant for subordinating himself to strong personalities.

"He was never a disciplinary problem in school, not even being sent to the principal's office," his mother Ruth later wrote. "He has always been well-liked by those he meets, and has always had many friends. Kevin sincerely believes that any problem or difficulty is solvable if the parties are willing to sit and discuss the issues." For the Andersons, hard work, coupled with respect and tolerance for others, were seen as sure pathways to success.

Later, a psychiatrist hired by Kevin's defense attorney was to note this strict upbringing in connection with Kevin's behavior under stress. Having learned from an early age to bury his resentments under a mask of pleasant and accommodating behavior, Kevin was therefore more vulnerable than most to succumb to a sudden, explosive rage that might erupt under sufficient provocation.

By all accounts, however, Kevin enjoyed a normal childhood, forming close and enduring friendships in the multiracial environment of Altadena. A core group of friends accompanied Kevin throughout elementary school, junior high and high school, and even to college. Later, this steadfast group would call themselves "the Altadena boys," and remain in contact for weddings, births of children, and vacations together. These relationships would remain steadfast, even after Kevin was arrested on a charge of murder.

If there was one thing that marked Kevin out from his contemporaries, however, it was his quick intelligence. Even as an elementary student at Audubon School, Kevin was tracked into a gifted students' program. Later, at John Muir High School in Pasadena, Kevin quickly emerged as one of the brightest students in the school.

And although some later tried to cast Kevin as a class nerd too shy to ask girls on dates—and implying that as an adult he would turn into some sort of sexual predator—that seems not to have been the case at all, at least according to his old friends. They recalled that Kevin played varsity soccer in high school, that he was popular and sociable, and that he dated regularly.

In the fall of 1977, Kevin enrolled as an undergraduate at Pomona College, one of the highly respected Claremont Colleges east of Pasadena. It was at Pomona that Kevin formed a number of new friendships that would endure well after his graduation in 1981. Many of those friends later came to Pasadena to testify for Kevin. Among them was a woman who would later become his wife, Natalie Profant.

After Pomona, Kevin was accepted into medical school at Howard University in Washington, D.C. There, too, the popular and easy-going Kevin made friends effortlessly. In the early 1980s, Kevin was married for the first time, to a woman named Gabriela Chenet, who was from the Carribean. For some reason the marriage was annulled after a few months.

After graduating from Howard's medical school in 1985, Kevin was accepted into a medical residency program at Martin Luther King Hospital in Los Angeles. The residency lasted until 1988. Following this, Kevin undertook a fellowship in neonatology—the care of newborn infants—at Harbor–UCLA Medical Center, also in Los Angeles, until 1990.

As the oldest of four boys, Kevin was particularly attracted to caring for children. It was, for one thing, less stressful than caring for adults, in part because illnesses suffered by babies and pre-teens were often less dire than those sustained by adults or the elderly. Some of Kevin's friends believed that Kevin had a difficult time distancing himself emotionally from his patients' medical problems, and that it was a bit easier to deal with children because the outcomes were usually good.

For the next two years, Kevin worked part-time at a clinic in Los Angeles. As he himself put it, he was a bit burned out after so many years of school, internship and residency. The part-time job allowed him to work for a month, then take a month or so off to decompress before starting in again. The occasional schedule also allowed Kevin the luxury of not becoming too emotionally involved with his patients. There was time, too, for Kevin to enjoy the outdoor pursuits that would continue for much of his free life—camping, waterskiing, hiking and amateur astronomy.

In the summer of 1991, Kevin married his Pomona College classmate, Natalie Profant. Years later, Natalie would still remember their post-marriage trip to Cabo San Lucas, because Kevin, without consulting her, had invited a number of his friends to join them. It was only when Natalie remonstrated with her new husband that Kevin relented and asked at least one of the invited couples not to come. This was typical of her relationship with Kevin, Natalie was to observe later: in inviting all the people to join in the Cabo San Lucas trip, Kevin was casting himself as the "good guy," Natalie said, leaving it to her to play the heavy.

At the same time he married Natalie, Kevin also purchased a house in his old Altadena neighborhood for $263,000. A daughter was born in the fall of the same year.

Kevin seemed in no hurry to nail down a permanent, lucrative position as a doctor; he found it more enjoyable to work sporadically, without responsibility for following up on patients' outcomes.

This began to change in the summer of 1992, when Kevin's stepfather, William Anderson, introduced him to a Pasadena physician, Dr. Randy Edmonds, who was a partner in Eaton Canyon Medical Group, a clinic next door to St. Luke Medical Center in northeast Pasadena. Initially, Kevin took over while Dr. Edmonds was on vacation. Then Dr. Edmonds fell ill, and later died. Kevin was asked to join the Eaton Canyon partnership on a permanent basis, and he agreed.

By the fall of 1993, the marriage between Kevin and Natalie began to falter. Kevin moved out of the Altadena house, and began dating Heidi Hughey, a spirited and attractive young nurse he'd met at the newborn nursery of

Huntington Memorial Hospital, also in Pasadena. Natalie
retained the Altadena house, which eventually went into
foreclosure when she was unable to keep up the payments.
Natalie was later to claim that Kevin had reneged on an
agreement to pay her $650 a month in alimony as one rea-
son the house was lost. At the same time, Kevin fell behind
in his $931 monthly child support payments—a circum-
stance that would, in the distant future, allow Kevin's prosecutors to suggest a possible motive for murder.

By the middle of the nineties, Kevin was earning $9,000
a month from the Eaton Canyon clinic; as he saw things,
the clinic's main partner, Dr. Lionel Ng, was getting on in
years, and Kevin hoped someday to take over the clinic. In
1998 Kevin got another remunerative appointment, this one
as the on-call neonatologist for St. Luke Medical Center
Hospital in Pasadena, where Kevin was on good terms with
the hospital's chief executive officer, Ken Rivers.

As the on-call physician for all newborns at St. Luke,
Kevin's contract paid him $10,000 a month to be available
twenty-four hours a day, seven days a week. To fill the
contract, Kevin was permitted by the hospital to hire other
physicians to cover for him if he couldn't be reached, provided that the hospital approved the qualifications of the
covering physicians. Kevin's seemingly close relationship
with Ken Rivers would also eventually emerge as a factor
in the murder he would be accused of committing.

By late 1998, Kevin's life had seemingly settled into a comfortable routine. He'd finally married Heidi, and the couple
had, with $38,000 of Heidi's money as a down payment,
purchased a new home in an upscale community east of
Pasadena, La Verne; he'd negotiated a new divorce agreement with Natalie, one that split visitation rights with their
daughter half and half, and also disposed of the old irritants
of unpaid child and spousal support; he was seeing babies
at the Eaton Canyon clinic and at two hospitals, helping
him accumulate a base of somewhere between 1,500 and
2,000 young patients; and was gaining renown throughout

the community as an up-and-coming young pediatrician, a
dedicated professional widely known for his easy manner
with kids, right down to his preference for ties festooned
with the image of Charles Schulz's cartoon canine, Snoopy.

Thus, the portrait of Kevin as a young doctor that
emerges—from his own account of himself, and from the
observations of his friends—is that of a caring, gentle man,
gifted in his ability to help children relax, and not particularly opinionated or even driven by ambition.

But for all his friendliness, there was a less attractive
side to Kevin. Occasionally, in fact, there were complaints
that Kevin seemed habitually compelled to proposition
nurses for sex. It was nothing particularly pushy, most
thought, but it could either be flattering or aggravating, depending on how one took it.

One nurse at St. Luke later told detectives that while she
liked Kevin and always found him cordial, he often managed to convey the impression that he was unhappy in his
marriage to Heidi; he frequently complained about Heidi,
in fact, and did so to most of the nurses who worked at the
hospital. (Heidi worked at Huntington Hospital, across
town.) Most of the nurses guessed that Kevin was simply
trying to win their favors by playing "the sympathy card,"
as this nurse later put it. One night, in fact, when she was
having problems in her own marriage, Kevin asked her how
her sex life was. When the nurse replied that it was non-
existent, Kevin suggested that the two "console each other."
The nurse pointed out that Kevin was married, and that she
wasn't "like that."

Still, as this nurse noted, Kevin was cool enough to take
no for an answer and move on to more promising prospects.
Rumors of Kevin hitting on the nurses began to surface,
however, and soon Heidi got wind of them. One of the
nurses recalled that Heidi—who held a black belt in ka-
rate—had supposedly threatened to "kick their ass" if any
of the St. Luke nurses were sleeping with her husband,
although Heidi denied saying anything like this.

Similar stories followed Kevin at Huntington Hospital

as well. There one nurse went so far as to complain to the hospital management that Kevin had on several occasions propositioned her, and on one occasion had rubbed up against her. A supervising doctor pulled him aside to warn him that there had been a complaint and suggested that he should watch his behavior in the future.

What few of the nurses knew was that during the fall of 1998—just when things looked so rosy for Kevin—Heidi had been having her own extramarital affair with a man she'd met at a local gym. According to both Heidi and Kevin, the "body-builder affair," as it became known during the trial, apparently devastated him. "I was just a blubbering blob of crying jelly," he said later. Kevin was also to blame Heidi's affair with the body builder for his failure to pass his pediatric board examinations that fall.

That Kevin's behavior with the nurses at Huntington and St. Luke was in retaliation for Heidi's infidelity cannot be ruled out. Still, the general ambiance that surrounded Kevin was that of a womanizer, albeit a particularly gentle, and almost needy one. As one St. Luke nurse later put it, Kevin was charming, non-threatening and always low-key. Even if he tried to cultivate the image as "a lady's man, seeking conquests," most of his would-be paramours saw him as somewhat hapless in the romantic department.

Yet this aspect of Kevin's personality was well in keeping with his overall lack of aggression. Just about the last thing that Kevin would be was confrontational. Instead, his colleagues and life-long acquaintances saw him as a person quite content to take almost everything in stride—everything, that is, except conflict.

Over and over again, Kevin's closest friends would remark on this aversion to conflict. Indeed, it was his nearly immutable habit to avoid angry exchanges, usually by simply absenting himself from the situation. This non-confrontational approach itself led to conflict, as first Natalie, then Heidi eventually pointed out to a defense investigator hired by Kevin's attorneys:

"Heidi stated that Kevin is a person with emotional

problems," the defense investigator reported. "She stated that he cannot stand any conflict, and does not realize that conflict is part of any relationship."

"Whenever we had an argument," Heidi told the investigator, "it was like the end of the world for him." Heidi told the investigator that when Kevin became frustrated with her, he simply left the room. "She stated that he never yells or gets physically violent. She described him as being 'passive aggressive,' and not speaking to her for weeks at a time, without telling her what was bothering him."

As a result, Kevin was the kind of person who attracted "weird relationships by being 'Mr. Nice Guy,' " Heidi continued. He made himself attractive to women by telling them what he thought they wanted to hear, and as a result, wound up attracting women who acted as "leeches," at least in Heidi's eyes.

The "leeches," according to the feisty Heidi, were always trying to take advantage of Kevin's malleable and non-confrontational personality; in short, according to Heidi, Kevin couldn't say no.

Seen from this perspective, Kevin was hardly the Don Juan–style sexual predator that prosecutors later tried to portray him to be. But if Kevin was inept as a Lothario, that did not make him any the less dangerous for someone who didn't have the first clue about American men.

4

India is a land of many colors—of races, to be sure, but also of cultures: of arts, foods, fabrics, customs, languages, sciences and religions. It is an ancient land, with a history that extends far back into the mists of man's earliest memories, from a time when the eternal cycle of birth, growth, decay and death held powerful resonance for every living thing. Over the centuries, India has been invaded countless times, each of the newcomers bringing with them their own traditions from both West and East, which are melded into the pre-existing social structure. It is, without a doubt, the world's original melting pot.

Today, India is the homeland of nearly a billion human beings—three times the population of the United States, in a geographic area that is one-third the size of ours. It is a country that speaks 16 major languages, which in turn are broken into as many as 1,600 distinct dialects. Its major religious groups are likewise fractured into a kaleidoscopic variety of sects and cults, many of them with traditions going back thousands of years. For these reasons, trying to explain and accurately summarize the world view of the average Indian would be both presumptuous and futile—in fact, due to the sheer variety of the subcontinent, such a description cannot exist. For a contemporary American—like Kevin Paul Anderson—to understand what makes a person who grew up in India inherently different from himself is nearly impossible, a fact which would later become vitally important as the events that propelled Anderson from physician to felon unfolded.

India's rich history extends back into the stone age—to a time even before civilizations first began in Egypt and the Euphrates Valley. At a time before the pyramids were even contemplated, the Dravidian people of the Indus

Valley on the border between present-day Pakistan and India had developed a highly sophisticated civilization that appears to have been centered on the Laws of Karma. This earliest civilization was primarily agricultural and, as far as anyone can now tell, almost exclusively vegetarian.

Beginning around 3500 B.C., the Dravidian civilization was invaded from the northwest (where present-day Afghanistan exists) by tribes of nomadic herders, the Indo-Aryans. These peoples were significantly different from the culture they conquered, being more militaristic, hierarchical, and given to the accumulation of material wealth. The invaders brought with them an ancient language, Sanskrit, and a cosmic view of bewildering complexity that placed most of its emphasis on adherence to the social order. Eventually, the culture of the Indo-Aryans metamorphosed into what today is called the Hindu faith, which is less of a religion in the Western sense than it is a method of social organization. Today, nearly 83 percent of the Indian population follows the Hindu world view; the word *Hindu* comes from the Sanskrit word for river, *sindhu*, indicating the Hindu view of time as an eternal flow.

Conflicts between the Indo-Aryan invaders and the indigenous population were many and bloody, according to most historical experts. One of the principal flashpoints was the invaders' predilection for animal sacrifices, and the consequent stockpiling of herds of cattle as a measurement of social standing; both practices were seen as violative of the Laws of Karma by the indigenous peoples. The Indo-Aryans also brought with them the raw forms of a caste system: a methodology of imposing social order, in which the highest caste, the *Brahman*, were priests; the second caste, the *Kshatriyas*, were warriors; the third, *Vaisyas*, were farmers and tradespeople. A fourth caste, *Sudras*, were servants. The castes were strictly maintained as a principle of *dharma*—the Hindi word that might be loosely translated as "way of life."

Thus, it was as much a part of the cosmic order for a farmer to always be a farmer, or a warrior a warrior, and

for his sons to likewise be farmers or warriors, as it was
for the sun to rise in the east—a way of nature that was as
immutable as it was unchallengeable. These castes were
imposed on the conquered people by the Indo-Aryans as a
vital part of the nature of reality, along with notions of what
was "good" behavior or "bad."

Nevertheless, the beliefs of the indigenous population
had a similar impact on the beliefs of the invaders. Over
time, the practice of animal sacrifice was dropped, for example, and the ideas about the Law of Karma were amal-
gamated into the Hindu way. Eventually, one's caste
became a matter of one's karma: actions in one life determined the one's status in the next. Going outside one's
caste—to marry, for example, to take up a trade unsuitable
to caste, or even to have personal contact with a member
of another caste—was considered a "bad" action in terms
of karma, likely to result in a lowering of caste in the next
life, all other things being equal. Adherence to caste was
"good," and therefore promised reincarnation at a higher
level in the next life. Thus the concept of karma became a
principal means of enforcing caste, which had the salutary
effect, from the Indo-Aryans' point of view, of maintaining
their control over society. Over the centuries, Hinduism
evolved into less of a theology than a social order in which
what one thought was less important than what one did.

Over the millennia, the four original castes were broad-
ened and subdivided to meet changes in society; today,
there are as many as 2,000 different castes in India, representing race, occupation, religious orientation and the
like. It has only been in the last sixty years, as India has
begun to emerge as a modern, independent nation, that the
barriers of caste have begun to break down.

Not all of the indigenous people were subsumed into the
Hindu way, however. While a considerable amount of conflict between the old ways of living and the new regime
unfolded in the thousands of years between the Indo-Aryan
invasions and the time around 1200 B.C., some of the original population managed to hold onto their beliefs despite

the pressures to conform. It appears that for some centuries these groups were tolerated as small minorities within the Hindu culture as a whole. Among them were the people who would later become known as Jains, and after them, the Buddhists.

As a general rule, the Jain peoples rejected the world view of the Hindus, particularly the pantheistic aspect of Hinduism holding that different lesser gods were manifestations of cosmic principles. The Jains were largely atheistic—that is, they did not believe in the gods of the Hindu system. Instead, they continued to adhere to the Laws of Karma, along with the belief that the soul was eternally reborn in situations that were more or less "auspicious" based upon one's own actions in his present life. Many Jains were tradespeople, and were thus thrust into the *Vaisyas* caste by the Hindu majority. But caste was never considered more than a social convenience by most Jains. Like Hindus, Jains recognized two distinct classes of adherents: householders, whose observance of Jainism might be seen as less strict, and those who were monks, whose pursuit of the tenets of Jainism was likely to be far more rigorous.

The principle objective of Jainism is to liberate the soul from the endless cycle of rebirths, much as it is in Buddhism. This objective stems from the Jains' essentially pessimistic view of existence. "Life in the world, perpetuated by the transmigration of the soul, is essentially bad and painful; therefore it must be our aim to put an end to the cycle of births, and this will be accomplished when we come into the possession of right knowledge," notes one historian of Jainism.[3] The way of attaining liberation is through moral acts that dissipate the accumulation of karma, Jains believe.

Among these moral acts are adherence to right conduct—not to kill, not to lie, not to steal and not to be driven by a desire for worldly possessions. Later, a fifth *Vrata*, or way of action, was added: not to indulge oneself in sensual plea-

---

[3]Bhattacharyya, op. cit.

sure. To achieve this liberation, a dedicated Jain advocated the practice of extreme (by our standards) asceticism—going without clothing, and even wearing a cloth over the mouth to prevent the inadvertent inhalation of insects to prevent their deaths. This image of the Jain holy man, naked, carrying a straw broom to sweep the ground to prevent crushing an insect by sitting on it, and the cloth covering of the mouth, remains the most common characterization of the Jain in the West, although such extremes were rarely practiced by the common Jain householder, even in the distant past.

To Jains, the universe has neither a beginning nor an ending, in that time is infinite; instead, time is divided into two cycles, one ascending, the other descending. In the first cycle, *utsarpini*, all aspects of life grow progressively better; in the descending cycle, *avasarpini*, things become progressively worse. At the conclusion of the descending cycle, the progressive cycle begins once more, to be followed eventually by the descending cycle, and so on, forever and forever. Thus, time is seen as cyclical, with "auspicious" beginnings and times to avoid undertaking risks.

Having been overwhelmed by the Hindu way and rendered into a relatively obscure sect even thousands of years ago, the practice of Jainism was continued by a tiny minority of India's population. By the middle of the 6th century B.C., Jainism, while followed by only a small fragment of the populace, nevertheless was to have a profound influence on world events. It was from the Jainist tradition that Buddhism is believed to have originated. Gautama Buddha is said to have been a contemporary of a legendary Jain *tirthankara*, Mahavira, and to have engaged in doctrinal disputes with him. And while the approach of the Buddhists to the problems of life found comparatively little favor, at least permanently, in India, the ideas of Buddha were to have lasting resonance in Tibet, China, southeast Asia and Japan over the subsequent 2,500 years.

About 200 years after Mahavira, in the midst of a severe famine, the Jains divided into two separate sects. According to Jains, many committed adherents left the area, and traveled to the southern part of the sub-continent. When they returned to northern India some twelve years later, they discovered that those Jains who had remained behind had begun to wear clothing; these *Svetembara*, as they are called, are the forerunners of modern Jains in India today. Those who continue the tradition of going without clothing are called *Digambaras*; not surprisingly, they are rather more conservative than their clothed brethren. The famed statesman Mohandas Ghandi is said to have based at least some of his famous philosophy of non-violence on the precepts of the Jains.

As an essentially ethical system of beliefs, Jainism posits no god—no central deity or deities separate from humanity—but rather a state of timeless beingness ideally within reach of any individual. Nevertheless, Jains believe that each age or cycle produces a holy figure—a *tirthankara*, or "bridge-finder," someone who is wise, and who rediscovers the Jain way. The *tirthankara* guides all living creatures in shedding the actions of karma, thereby liberating the soul from the cycle of endless rebirth. For many Jains, a pilgrimage to a place associated with a *tirthankara*—often a high place—has the effect of exposing the pilgrim to the holy actions of the masters from the past, and reconnects the ordinary person with the ethical precepts necessary to free oneself of the cycle of rebirth in a ritual purification.

"Your mind feels sudden joy and teems with bright thoughts," reports Jainism's Web page, jainsansaronline.com (yes, even ancient religions have web pages these days). "You recover from greed of money and spend[ing] it. Fellow feeling is promoted and pilgrims of different nations and cities live with love. Wonderful is the influence of sacred places. Go to Mt. Shaturnjaya. When you reach its foot, you feel the eagerness to see God and give him gifts and gain piety. The voice from within comes resounding, 'Let me sing your virtues and praise you. From a distance I have come, please appear before me.' " Such holy places, scattered across India's northern third, are frequently attended by large pilgrimages of believers; and as such, would come to play an important role in what was to befall Kevin Anderson and Dr. Deepti Gupta, a Jain believer, and eventually Kevin's victim.

5

Deepti Gupta was born October 8, 1967, the daughter of a well-to-do Jain couple intent on insuring that their children were throughly well-educated and prepared to prosper in the modern world. The India that Deepti was born into was an old world striving valiantly to become a new one, just as Deepti herself would be fated to be thrust willy-nilly into a modern era.

The India of Deepti's birth was a curious, sometimes startling admixture of the ancient and modern, in effect a distillation of new solutions into old bottles. After two centuries of dominance by the British Empire, the newly independent nation was striving to hurl itself into the contemporary era. With only a fraction of the population literate, one of the most important tasks was to improve the educational system. New universities were opened, and the disciplines of science and engineering were emphasized. As one result, the India of today is on the leading edge of a great deal of scientific research, and has developed as one of the world's most important centers of computer software development. But this was still to come at the time of Deepti's birth, when the nation was still emerging from its experience of British colonization.

Even after independence, the millennia-old traditions such as caste and religious beliefs were not so easily swept aside. The result was an atmosphere of flux, as old traditions were made to fit into new circumstances wrought by the advance of technology and the needs of developing a largely rural nation into a modern industrial state.

One of the oldest of traditions of India has continued despite the changed social environment. This was the practice of arranged marriages. In a society where adherence to caste was long considered paramount, the decision to marry was fraught with far more significance than in the West, with its romantic ideals about mere love. Matchmaking was more than just putting a likely young couple together; there had to be considerations of caste, religion, social obligations, family backgrounds, indeed a whole panoply of considerations that at times took on the coloration of a business merger as much as anything else. Moreover, in India, marriage was considered sacred; divorce, while legal, was extremely rare. Even more rare was adultery, while pregnancy in an adulterous relationship was almost unheard of. Becoming pregnant in an adulterous relationship with a person from another caste was considered anathema.

Like many traditional societies, India is a male-dominated, even puritanical culture. Men are widely considered to hold authority over their wives. And while the husband must do whatever he can to further the endeavors of his wife, the final say-so belongs to him.

In the world of emerging India, however, many of these aspects of married life came under the pressure of modernization. As upper-caste women gained more education, for example, fewer were willing to subordinate themselves to their husbands, and more likely to dispute them. Relations with in-laws—always a tricky business even in the old days—became more difficult under the stresses and strains of modern life.

Another ancient tradition that survived into modern Indian society was the widespread practice of astrology. Even today, many Indians of all castes consider astrology an important part of their lives, and continue to make important life decisions based upon it. Indian astrology—*jyotisa*, or Vedic astrology, as it is called—combines aspects of both Western (Greek and Arabic) astrology with Chinese lunar astrology. As a result it is a rather arcane discipline, involving complicated mathematical calculations based upon a person's astrological period of birth, the relative positions of the moon and planets, and one's *dharma*, or life path, which of course has much to do with caste and karma. Much of the practice of Vedic astrology, in fact, is concerned with the Laws of Karma, and with determining the most propitious moment for such activities as marriages, career decisions, births, and similar life-altering questions. And while some modern Indians have dismissed *jyotisa* as nonsense, others, even the well-educated, continue to rely on it.

This, then, was the India that formed Deepti Gupta as she was growing up—a land rich in tradition, but one torn by the stresses of birth into a modern age. In time Deepti would have to confront these contradictions in the most personal way.

By the late 1980s, Deepti had matured into a most beautiful young woman. Five feet five inches tall, slender, with dark silky hair, she was gifted with great intelligence and a charming manner—in short, a prize for any prospective husband. Deepti had grown up in the north central Indian center of Kanpur, a major commercial and industrial city of about 2 million on the Ganges River. By some accounts, Deepti was raised in a sheltered environment; certainly she was later described as largely innocent to the ways of the world. Deepti graduated from Kanpur University, continued in medical school, and by 1991, was in her internship as a physician there.

In many ways, Deepti's very success as a medical student is reflective of her unusual qualities. Even with the emphasis on education, relatively few Indian women, even in the 1980s, had the advantages of a university education. Far more rare, even exceedingly so, were women who not only were accepted into medical school, but who actually became doctors. The fact that Deepti did so—and that later, so did her younger sister, Anshu—demonstrates at least two facts: that Deepti was enormously talented, and that her family, doubtless influenced by Jain traditions, was unusually forward-thinking, at least in some respects, for India.

In other areas however, Deepti's family adhered to older traditions. For one, Deepti continued to place reliance in *jyotisa* for choosing propitious moments for important life decisions. And in another, Deepti's family believed in the concept of arranged marriages.

In the summer of 1991, Deepti's family introduced her to Vijay Gupta, a young engineering professor with excellent prospects; Vijay had some time earlier joined a growing exodus of talented young Indians to the United States, where opportunities in engineering and computer science seemed boundless, at least from the Indian perspective. By 1991, Vijay held an instructorship in engineering at Dartmouth University in New Hampshire.

Vijay was about eight years older than Deepti, who was then 23, and in the tradition of arranged marriages in India, was introduced to Deepti and her family by his own parents. Because the concept of arranged marriages was unfamiliar to most Americans, Vijay was later asked to explain:

"Basically, a lot of marriages [in India] are arranged in the sense that parents will help you meet your prospective spouse," he said. "But you can still say no if you don't think that this is the person for you. There is no pressure to marry the person. About fifty or a hundred years ago, you didn't have a choice. You just had to marry the person. But in our case, we had full freedom to say no."

Vijay and Deepti agreed to have each other as husband and wife, and a six-month engagement ensued. In this time, Vijay and Deepti grew closer. Among other things, they had in common a familiarity with things medical: while Deepti was becoming a doctor, Vijay was becoming a well-known expert on soft-tissue injuries resulting from accidents, and in fact, would later go on to become an expert witness on the subject in American courtrooms.

In early 1992, Vijay and Deepti were married in a traditional Indian wedding ceremony. Deepti affectionately nicknamed her new husband "Guddu," and, following the marriage, moved with Vijay to Dartmouth. There Deepti passed her medical board examinations, and was accepted for a medical residency at Dartmouth–Hitchcock Medical Center for the 1993–1994 term. Deepti decided to specialize in pediatrics, particularly the care of adolescent girls.

While at Dartmouth, Vijay and Deepti formed a number of close relationships with others in both the engineering and medical school faculties, who were later to express complete shock at the turn of events that was to claim her life. Many saw Deepti as sweet and innocent, although her intelligence and dedication to medicine even then marked her as a person of unusual determination.

In June of 1995, Vijay came to the University of California at Los Angeles to attend an engineering conference. About the same time, Vijay received an offer to join the Mechanical and Aerospace engineering faculty at UCLA. At Deepti's insistence, she and Vijay consulted a Vedic astrologer in the Los Angeles area, one Anil Sharma, for the purpose of considering whether to accept the new position, and whether to make the move. Vijay himself didn't put much stock in the forecast, which was calculated to determine whether such life-changes might be implemented under "auspicious" celestial circumstances. Still, this was an important aspect of his wife's life, and Vijay resolved to go along with it, even if he had his doubts—and later, even a little resentment—about Sharma, who characterized himself as a *Brahman* and a "spiritual counselor."

"We believe in the theory of karma and reincarnation," Sharma said later, "which means that, just do a good deed and do not expect anything in return, because whatever you do now, you will get returned, either later in life or in your next life. We firmly believe that good things and bad things in this life is because of what we were in the past life."

Apparently the signs were auspicious for the transition, because Vijay accepted the UCLA job, and Deepti applied and was accepted for a second-year residency at Los Angeles County–University of Southern California Medical Center, probably the largest public hospital in Los Angeles. In December of that year, after some initial difficulty with her visa, she resumed her training in pediatrics.

Deepti's medical talents were immediately evident. As

far as her supervisors at County–USC Medical Center were concerned, she could do no wrong.

"Dr. Gupta was a wonderful pediatrician," wrote Dr. Carolyn Lytle, one of Deepti's program directors, who was involved with her on an almost daily basis. "She was calm, soft-spoken, polite, gentle and dedicated to her patients . . . she was conscientious about patient care and eager to learn everything she could about pediatrics so that she would be well prepared when it came time to enter a practice after residency."

That was how others came to see Deepti, as well: serious about her chosen profession, but always open and friendly—in short, a joy to be around. After her death, in fact, praise for Deepti's gentle, non-violent beliefs, her nurturing good humor, her loving nature and her honesty poured into the court of the judge who was assigned to pronounce sentence on her killer. The idea that, even apart from her Jain upbringing with its enormous tradition of non-violence, Deepti Gupta could ever threaten to do harm to another human being, let alone a child, seemed utterly ludicrous.

But in the end, that was what a jury was asked to believe; and to the extent it did, Kevin Paul Anderson was able to escape the death penalty. Just how it all came about, however, was enough to make almost anyone believe in the power of karma.

6

Years later—after she was dead—the defenders of Kevin
Anderson would make a concerted effort to depict Dr.
Deepti Gupta in a less than favorable light. As Kevin's
prosecutors worked diligently to portray him as a predatory
Lothario, so his defense worked just as hard to paint Deepti
as a woman who pursued him beyond the point of all reason.

In the aftermath of the trial, in fact, it was almost as if
there were four different people involved: Dr. Kevin Anderson, the gentle, inoffensive, dedicated professional who
always made it a point to walk away from a fight, versus
Dr. Deepti Gupta, a scheming, ambitious sex siren who
simply wouldn't take no for an answer; or, if one preferred,
the warm, wonderful, innocent and dedicated Dr. Gupta,
versus the seducing, lying, manipulative, "animalistic" Dr.
Anderson. The truth, as is usually the case, lay somewhere
in the middle.

Some of Kevin's personal shortcomings have already
been mentioned. Chief among them was his penchant for
tailoring his own personality to match what he believed
others wanted him to be. That he would later be seen as
"calculating . . . [and] manipulative" was only the inevitable
result of these efforts to find the least confrontational way,
even when his own best interest dictated otherwise.

And while Kevin's eventual defender, lawyer Michael
Abzug, said it pained him to point them out, there *were*
flaws in Deepti Gupta's character—but whether those flaws
were the result of innate shyness in a foreign culture or of
formalism that many instinctively took for snobbery, is a
matter that can no longer be judged.

To some of the nurses who came in contact with her,
Deepti could be overbearing, even sanctimonious. As a

woman from a country rigidified by a caste structure, she could also seem to be condescending to people she thought were her inferiors. She was often seen to be fixated on her goals, and simultaneously oblivious to others' feelings. She could be petulant and manipulative if she was thwarted in getting her way. While to some she was dedicated, to others, the same quality of personality was seen as ruthlessness.

But these were mostly judgments rendered later, after Deepti was dead, and as Kevin's defenders were looking for even the remotest justification for his acts.

In September of 1996, Deepti became pregnant by means of artificial insemination.

Much later, after the tragedy of Deepti Gupta and Kevin Anderson had received widespread publicity in the Los Angeles area, that fact seemed to be one of the most bizarre of the many strange circumstances that lay behind the murder. To the average American mind, the idea that a normal, healthy heterosexual married couple would resort to artificial means of conception suggested all manner of possible speculations: that it was proof that Deepti detested her husband Vijay; that Vijay was a cold, unfeeling, calculating man; that Deepti was driven to the arms of Kevin Anderson because Vijay had no feeling for her at all. Even the Los Angeles County Sheriff's Department came to see Vijay as some sort of sexless figure, his head so far up in clouds of equations and stress formulas that he simply had no interest in making love to his wife.

In all fairness, however, this reflects more of our own cultural attitudes about sex and procreation than it does anything meaningful about Deepti and Vijay Gupta. When he was asked about this at the trial of Kevin Anderson, Vijay simply and effectively told the truth: he and his wife planned the pregnancy, and planning meant control over the moment of conception. What Vijay did not explain—because he wasn't asked—was that Deepti's belief in "auspicious cycles" in such important matters as pregnancy and birth made such a means of procreation very nearly ideal;

it was not that Vijay didn't love his wife, or that he was physically distant from her, despite the insinuations mounted in the area's mass media. Indeed, throughout the summer before her death, Vijay later said, he and Deepti had been attempting to have a child the regular way, an effort that was suspended around the beginning of October because the "cycle" had passed. That didn't mean they didn't have physical relations any longer, Vijay said, but only that they resumed using birth control methods.

None of this is to say that Deepti and Vijay had a marriage filled only with bliss. Like any other couple, they argued. "Every marriage has discussions," Vijay said later. "She was not a woman from a small village in India. She was a well-educated woman, a doctor. She had her own mind, and we discussed things, and arguments were there." Voices were sometimes raised, Vijay admitted, and on some occasions Deepti cried. On several occasions she complained to Sharma, the astrologer, that Vijay was "abusive" to her, especially during the pregnancy. At least some of the trouble was over in-laws—it appears that neither of the couple's families thought much of the other, despite their earlier introduction for the purposes of arranging the marriage. But at no point did Deepti ever seriously consider leaving Vijay, and the couple continued to live together in a pleasant, upper-middle-class, hillside neighborhood of suburban Glendale, surrounded by friendly neighbors, some of them also Indian expatriates.

After giving birth to a daughter in early May of 1997, Deepti mulled over not returning to work, according to the astrologer Sharma, but eventually decided to complete the pediatric training program. She and Vijay hired a live-in housekeeper–nanny to help out while both maintained their busy schedules. On September 1, 1998, Deepti completed the training program, and, after passing the rigorous test, became board-certified in pediatrics in January of 1999. That certification qualified her to hold contracts with most health maintenance organizations, and would soon come to play a role in her murder, or so Kevin Anderson's prosecution would argue.

Even before gaining her board certification, Deepti was actively circulating her résumé among pediatric clinics. She was still looking for the right situation when a copy of it came across the desk of Dr. Lionel Ng, managing partner at Eaton Canyon Medical Group, where it was favorably reviewed by Dr. Kevin Anderson.

The way Kevin recalled it, Deepti's résumé had inadvertently landed on his desk in the office he shared with Eaton Canyon's business manager, Konrad Sadek. Kevin looked over the papers, and thought that it might be a good idea to hire Deepti. He had never met her, but her qualifications looked excellent.

"She was young," Kevin recalled. "She seemed like she was a good doctor. And we needed another physician, for one thing." Kevin believed that the other doctors then working at the clinic would soon begin to think about retirement, since all three were somewhat older than he was. "As time went on, the younger doctors would be able to take it over," he said. "We could run it the way we wanted to run it, and maybe we would have a little bit more say. So she seemed liked a person [who] could be in there for the long haul."

Kevin suggested that Deepti be asked in for an interview, and in October of 1998, he was introduced to Deepti by Dr. Ng, who subsequently agreed to hire her for the clinic. As far as Kevin could recall, she began work in either November or December of that year.

Deepti's arrangement with the Eaton Canyon Medical Group was later to provide the grist for a great deal of dispute, not only between her and Kevin, but also at Kevin's later trial. As Vijay recalled it, Dr. Ng's written, six-month contract with Deepti called for her to be paid $50 an hour to see patients, both those of existing physicians who were otherwise busy, as well as new patients who came to the clinic.

In fact, it was Vijay's understanding that *all* of the new patients who came to the clinic would have Deepti listed as their physician; that way, at the end of the six-month period, she would have her own patient base. Once Deepti had her own patients, she would enter into a regular arrangement with the clinic, in which she would be responsible for the clinic's overhead, along with the four other physicians. The idea, therefore, was to help Deepti establish her own patient base. This arrangement later became the crux of Kevin's prosecutors' initial contention that he had killed Deepti Gupta in a dispute over "the list" of patients, which soon became another bizarre aspect of the publicity over the tragedy. The contract also contained Deepti's agreement not to solicit the clinic's patients for any competing clinic, and to keep the clinic's "medical records" confidential.

Deepti began her work at the Eaton Canyon clinic with a great deal of enthusiasm, and in truth, she had plenty of reasons for optimism. She was young, at 31, was married to an upwardly mobile professor of engineering, held a board certification in pediatrics and was making good connections in the medical community. Based on the flow of patients to the clinic, Deepti had a good chance to establish the foundation of what promised to be a long and rewarding career in medicine.

Sometime in February of 1999, Kevin took Deepti over to St. Luke to help her obtain floor privileges there. As the hospital's on-call neonatologist, Kevin's $10,000-a-month contract called for twenty-four hour coverage, seven days a week. It was up to Kevin to find qualified doctors to fill out the on-call rotation for which he was responsible, and when he asked Deepti if she was interested in going to work for him, she responded enthusiastically. This, too, was another way to build a patient base: by treating babies at the hospital, Deepti could become known in the community, and expect that at least some of the patients might eventually find their way to the Eaton Canyon clinic in future years. The contract required Kevin to "proctor" Deepti's performance for some period of time, which in effect made Kevin Deepti's supervisor.

It was while waiting for Kevin at St. Luke one day in February that Heidi Anderson met Deepti for the second time, the first casual encounter having taken place at an Eaton Canyon staff Christmas party two months earlier. On this occasion at St. Luke, however, Heidi and Deepti fell to talking about their marriages.

Heidi later recalled that Deepti had told her that her marriage had been arranged by her parents, as was customary in India. Heidi seems to have been intrigued by this disclosure.

"I just talked to her about the fact that . . . she was in an arranged marriage, and what it was like. It was interesting. We talked about—we were both kind of newly married . . . she said she was unhappy," Heidi said.

The idea that Deepti was unhappy in her marriage with Vijay—that he was the pursued and Deepti was the pursuer—establishing that Deepti might have had a motive for chasing Kevin was crucial to the picture Kevin's defenders wanted to put forth and formed the linchpin of Kevin's later defense. But the circumstances of this supposed conversation—no witnesses other than Heidi—led some to doubt that it ever really occurred. Asked about this supposed remark, Heidi insisted that Deepti *had* told her that she was unhappy with Vijay.

"And she shared a very intimate detail with you concerning her marriage?" Heidi was asked, skeptically.

"Yes," Heidi said.

The tone of the question made it clear that at least in the minds of Kevin's prosecutors, Heidi had made the story up to help her husband.

Whether Deepti was happy in her marriage or not, one place where she soon came to be really and truly unhappy was at Eaton Canyon.

Later, it was difficult to sort out what exactly was going

on at the clinic. According to Kevin and some of the other employees, a number of changes had been made at the clinic in 1998, both in working conditions and in the level of care provided to patients. Some of these changes appear to have been related to the changing nature of health care financing. As more and more Americans became covered by health maintenance organizations (HMOs) in place of traditional medical insurance, clinics like Eaton Canyon came under increasing pressure to contain costs.

One of the changes reduced Kevin's pay to $5,000 a month. (About this same time, however, Kevin got the $10,000-a-month St. Luke "on-call" contract, which had the effect of moderating or even exceeding this loss of income.) He put up with this pay cut and the other changes, Kevin said, because he hoped to one day "inherit" the clinic from Ng and the older doctors, in which case he would have the power to make changes in the way the clinic did business. He first envisioned Deepti as a potential future ally, once the older doctors at the clinic began to retire, Kevin said.

But Deepti soon became restive at her new employer. She first crossed swords with a medical assistant over a prescription she had written. Deepti had been treating an asthma patient when her effort was criticized by the assistant, who re-wrote Deepti's prescription. The assistant told her that the patient's HMO required a less-expensive medicine, but Deepti was not placated. There followed an argument over who was the doctor, and who the assistant, which was reported to Dr. Ng. Ng criticized Deepti's treatment of the patient in front of the assistant, and backed the assistant in the dispute. Deepti felt humiliated. The seeds of a personality conflict were sown.

Later, Deepti discovered that the same medical assistant was "timing" her—that is, keeping track of the amount of time Deepti was spending with each appointment. The clinic's profit margin was based on the number of patients seen on a daily basis, and the HMOs all had standards for the time a doctor might average with a patient that had to be met to keep the HMO contract. Deepti was apparently exceeding those averages. Deepti again complained to Ng, but Ng refused to admonish the medical assistant, which Deepti took as another insult. She refused to see any more patients until the matters were resolved. She would quit, she insisted, before a medical assistant would have the power to tell her how long she could see a patient, or tell her what medicine she should prescribe. She went home.

If Deepti was offended by the clinic's stance, Dr. Ng was likewise offended by Deepti's attitude. He thought she had been rude to him. Kevin soon learned that his protégée and potential future ally had quit.

"I called her on the phone and I said, 'Well, what happened?' And she said, because Dr. Ng is doing this and doing that," Kevin recalled. Kevin checked with Ng.

"If I remember correctly," he continued, "he [Ng] didn't like the way she spoke to him. He felt she was being disrespectful or not showing the proper respect for him in his position. And she was abrupt, and he didn't like the way she was treating some of the patients."

Kevin told Ng that finding a competent doctor wasn't all that easy. He suggested that Ng try to work out some sort of compromise with Deepti. "He insisted that she apologize to him," Kevin said. This, of course, was classic Kevin: avoid confrontation, mollify everyone. Kevin later told Heidi that Deepti was having trouble with Dr. Ng, and that he'd had to intercede on Deepti's behalf with the managing partner.

Meanwhile, Deepti had come home from work very upset. When Vijay asked what was wrong, Deepti told him. "She looked visibly disturbed," Vijay said later. "She was disturbed, she was depressed, and she told me what was bothering her." Apart from the dispute over the medical questions, Deepti felt that Dr. Ng had treated her with condescension, which was made worse by the fact that he had done it in front of the medical assistant.

As a result of his wife's distress, Vijay said, he arranged a meeting with Dr. Ng, Deepti and the clinic's business manager in early March of 1999, where the issues about the medicine and the timing were raised by the Guptas, and presumably, Deepti's sudden departure from the clinic, which Ng saw as unprofessional, was cited by Dr. Ng. Ng admitted that the medicine had been changed, but explained once more that it was because the HMO wouldn't agree to the more expensive prescription.

As for the "timing" issue, Dr. Ng explained, everyone at the clinic was being timed, not just Deepti, to help the clinic comply with HMO directives. And for his part, Dr. Ng continued, he had his own problems with Deepti: her refusal to see any more patients until Ng had acceded to her demands was unprofessional, he said, and he thought it showed that Deepti had a disrespectful attitude. He thought Deepti owed him an apology.

Apparently Deepti apologized to Dr. Ng, and Vijay, at least, was mollified by Dr. Ng's explanations at this meeting, because Deepti soon returned to work at Eaton Canyon. Yet she was still unhappy; it bothered her that the bureaucrats and paper-pushers had as much say as she did about the standard of medical care. She told Vijay she still intended to quit, once she got something else lined up. Vijay was not happy to hear this. He then had another meeting with Ng—this one without Deepti's knowledge. The issue of the medicine came up again, and again Ng explained about the HMO's requirements.

Vijay returned home and told Deepti that he'd tried to iron out the differences. "I told her that I met with Dr. Ng," Vijay recalled, "and I wanted to have her work there, and make it a place where she could comfortably work, if I could work it out for her. And she didn't like that. She said she will not work in a place where she's told what kind of prescriptions she should write, and she became very angry at me. Why did I go behind her back and meddle in her professional affairs?"

While the dust-up with Ng and the Eaton Canyon clinic wasn't directly related to Deepti's subsequent murder, the episode is interesting for what it shows about several things. First, it seems clear from the events that Deepti was hardly a shrinking violet. She was willing to go toe-to-toe with anyone, even her boss, if she believed she was in the right. Second, the events show Deepti as someone who was willing to tell her husband where to get off when she believed he'd exceeded his proper role, as Vijay had done in seeing Ng on his own. These aspects of Deepti's personality were hardly consistent with someone who was "sheltered" and naive, as Deepti was later portrayed by Kevin's prosecutors.

Deepti now arranged to obtain part-time employment at two other clinics, one in Tarzana and the other in Montebello. She gave notice to Dr. Ng in early April, and her last day was April 10. But this wasn't all.

Based on who one chooses to believe, it is possible that Deepti at this time began to contemplate opening her own clinic—an endeavor she would mount by recruiting Dr. Kevin Anderson as the "rainmaker."

Or at least, that was Kevin's version of the story.

"She called me out of the blue," Kevin said later. "And she said, 'You know what? Are you considering staying at that place forever?' "

And Kevin, in a fateful if not karmic response, said no.

"Why don't we go into practice together?" Kevin said Deepti asked.

"I have to think about it," Kevin said. Which is what he should have done.

7

About the time that Deepti decided to quit Eaton Canyon, Kevin had been having his own second thoughts about the place where he'd worked for the previous six years. As Kevin put it later, he'd been having some doubts as to the "competence" of some of the clinic personnel for some time, even before Deepti was hired. That in fact was one reason why he wanted to bring Deepti aboard, as he said— he'd thought he and Deepti would eventually "inherit" the clinic, and once in control, they could make changes that would be more to their liking.

Even before Deepti had walked out, Kevin had a conversation with Ng about the future. That was when Kevin discovered that Dr. Ng had no plans to step aside.

"So I talked to him about that," Kevin said later, "and he apparently changed his mind. And since we didn't have a written contract, I had nothing really to fall back on. He said, 'No, I think I'm going to just stick around, work maybe one month out of four, and then you just cover for me for the other months.'"

Kevin went home to La Verne and discussed the situation with Heidi. For some time, Heidi had been encouraging Kevin to start his own clinic, and now that Ng had told Kevin that he planned to stick around for years to come— as long as he had Kevin to "cover" for him—perhaps the time was right to consider some other options, Heidi suggested.

Then came the call from Deepti—at least, according to Kevin and Heidi.

That wasn't so, Vijay said later—it was Kevin who had called Deepti in an effort to recruit *her*.

* * *

The idea of a partnership between Kevin and Deepti seems to have been a felicitous one, at least on paper. Each brought to the table some distinct and complementary advantages.

First, Deepti held board certification in pediatrics; Kevin did not. (As noted, he had failed to pass the board certification test in the fall of 1998.) As the economic landscape of medical care was changing, increasingly HMOs were requiring doctors who wanted to get paid by them to hold board certifications. If a start-up practice was to succeed financially, having a board-certified pediatrician would almost be a necessity.

Second, Deepti had about $100,000 in a savings account. This was from the income she had earned while a resident at County–USC. While Deepti had been completing this residency, according to Vijay, he had been paying all the bills. That left Deepti with a substantial fund to help get a start-up medical practice off the ground. Kevin had very little savings of his own. So Deepti had two things that were of great value to him if he wanted to start his own pediatric practice: the board certification, and a lot of cash.

As for Deepti, partnering with Kevin brought advantages to her. For one thing, Kevin had been in practice in Pasadena for almost six years. He was an established pediatrician with somewhere between 1,500 and 2,000 young patients who saw him regularly. At $10 per patient per month (the average payment made by HMOs to medical groups), that experience represented the potential of somewhere between $15,000 and $20,000 a month in gross business income.

In addition, Kevin was very well connected with the medical establishment in Pasadena. He was close to the St. Luke administration, and knew virtually all of the other pediatricians, and more importantly, through Heidi, had good connections with most of the obstetrician-gynecologists—from whom, of course, referrals to pediatricians often came.

Finally, not to be discounted was the sweet revenge factor: if Kevin and Deepti could somehow get all of Eaton Canyon's pediatric patients away from Dr. Ng, doubtless causing Ng considerable financial distress, Ng might rue the day he had humiliated Deepti, even as he might sorely regret treating Kevin as a hired hand.

In early May, Kevin pulled Dr. Ng aside and told him that he was quitting: his last day, Kevin said, would be August 18, 1999.

At first Heidi was enthusiastic about the proposed partnership between Doctors Gupta and Anderson. "I was very supportive," Heidi said later. "I was very encouraging to him. It was a good idea."

The way Heidi saw the proposed partnership, it would be Kevin's patient base—assuming he could convince the Eaton Canyon patients to follow him to a new location—complemented by Deepti's money, and her board certification. Heidi herself would help out around the office, and with bringing in new business from the OB/GYNs she knew at Huntington. Together the three medical professionals would go, arm-in-arm down the gold-paved pathway to a dazzling financial future.

But Heidi was swiftly disabused of this fantasy.

For one thing, she quickly came to the conclusion that Deepti didn't like her—or at least didn't think much of her. Some of this antipathy first surfaced at a medical conference attended by Deepti, Kevin and Heidi in Dana Point, on the Orange County coast about halfway between Los Angeles and San Diego.

At the conference, Heidi ran into Deepti.

"I saw her," Heidi said, "and she was just . . . I walked up and she looked at me and I looked at her. We didn't— She didn't say very much. It wasn't very pleasant. I just felt like she kind of sneered at me. Kind of like, 'Why are *you* here?' That's the feeling I got." She decided that Deepti thought she was better than Heidi because Deepti was a doctor, while Heidi was only a nurse. Deepti, she said, had refused to shake hands with her.

Later, said Heidi, Kevin told her that Deepti was offended because *Heidi* had refused to shake hands with *her*. Heidi said it had been the other way around, but Kevin didn't seem to believe her. In an attempt to make peace, Kevin invited Deepti to have dinner with them, but Deepti declined. Later that night, Kevin chided Heidi for coming to the conference with him. It was almost as if she didn't trust him.

"Look at Gupta," Kevin said. "She doesn't bring her spouse."

Things went downhill from there, at least between Heidi and Deepti.

By the middle of May, planning for the new Kevin–Deepti medical partnership had begun. Kevin began keeping written notes in a notebook he carried around; later, the jottings would form the basis of his prosecutors' attempts to show that Kevin had never really been intending to go into partnership with Deepti, but that he had only dangled that as a fabulous prospect before her eyes as part of an elaborate attempt to seduce her.

In retrospect, this analysis appears to be, paradoxically, both too complicated as well as too simplistic. Complicated, because all the effort and time spent by Kevin from May through August on the prospective partnership seems to indicate that he took the idea of a business with Deepti Gupta seriously, not just as a seduction ploy; and simplistic because it leaves out the psychological dynamic between Kevin and Heidi that the partnership and, eventually, its more carnal embodiment tends to illuminate.

In going into business with Deepti, Kevin was delivering a non-verbal, perhaps even subconscious message to his wife: *I can punish you by making you jealous. I can leave you behind. I don't need you.* In that sense, it might be argued that the prospective business with Deepti Gupta was more designed to get at Heidi than Deepti. And it worked— at least until it all spiraled out of Kevin's control.

There is little doubt, however, that Deepti was entranced

by the prospect of starting a pediatric clinic with Kevin. According to Vijay, Deepti told him that it had been Kevin who had solicited her to go into business, not the other way around. To Deepti, the chance to open up a new office with an established doctor like Kevin Anderson was a golden opportunity, and one that she did not intend to pass by.

"She told me," Vijay said, "that he [Kevin] was very unhappy at Dr. Ng's practice because he was bringing in a lot of patients and he was not getting enough compensation for that, and he wanted to go into private practice with her."

Kevin, Deepti explained to Vijay, was pediatrician to somewhere around 1,500 to 2,000 patients at Eaton Canyon. That was an enormous base to build a possible practice on. Besides, Deepti said, Kevin was an important person, someone who could open a lot of doors for her. Based on Vijay's description of his wife's enthusiasm for the joint practice with Kevin, and on Deepti's subsequent conversations with the Hindu astrologer, Anil Sharma, it appears that Deepti saw the proposed partnership as her main chance, one that she was determined to seize. Even when Kevin began emitting signals that he was vacillating on the idea, Deepti continued to press forward, almost as if she could will the clinic into reality. This persistence was very nearly unaccountable, given the circumstances; some would say, in fact, that it was almost karmic.

8

Sometime around May 15, 1999, Kevin and Deepti held their first meeting on their proposed partnership. The first order of business was, naturally, customers—patients, that is. While Kevin's name was familiar to the 1,500 to 2,000 Eaton Canyon patients he had seen over the years, there was no guarantee that any would follow him to a new office. If most did, they would be set. But if the vast majority chose to stay at Eaton Canyon, Kevin and Deepti's new venture would sink like a stone.

And while Deepti had contractually agreed not to "solicit" Eaton Canyon patients after she no longer worked for Dr. Ng, no such proviso applied to Kevin. Nor was there anything to prevent them from sending simple announcements to everyone saying that they were opening their own clinic. The plan was to send the announcements to all of the patients listed on both doctors' Eaton Canyon appointment calendars for the months of January, February, March and April—approximately covering the same period Deepti had worked at the Eaton Canyon clinic. In Deepti's case, this might have amounted to fewer than 100 names; in Anderson's, rather substantially more than that. But some percentage of Kevin's patients had actually been seen by Deepti while she was at Eaton Canyon.

These appointment calendars, or "patient logs" as Kevin referred to them, were eventually transmuted by prosecutors into the fabled "patient list" that Kevin and Deepti were reputedly squabbling over when the murder occurred.

In actuality, however, there never was a "patient list"—nothing like a voluminous listing of patients' names, addresses, telephone numbers, insurance particulars and firm commitments to have either Deepti or Kevin as their doctor, as the prosecutors attempted to suggest was at the core of

Kevin's murder of Deepti. The so-called "patient list" was simply a collection of monthly calendars with appointments, with the patients' names color-coded to denote the doctor they were scheduled to see. And as Kevin and Deepti soon discovered, matching the names on the calendars with real addresses, to mail announcements of the new practice, was very difficult indeed. What the "patient list" did come to represent, however, as the months wore on, was a symbol, almost a codeword, for the on-again, off-again proposed partnership arrangement that would eventually come to obsess Deepti Gupta, and, if his defenders were right, drove Kevin to near madness.

But in the beginning, while Kevin and Deepti were still dreaming, getting the appointment calendars seemed like a natural place to start organizing their new enterprise. It also seems that Kevin indicated to Deepti that those of "his" patients that had actually been seen by her during the months from December to April might be directed to Deepti's care when the partnership got going. Certainly Deepti thought of these patients as "hers," even though the records indicated they were originally seen by Kevin. This confusion was to cause a great deal of difficulty in the future, particularly since Deepti believed that Kevin "owed" her those patients, since she had seen them.

Kevin's notes from the meeting show several other things. One phrase, "time to contact," is in reference to the appointment calendars. Here Kevin wrote "August," meaning that he and Deepti intended to send their announcements out in that month in order to be ready to open in September. Kevin's notes also list four possible locations for the new clinic, and jottings suggest that he was going to contact the private insurance companies he held contracts with to amend them to include Deepti as his new partner. So far, things were going swimmingly.

A week later, Kevin and Deepti held their second meeting. This one was devoted to financial considerations. Each doctor agreed to put some amount of money into the pot to get the clinic rolling. This gave Kevin some pause; he didn't have a lot of ready cash to invest. Deepti assured him that she had plenty of money, and that they would be able to negotiate some arrangement that would enable them to go forward. Kevin put the worry aside for the time being, and told Heidi that one reason he wanted to go into business with Deepti was that Deepti had a substantial amount of money available to invest in the proposed partnership, which seemed to make it financially feasible.

As May turned into June, Kevin and Deepti began spending more time together—often visiting places they were thinking of leasing for the clinic offices. At first, Heidi went with them, but she soon began feeling like a spare wheel on a bicycle. In her view, Deepti continued to act condescendingly to her.

On one occasion, Deepti came to the Andersons' house in La Verne before going to look at possible clinic sites. Heidi recalled giving her a tour of the house: "[I] tried to be friendly," she said. "And then we got in the car and went to look at office buildings. I told her to go ahead and sit in the front seat." Heidi thought that giving her the chance to sit next to Kevin would enable Deepti to discuss matters more easily with him.

"We went to a couple of offices," Heidi said. "She just seemed kind of rude to me. When I would join in the conversation, she would just cut me off, or just kind of, you know, 'What do *you* have to say about it?' I just felt really bad about it."

By early June, Deepti had staked out an office location she believed would be ideal. Located on Green Street in downtown Pasadena, the Thatcher Building was used by many of Pasadena's medical professionals. The location had been suggested to her by Marvin Cooper, a certified public accountant used by a number of medical professionals in the area. Deepti had been referred to Cooper by a malpractice insurance representative she had contacted to line up insurance for the proposed venture.

At the Thatcher Building, Kevin and Deepti were met by the leasing agent, Tracy Thomas. Thomas showed the two doctors available space on the building's second floor, which was due to become available about September 1. Deepti and Kevin both submitted required bank statements, tax returns and an authorization for a credit check, which would seem to indicate that, at least in early June, Kevin was serious about the proposed partnership.

Three days after showing Kevin and Deepti the space in the Thatcher Building, Thomas gave a written lease proposal to Deepti, and faxed a copy to Kevin. The deal called for a five-year lease at $2.20 a square foot. At a little over 2,000 square feet, the monthly office rent would be about $4,500.

Kevin thought the price was too high. He wanted to continue looking. Deepti didn't agree. She signed the lease on June 18. Kevin was not happy.

Up to this point, the proposed partnership had been coming along well. Each doctor had responsibility for lining up various aspects of the business. Kevin, for example, was responsible for assembling the names of all the Eaton Canyon patients, and later contacting them, to let them know he and Deepti would soon be in business together. Deepti was responsible for drafting the partnership agreement, and for contacting insurance vendors and the like. Both were to be jointly responsible for finding the new clinic's office space.

But the more Kevin considered the commitment they would have to make at the Thatcher Building, the more worried he got. He wasn't sure that they would get enough patients from Eaton Canyon to make the lease payments. He suggested to Deepti that they keep on looking for less expensive offices, but Deepti seemed infatuated with the Thatcher Building. To Kevin, the Thatcher Building seemed a more upscale location than he was comfortable with; many of his patients were lower income, and he worried that spending too much on rent might make it harder to practice medicine. Deepti, on the other hand, was less enthusiastic about having mostly poor people for patients. She wanted to have more privately insured patients, who might be more comfortable in the Thatcher Building.

This division of opinion was more than just a matter of taste, it appears. Instead it went to the heart of both doctors' views of themselves and their ambitions. Where Kevin wanted to practice comfortable, low-stress medicine, Deepti seems to have been more ambitious—she wanted to create a big-time clinic. The space in the Thatcher Building, for example, had either four or five examining rooms, depending on the configuration.

The difference in outlook was subtle, but profound, and had a lot to do with how Kevin and Deepti each saw themselves. It was, in fact, a major difference between their personalities, one that would crop up with increasing frequency as the summer wore on.

Kevin's diffidence about the plusher digs (and what they said about Deepti's goals) was almost immediately apparent to Heidi. By the middle of June, Heidi was pretty sure she didn't like Deepti, and it wasn't difficult for her to find reasons for her dislike.

Still trying to involve herself in the new clinic, Heidi had drafted a proposed announcement to send to the Eaton Canyon patients shortly after Kevin and Deepti had first looked at the Thatcher Building offices. Heidi suggested that the new clinic be called Green Street Pediatrics, after the address. The announcement misspelled Deepti's name.

"I showed that to Dr. Gupta," Kevin said later, "and Dr. Gupta didn't like that. She thought the name was stupid. She didn't like the format of the whole thing. I took that back to Heidi and told her."

When Kevin told Heidi that Deepti had rejected both the proposed name of the clinic and the draft announcement, Heidi got upset. She and Kevin then got into a nasty argument about Heidi's involvement with the project, with Kevin telling her that his business was his business, and that she would have no say in it. Now Heidi was not happy.

As the end of June neared, Heidi began resenting the claims that Deepti was making on Kevin's time. Deepti began frequently calling Kevin at the La Verne house, according to Heidi, and was usually curt with her if she answered the telephone instead of Kevin. Deepti, at least in Heidi's view, was becoming more and more demanding and controlling of Kevin—in short, in Heidi's mind, Deepti was becoming another one of the "leeches" who took advantage of him because he couldn't say no. And when Kevin wasn't available, or if he took time off, Deepti would chastise him, and suggest that Kevin was lazy, that he wasn't doing his part to get the clinic up and running.

"She would be very upset about the time Kevin wanted to spend away from his work," Heidi recalled. "She seemed very manipulative and controlling of his time, and what he did with his family and friends. Her tastes and what she seemed to want out of a practice seemed to differ from Kevin's."

Heidi was asked to cite an example.

"She was much more, in my opinion, materialistic than Kevin. She wanted to have an office, starting out, in what I think is a high-rent area of Pasadena . . . whereas, you could start somewhere that isn't as pretty or nice, but just as good, which, knowing Kevin, that would be okay with him."

And always, in Heidi's view, there was this relentless pressure on Kevin from Deepti to get moving.

9

The proposed September 7 opening date for the clinic had more meaning for Deepti than either Heidi or Kevin realized. As early as late May, after Deepti and Kevin had met several times to work out some of the preliminaries of the proposed partnership, Deepti and Vijay had gone to see Anil Sharma, the Vedic astrologer, to get his views on the new business.

Sharma had a small office on Pioneer Boulevard in Artesia, southeast of downtown Los Angeles, in a neighborhood where many Indian expatriates had established businesses. He'd been advising Deepti since she and Vijay had come to southern California in the spring of 1995.

"Many people," Sharma later explained to two detectives from the sheriff's department who came to interview him, "go astrologically. They go for a good date. Among Hindus, Indians, they normally do a thing on a good date. They want a particular time to start a new business, or a particular date to start a new job. And, normally the priest tells them: this is a good time, this is a good lunar day to start."

Sometime in late May or early June, Sharma said, Deepti and Vijay came to ask about the proposed new business with Kevin Anderson.

"She came," Sharma said, "and indicated to me that there is a major change that's going to happen in her career field, and that there is this Doctor Kevin who has told her he's going to team up with her. And he's a big source. A very important source for referrals, and sending patients, as well as making things happen for her. The way she put it is, that this guy is the guy in charge of many things. And he's holding a position, I think, of chairman of the board in a couple of places." (Kevin was a member of the medical executive board at St. Luke Medical Center, as well as head of the hospital's neonatology directorate.)

Deepti wanted Sharma to tell her how things looked astrologically for the new venture, and for her life. "And I told her that . . . certain dates were favorable, and certain dates will make it happen. In the past, I have been really accurate by telling them some event is going to happen in their life. And normally, it happens."

Following this forecast, Sharma said, Deepti began calling him regularly—until just before the end. By then she was making so many calls to Sharma that Sharma told her she was out of control. But by that time a lot of other things had happened.

Vijay, for his part, was not a believer in Vedic astrology. And while Sharma told the police, and later testified that he was a "Hindu priest," Vijay was more skeptical.

"He's an astrologer," Vijay said. "She wanted to—She believed in all this stuff. And she [would] seek his advice from an astrological point of view, [like] the right time to have a baby or not the right time, the right time to go into business, or things like that. I don't think he was in the category of a Hindu priest."

He'd gone with Deepti to see Sharma, Vijay said, but not for his own purposes. And while he was there, he'd asked about his own future—but just out of curiosity, "just like anybody else."

Sharma was never asked, either by the police or at Kevin Anderson's trial, just what advice he had given Deepti Gupta.[4] But given Deepti's increasingly strident insistence that the clinic open for business on September 7, the chances are excellent that that was the "auspicious" date he recommended.

If this was the case, it sheds a great deal of light on Deepti's subsequent attitudes and actions as the summer of

---

[4] Anil Sharma agreed to be interviewed by the author, but on the day of the interview left a message saying he had to go out of town.

1999 unfolded. As time before the crucial September 7 date dwindled, Deepti became more and more demanding of Kevin—and likely, more willing to enter into risks that ordinarily she would have bypassed, all to insure that the September 7 "auspicious" opening date could be realized. Certainly Heidi never knew this; and if Deepti had confided the reason for her sense of urgency to Kevin, it did not seem to be something that struck him as important. Here was yet another example of how the cultures and belief systems of the two doctors were mismatched, with eventually fatal results.

10

Besides seeing Anil Sharma, the Guptas also consulted with Marvin Cooper in preparation for the new business. This took place in late June, according to Cooper, who said he had been recommended to Deepti as a business planner by the malpractice insurance representative Deepti had contacted early on.

Cooper had offices in Encino, in the San Fernando Valley. As a CPA, he had numerous medical people among his clients, and was well versed in the financial considerations necessary to starting and operating health care practices. Deepti and Vijay wanted Cooper to draft a proposed agreement that would outline the business relationship between Deepti and Kevin in the new partnership. Deepti had some definite ideas of what the proposed "practice formation agreement" should contain. One of the most important was her insistence that she and Kevin be equal partners in the new clinic. Cooper was quite clear on the concept: Deepti did not want to feel as though she were Kevin's employee.

Cooper went to work roughing out a working draft of the proposed partnership, a document that would set out just who would do what, and how the profits and expenses were to be split, which he subsequently faxed to Kevin on July 15, while Deepti was out of the country. As Deepti insisted, everything was fifty-fifty.

Meanwhile, Kevin was consulting with *his* accountant, Steven Sorrell. Sorrell had prepared Kevin's tax returns for the previous two years, including one for a corporation that handled the income and expenses for the $10,000-a-month on-call contract for St. Luke. In late June—it isn't clear whether this meeting took place before or after Deepti and Vijay's meeting with Cooper—Kevin scheduled an appointment for himself and Deepti to take place at Sorrell's house. The purpose of the meeting was to discuss the formation of the partnership.

Thus, it appears that as of late June of 1999, Deepti and Kevin were each meeting with their own business planners, although Kevin included Deepti in his meeting, while Deepti met with Cooper without Kevin; it doesn't appear that either of the business planners knew of the activities of the other. At least, Sorrell said, he never knew about Marvin Cooper's services for Deepti Gupta.

At the meeting, held in early July before the Guptas left the country on a previously planned trip to Europe, one of Sorrell's first questions was whether Kevin and Deepti had a partnership agreement. The two doctors said they did not have one. Sorrell was shocked.

"I actually went on at some length," he said later, "and suggested to them that it was important in a partnership that they discuss in advance some of the issues that come up often in partnership. Things like division of profits and relative efforts of each party, and vacations and things like that . . . that there were quite a number of issues that come up during the course of a partnership that people don't always think about going in. And that it was important to think about them and memorialize them." Sorrell thought such arrangements should always be put into writing.

Sorrell was asked if Kevin had told him how the partnership was going to be organized.

"Yes," Sorrell said. "They were going to be equal partners."

The way Kevin saw the arrangement, Sorrell said, Kevin was going to contribute "receivables"—that is, either patients or funds owed to him by various insurance companies—and Deepti was "going to provide more of the working effort, initially."

As the discussion unfolded, Kevin was by far the more vocal, Sorrell recalled. And when Sorrell discussed some of the pitfalls that awaited an unwritten partnership, it was

clear to the accountant that neither Kevin nor Deepti had
thought such matters through.

"It was clear they had not considered any of the issues,"
Sorrell said later. "Dr. Anderson was, say, more interested
in getting through the tax issues, and did not seem to be
particularly perturbed by those issues that I raised. Dr.
Gupta was actually fairly quiet during most of the meeting.
I had to kind of prod her from time to time to make sure
she was understanding it. Because I wasn't sure from her
reaction . . . they did seem to somewhat gloss over the issues that I thought were important for them to consider."

As Sorrell continued to discuss the possible problems in
partnerships, Kevin seemed indifferent. "He did not seem
to think it was important. It was sort of, 'We're not worried
about that, it will be okay.' I was particularly concerned
about the fact that they were not making equal contribu-
tions. Because, in my experience, in many partnerships, if
the two partners don't have a clear understanding of the
contribution that each is supposed to make, down the road,
that tends to lead to tension, with one partner believing he
or she's putting in more, relative to what they're taking
out."

Kevin's supposed indifference to the possible problems
of an unbalanced partnership was later pointed to as evidence that he never really intended to go into a real partnership with Deepti, that it was all some sort of con game
to lure Deepti into an intimate relationship. What it more
likely reflects, however, is the gulf between Kevin's per-
ception of what was going on and that of Deepti Gupta.
While Kevin could, in his agreeable, non-confrontational
way, *say* it was perfectly okay with him to go equal partners
with Deepti, in his own mind he knew that he would be
providing most of the patients for the new clinic—"the receivables," as he put it.

Just why Kevin would agree to an equal partnership—
sharing expenses and profits fifty-fifty—when he had 90
percent of the business was perplexing. That was what Sor-

rell was trying to point out, and what Kevin didn't seem to be hearing.

And here was where Kevin made his first fatal error: agreeing to honor Deepti's request for an equal partnership, with equal say-so over all decisions, when the vast majority of the anticipated patients were his, simply made no sense. It would have been far better if Kevin had just said no; that Deepti, as the junior in both patients and experience, should join the clinic as an associate, gaining equity in the enterprise as her own patient base grew over the years until equality was both real and practical.

But, as Kevin explained to Heidi, Deepti was the one with the money; and besides, Deepti was insistent that she didn't want to work for anyone, she wanted to be her own boss, and this was Kevin's noodle-ish way of keeping everybody happy. Kevin's notes for the meeting, dated July 4, indicate that each partner was to contribute $17,000 to the start-up, and if either party was short of that amount, that they would "negotiate the difference." That made it sound as if Kevin would trade some of his "receivables"— anticipated patients—to Deepti as an "in-kind" contribution to the anticipated total start-up cost. That was one way, he said later, that Deepti could have an equal say in running the clinic. "I knew that was her wish," he said, "and that was okay with me."

It was okay with everybody except Heidi. She didn't understand why, if Kevin had almost all of the patients, Deepti should have an equal partnership. She was already suspicious that Deepti was taking Kevin for a ride like one of the "leeches." Even worse, she was beginning to suspect that Kevin was falling in love with Dr. Gupta.

This suspicion first arose, at least in Heidi's mind, early in July. The telephone calls from Deepti, had, if anything, increased. And as Kevin talked to Deepti on his home telephone, Heidi was aware that Kevin seemed to be saying whatever he thought Deepti wanted to hear.

"The way he would talk to her," Heidi said, "the part I

heard, he was just placating her. 'It's going to be okay. Don't worry.' It was so annoying to me. I thought, it's taking up so much time, and he has to constantly placate her with this encouragement and stuff. I finally said to him, 'Where's her husband? Why isn't he taking some of this? He should be doing this rather than you.' "

Heidi had no way of knowing, of course, that Deepti had become "furious" with Vijay when he'd tried to help her at Eaton Canyon. But even if she had, she thought Deepti was intruding far too much in their personal lives.

On July 8, just as Heidi and Kevin were getting ready to go to the Colorado River for a weekend-long waterskiing trip, Deepti called and blew her stack that Kevin was leaving town.

"On probably Thursday or so," Kevin said later, "right before we left, I had talked with Doctor Gupta, and Deepti was very upset. She did not feel it was appropriate for me to go out of town without notifying her first. She felt like—these vacations, as she called them, were taking away time I could be spending, putting forth energy into the practice. She felt like I wasn't devoting the amount of time that I should. I was taking too much time to have fun. And Heidi felt that this was really none of her business, what we did on the weekends ... [Deepti] just didn't understand why that was an issue."

Deepti was so upset, she was yelling at him over the telephone, Kevin recalled. " 'You can't keep taking time off. You simply can't. I mean, we need to get this practice going. We have two months to get it up and going, and you're off running around having fun.' "

By this point, as a man in the middle between two women who didn't like each other, Kevin did what came naturally: he soothed Deepti's concerns by telling her everything was working out, that she didn't need to worry; and complaining about Heidi's "interference," then putting the telephone down to complain to Heidi about Deepti's "demanding" behavior. Split between two women, trying to satisfy each, Kevin probably saw this behavior less as disloyalty to either woman, but more as the sort of little white lie that wouldn't harm anyone. But in a larger sense, Kevin was no longer being true to anyone, but most of all to himself.

And when Heidi told Kevin she believed that Deepti was trying to start an affair with Kevin, Kevin told her she couldn't be more wrong—even as he kept secret his growing attraction for the young Indian doctor.

The next day, on the trip to the Colorado River, Heidi and one of the Andersons' mutual friends tried to talk Kevin out of going into the partnership with Deepti. Heidi told Kevin that Deepti was "too bossy," and Kevin seemed to acknowledge the criticism. But Kevin continued to insist on going forward with the deal, saying that Deepti was a good doctor, and that she would be a valuable asset to the start-up practice.

On their return from the Colorado River, Kevin wrote a four-page letter to Deepti. The note was inside a greeting card that showed a young boy walking through a forest toward daylight. Below Kevin had written: "I hesitate for only a moment before going toward my destiny, but there I must go."

In the enclosed letter, Kevin wrote:

Deepti,
    As I cannot sleep, I must write this message to you. I want you to know, first of all, that I greatly respect you as a physician, mother and person. It is because of this respect that I write to you now. After our first phone conversation, I had a serious talk with my wife. It was very heated, with threats to leave and hurt egos. Suffice it to say she will not be a factor in any business decision I make. While she may have ideas that may help me, any decision is not in her hands; and if she is to be with me, that is fully understood. I was wrong to give the perception that she was having more input than was appropriate. For this I apologize. Just as I run the finances of the home, I will run the business decisions.

*This will be a line that will not be crossed, whether I'm
in business with you, Mickey Mouse or alone.*

Apparently in their telephone conversation of the week
before, Deepti had flailed Kevin for giving Heidi too much
influence over him, and had said she doubted Kevin's commitment to their new enterprise. This latter criticism appears to have stung Kevin, who now took pains to assure
Deepti that he had just as much commitment as she did.

*Commitment. As you pointed out, this is very important.
I have always, as I know you have, taken this very seriously. Just by the fact that we are physicians demonstrates our commitment at the highest levels. You calling
this into question was [un]justified and hurtful. One
must have no doubt about the other half, their other half.
To reach a higher level one must be committed. I have
never doubted my own commitment to my profession or
this endeavor. Outside of covering for St. Luke I plan to
have no other endeavors. I feel I have been meticulous
in organizing and preparing for a smooth transition for
my patients and securing the most efficient path to prof-
itability. Your reassessment of our terms of partnership
is distressing. You are correct in saying that I don't have
a baby. But I do have a lovely daughter whom I groom,
feed and prepare for her daily activities seven days a
week. I do this with little help.*

Kevin continued for a bit about his responsibilities to his
daughter, noting that while Heidi helped, the task of raising
the child was his responsibility, not Heidi's. Then he returned to the subject of the new practice:

*As for this new office, it has become my life. If you
choose not to get involved at this time, I will respect
your decision. For me, however, I cannot turn back. I
will succeed at this, alone if I have to . . .
I also feel that I should mention something about my*

*trips. We haven't been scheduling things on weekends
so I did not feel this weekend (July 10th) was any different . . .*

*As I told you, my life was at a low point last summer
and fall. My relationship [with Heidi] was essentially
over. Not only was it loveless (which in relationships I
was getting used to), but my wife was openly with another . . .*

*This is very difficult to say, as I wish I could state
these things as facts. But the truth is, while I write this
letter, as you say, with all emotions aside, I can't help
but know I'm still in love with you. I am determined not
to let that interfere in what must be done or said, however, and I have learned to be very good at burying my
feelings and so I will from this day onward.*

Kevin now asserted that his failure in the 1998 board
certification exam for pediatrics—he claimed to have
missed passing by just five points—was due to Heidi's
"body-builder" affair.

*I felt her actions had interfered with my career, and this
was what angered me the most. She is free to do what
she wants in her life. I claim to control no other person.
Emotions are not always in our control, and to expect
otherwise is to have a life filled with frustration and
disillusionment . . . We are what we are . . .*

Kevin referred to the Guptas' trip to Europe, and suggested that when they returned that he and Deepti get together to consider their future.

*I will then choose to remember you as I last saw you.
That is my prerogative. The boy on the card is very
meaningful. As he walks down the path from darkness
to light, he does so alone. I am determined to get to
where I know I belong . . .*

Kevin praised Deepti for her determination, but just as with the notion of commitment, he said he could be just as determined as she was. And, he added, if they went forward with the new practice, he was determined to contribute an equal financial share as Deepti:

> *In no way should you overcontribute. And I promise you with my word that I will contribute equal finance or I won't join you. Never will you do all the work while I play. This has never been my intention . . . I have never not carried my own weight, and I won't start now, and that I say in the strongest of terms. On this you have my unwavering promise.*
>
> *Well, now my soul is feeling more at ease and the sun is coming up. I must go. This was a difficult letter under difficult circumstances. I hope you understand.*
>
> *Kevin*

The tone of the letter is striking for what it indicates about Kevin's personality, particularly his sensitivity to Deepti's apparent criticism that Heidi had too much control over him. He seemed resolute to assure Deepti that she had him all wrong—that he was the one who made all the important decisions in his household. And it is also interesting for its unintended prophecy, words that, at the time they were written, no one, least of all Kevin, could ever have envisioned would have such terrible meaning: *I will then choose to remember you as I last saw you . . . I am determined to get to where I know I belong . . .*

And further: since Kevin seemed to be suggesting, without taking responsibility for it, that he would understand if Deepti called the whole thing off, the terrible irony is that Deepti did not do exactly that—because if she had, the chances are she would be alive today.

Still, whatever Kevin's motives and intentions—whether he wanted Deepti in the fold because of her saved $100,000, or because he was succumbing to a growing attraction to her—by early July there was yet another factor in the decision: the prospect that Deepti might be eligible for a $10,000-a-month "relocation assistance grant" from St. Luke to help her start a new practice.

Later—much later, after Deepti was dead, and Kevin was on trial for her murder—the exact circumstances surrounding this potential source of $120,000, what was to be done with it, and how it affected the arrangements between Deepti and Kevin was shrouded in confusion. Much of the information surrounding the potential grant was never nailed down with precision—such as when it was first discussed, by whom, and why it ultimately wasn't approved. As things turned out, however, the loss of this substantial sum of money was to emerge as one of the most significant bones of contention between Deepti and Kevin in the days just before her murder. Although Kevin denied that he had anything to do with the denial of the grant, the outlines of a case to the contrary are apparent. The money, its loss, and the circumstances of how the two doctors tried to get it, suggest that Kevin may have had a good reason to see Deepti dead.

As envisioned by the hospital, the $10,000-a-month grant, federal money, was to be used to recruit new physicians interested in starting a medical practice in the hospital's service area. There were several conditions that had to be met for eligibility, however: the recruited doctor had to be less than a year out of residency; there had to be a need for the doctor's specialty in the hospital's service area; and the eligible doctor could not have a previously established practice in the area.

Since she had completed her residency at County—USC Medical Center in September of 1998, Deepti easily met the first criterion. The other two, however, were more problematic. First, there was an abundance of pediatricians in the St. Luke area, so it wasn't as if a relocation grant was needed to bring in one more; and second, Deepti had at least some patients from her four months at Eaton Canyon, and if the partnership with Kevin came off, she would have access to many more. Still, both Deepti and Kevin believed that she might be eligible for the grant, which would have the effect, at least in Kevin's mind, of insuring that the partnership was financially feasible.

Deepti, for her part, apparently came to believe that with Kevin in her corner, the grant was a done deal. She believed that Kevin had so much pull at St. Luke the grant was in the bag, and said as much to both Vijay and Anil Sharma, the astrologer.

Even Kevin thought that obtaining the grant would be no problem, at least initially.

"She would qualify for that, just barely," Kevin told the detectives on the night of his arrest. "They would kind of have to budget a little bit, but because I had worked there for a long time and they knew we were going to work together, they were going to grant her that, and that money would go into the practice in general. So that would pretty much float the practice for the first year. They guaranteed us a year, and it was, I think, $10,000 a month."

This statement by Kevin is one of the most intriguing he made during the entire case, both for what it suggests, and also for how its significance slipped by the detectives, and later, Kevin's prosecutors. For one thing, it appears to have initially been inaccurately transcribed. The words "budget a little bit" were actually "fudge it a little bit," at least according to the transcript later used at Kevin's trial; and Kevin agreed that that was what he'd actually said.

There's a significant difference between "budgeting" something and "fudging" it, as anyone can see. What Kevin seemed to be suggesting on the night of his arrest, at a time when he was under tremendous stress, was that his associates at the hospital might be willing to bend the rules to see that Deepti got the grant—"because I had worked there a long time, and they knew we were going to work together."

Although accounts were later contradictory, it appears likely that Kevin and Deepti first learned about the possible grant sometime in late June of 1999 as they were working out the initial details of the proposed partnership, although Kevin later insisted that the first he'd heard of the prospective grant was in mid-August, and even then from Deepti and Marvin Cooper.

"I hadn't known about that before," Kevin said. "That was the first time I had heard it mentioned . . . this is all what was told to me. I had never heard of it before." Deepti, Kevin said, asked him to use his influence at the hospital to get the grant for her.

"She asked me if, because the person that would apparently know about it at St. Luke would be the head of St. Luke, and I knew him," Kevin said, referring to the hospital's Chief Executive Officer Ken Rivers. "And she asked me if I would introduce him to her and get her into a meeting with him, and then she could pretty much do the rest, she said."

Here Kevin clearly was not telling the whole truth, because even Heidi said that that possible grant was part of Kevin's business calculations in July, before he'd ever met with Marvin Cooper. Heidi said that initially Kevin had looked into the grant's availability for Deepti, only to learn that it wasn't available, which was one reason why he was cool toward the partnership that month. It was later that he learned it might be available after all, and this apparently restimulated his interest in going into business with Deepti.

Marvin Cooper, for his part, agreed that he had been the person who first raised the possibility of Deepti's eligibility for this bonanza. Since Cooper first met with the Guptas in late June, it's possible that the potential grant was initially brought up at that time. Cooper later acknowledged that he was familiar with the grant and its process, both at St. Luke and at other hospitals.

Ken Rivers later said that he and Kevin "had a couple of conversations" about the proposed grant for Deepti. Just when the first of these conversations occurred was never made clear, but it certainly had to have taken place before August 8, which was Kevin's last day of work at Eaton Canyon. "One of the conversations," Rivers said later, "he . . .

wanted to move out on his own. He was with a group. He wanted to move out on his own and wanted to know if the hospital was willing to talk to him about bringing in a potential partner." At least initially, Kevin did not mention that Deepti was the potential partner he had in mind, according to Rivers.

But Kevin clearly had his eye on the grant as one way of making the partnership work, both at first, and then later in the summer as the events surrounding the formation of the partnership were to reach a climax. As eventually proposed in a partnership formation draft agreement written by Marvin Cooper, Deepti was to agree to turn over $3,000 of the $10,000 a month she would receive from the grant as a contribution to the partnership. In addition, Deepti was to agree to assign to Kevin the first $2,000 of each month's clinic profit to Kevin's side of the ledger. Thus, exactly half of the desired $10,000-a-month grant would accrue to Kevin's advantage, and $2,000 a month in cash. This was probably what Kevin meant when he had told both accountants, Sorrell and Cooper, that his contribution to the start-up would be "negotiated." But seen from another angle, the division of the grant that "would have to be fudged" to be obtained has a striking resemblance to a sort of finder's fee for Kevin.

Later, the timing of this maneuvering over the possible grant would be cited by prosecutors of Kevin's profligate manipulation of Deepti—that, in fact, he had held out the pot of gold represented by the grant as part of his campaign to get her into bed, and that he knew and always had known that Deepti would never get the grant. It was all some sort of come-on, they maintained. Indeed, prosecutors tried to show that Kevin even used his influence with Rivers to make sure that Deepti *didn't* get the grant, once he'd had his way with her, because he didn't want Deepti around as a competing pediatrician.

In retrospect, this notion seems to be another simplification of Kevin's motives, because the facts were to show that Kevin continued trying to get Deepti the grant even into the days just prior to her murder. And while Kevin's prosecutors insisted that he did this only to keep her in his bed, the truth seems to be rather more convoluted: again, Kevin just couldn't tell someone something they didn't want to hear.

In spite of her pressuring Kevin to get busy on their proposed partnership, Deepti took her own vacation in July.
She, Vijay and their daughter flew to Europe on July 8, the
same day she'd blown up at Kevin for his waterskiing trip.
Vijay was attending a conference there, and they'd decided
to tour some of the European countries. On this trip, Vijay
and Deepti stopped in Portugal, where Deepti bought a
present for Kevin's seven-year-old daughter from his second marriage: a religious icon, a statue of Our Lady of
Fatima.

The Guptas returned from Europe on July 24, and the
effort to get the partnership together resumed.

By this time Kevin had received a fax of a proposed
partnership agreement from Marvin Cooper, which Cooper
said he'd sent on July 15, while Deepti and Vijay were out
of the country. The proposed agreement identified the partnership name as "Anderson—Gupta Pediatrics," and gave
Deepti a full fifty percent of the ownership of the business.
It does not appear that Kevin responded to this proposed
agreement; apparently Kevin had decided to wait until
Deepti had returned before doing anything about it.

At the same time, according to Kevin, he was considering some other options. He'd already told Dr. Ng that his
last day at Eaton Canyon would be August 18. He had
desultory conversations with several other Pasadena-area
doctors about leasing space in their clinics, but hadn't found
anything that seemed suitable. Deepti hadn't been im-
pressed with those locations. To Kevin, she seemed adamant about locating in the Thatcher Building.

Sometime in July, while Deepti was still in Europe,
Kevin and his step-father had dinner with Dr. Rodney Richard, another Pasadena pediatrician. Dr. Richard was think-

ing about retiring, and mentioned this to both Kevin and his step-father, and as a result, a seed was planted in Kevin's mind, and even more firmly, in Heidi's.

By this time, Heidi was absolutely convinced that a partnership between Kevin and Deepti would be a disaster. Deepti's determination to pull the clinic into existence by sheer willpower appalled Heidi. She envisioned a future in which Deepti would be calling Kevin at home every night, either to "leech" emotional support, or to berate him for some oversight. Heidi saw the whole casual lifestyle she had worked so hard to create with Kevin—the camping trips, the expeditions to the Colorado River, the easy-going schedules that gave both a significant amount of leisure time—all going up in smoke as the ambitious Deepti took over. But Kevin was reluctant to terminate the discussions with Deepti.

When the Guptas returned from Europe, the involvement between Kevin and Deepti seemed to get worse, at least in Heidi's eyes. Harsh words were exchanged between Kevin and Heidi as he began spending even more time with Deepti, either on the telephone or in business meetings that now excluded Heidi.

"What is it with her?" Heidi demanded of Kevin. "Are you attracted to her, that you have to work with her so much?" Heidi told Kevin that Deepti had a romantic interest in him, and again Kevin denied it. He told his wife that Deepti's intentions were strictly professional. But he wasn't telling the whole truth, at least about himself.

"Over the summer," Kevin said later, speaking of Deepti, "we spent a lot of time together. We had a lot of meetings. We started getting closer. We started sharing some confidences in late July. When we would meet, instead of shaking hands, we would hug before we parted. By the time August rolled around, we were . . . becoming romantically involved. And by that time, by mid-August or so, we were pretty involved with each other."

Kevin was asked whether any of the "confidences" he shared with Deepti involved each other's spouse.

"She told me on several occasions different things," he said. "She said there was really not a lot of love in their relationship, that he was abusive to her during her first pregnancy, that she was basically sticking it out . . . because of a family commitment. Because they had an arranged marriage, a lot of family issues going on there. It was affecting her sister, who was going to be married, and she [Deepti] just didn't seem very happy."[5]

And the out-of-marriage talk was reciprocated by him, Kevin admitted.

"I told her about my relationship. I told her mainly about problems we were having in the relationship. With Heidi. Myself and Heidi. I told her some instances where I had been hurt—things like that. Both of us shared, I think, a lot of it was sharing hurt, and sharing painful things that we had happen in our relationships."

Kevin claimed that it was Deepti who first suggested the idea of getting romantically involved. It was while they were discussing Heidi, in late July, after the Guptas had come back from Europe.

"She asked me, 'Why don't you want to be with me? Because, when we have our business set up we're going to have our own time to be by ourselves in our business. When you are at home, that's one thing. When you are at our business, that's our time.' She had an idea that being romantically involved at work would be an okay thing. I said I wasn't a hundred percent behind that. I thought we could keep business and personal stuff separate. I was definitely a fan for that."

But, Kevin continued, "I was torn. I was becoming attracted to her and . . . I didn't totally reject the idea, but I didn't feel comfortable with it."

Viewed from a distance, this description of the events seems forced. What Kevin was really saying was that the

---

[5]Deepti's sister was actually married in December of 1998, so this appears to be a conflation of events on Kevin's part, possibly to make himself look better.

love affair was all Deepti's idea, and that he was the one seduced, not the seducer. "I wasn't a hundred percent behind that." In fact, putting the responsibility for their affair on the person who was dead had all the earmarks of blaming the victim—quite easy to do when the person who has been killed is no longer around to offer a contradiction.

But in truth, trying to get a fix on Deepti's personality, particularly at this stage, is very difficult because of so many seeming contradictions in her behavior. The confusion would later be heightened by Kevin's prosecutors, who attempted to portray Deepti as an innocent victim of Kevin's manipulations, an unworldly, naive, easily led and starstruck protégée who was lured into Kevin's carnal ambitions, and who later was murdered when she became "inconvenient," as the prosecutors would put it.

The trouble with the portrait, however, is that it is largely inconsistent with other people's descriptions of Deepti Gupta as smart, ambitious, determined and demanding. There is likewise a suggestion that Deepti knowingly became involved in a physical relationship with Kevin to tie him closer to her as a means to make use of his contacts in the medical community, to get the partnership into being, and to help make sure that the grant was awarded. All of this seems to have taken place without Vijay suspecting it. He later said he had no idea that Deepti was having an affair with Kevin until after she was dead.

There is at least one witness who sheds some light on Deepti's attitudes during this period, however, and that is the Vedic astrologer, Anil Sharma.

In an interview with the sheriff's detectives a little more than a week after Deepti was killed, Sharma left the distinct impression that Deepti had fallen in love with Kevin.

At first, Sharma said, Deepti saw Kevin as someone who could help her realize her ambitions.

"This was business," Sharma said. "As far as I know, there was nothing else, except business, at that time. And after some time, she's calling me maybe every three, four days—or maybe once a week. And she started sounding desperate, saying that . . . Kevin is pulling out."

As time went by in the summer of 1999, Sharma said, he noticed that Deepti stopped referring to Kevin as Dr. Anderson and began referring to him as Kevin. Sharma thought this was significant. "I could sense this change in her," he said.

"And then," he continued, "after a certain point in time, she started hinting that this person is interested in her. And he's a very nice guy. And 'We get along very well.' " According to Sharma, Kevin plied Deepti with stories about being unhappy in his marriage to Heidi.

Deepti told Sharma, "He [Kevin] has a lot of problems at home. And we can talk well. We can talk to each other . . . he's unhappy. He has one ex-wife with one child. And that's one case. And now, this woman [Heidi] is not a good woman. She hooked him for money. And he doesn't love her. [But] when he hinted at leaving her, she told him, 'I'll clean you out. I'll see that you are on the street.' And he said, 'I can't leave her because my financial and my professional reputation will be finished.' He's very scared of his wife."

As time went on, Sharma realized that Deepti was growing infatuated with Kevin—caught up on the roller coaster of her own ambitions for the clinic, her realization that a man she saw as a powerful and influential contact was interested in her, and Kevin's woeful tales of not being appreciated at home. And here the cultural gap asserted itself once more: a woman raised in the United States would be more likely to see this picture as a possible recipe for disaster, not to mention a likely lie, but Deepti was not cynical, or at least not cynical enough.

Every time Deepti talked about Kevin, she praised him, Sharma said, even when Kevin seemed to be pulling back from the partnership. It was almost as if Kevin kept teasing her with the prospects of success, only to pull back and play hard to get. She asked Sharma to perform some prayers for her, or give her some mantras to chant, to help make sure that she could continue to be with Kevin. It wasn't too long before Sharma realized that this was more than just business.

"And that was very ambiguous. 'I want to be with this person' was very ambiguous. [But] after some time she started hinting to me that he is pressuring her for a physical relationship." Deepti told Sharma that she wasn't interested, but even Sharma could see that she was wavering. Still, Sharma was quite convinced that Deepti never would have initiated any physical affair.

"I have a feeling," he said, "that he started hitting on her. Because I know Deepti personally. She wouldn't go after a man. Or she wouldn't just let somebody—she's not a loose moral person. Indians are very difficult. Indians are very conservative on sex with a man. And even with the husband, they are very conservative on what kind of sex act they do. It's very traditional."

And then, around the middle of August, Sharma said, there was a period of silence from Deepti. Suddenly there were no more calls.

He guessed that Deepti had slept with Kevin, and was avoiding Sharma so she wouldn't have to admit it.

12

In early August, Kevin informed Eaton Canyon that he'd reconsidered his departure date. Instead of August 18, he said, he intended to pack it in on August 8. As he put it later, he was getting a lot of pressure from Deepti to get moving on the clinic, and he decided to leave early so he could get the arrangements together. Dr. Ng was in Taiwan visiting a sick relative. He had to come back early to cover for Kevin. He wasn't happy about it, either.

As for Kevin and Deepti, the major sticking point was still the office lease. Kevin didn't like the Thatcher Building. He kept insisting to Deepti that they could find some place that was less expensive. But Deepti found something wrong with every place they looked. Kevin continued to worry that the new partnership wasn't going to be financially feasible—at least for him. The $4,500-a-month rent at the Thatcher Building was giving him a case of nerves. There was no guarantee that *any* of the Eaton Canyon patients would follow him to a new clinic, let alone enough to afford the rental payments.

Another matter to be resolved was the partnership agreement. On August 8, Deepti faxed a handwritten set of points to Marvin Cooper, representing things she wanted to see in the agreement. By this point, the opening for the new clinic had been pushed back to October; there simply wasn't enough time to get everything done for a September 7 inaugural. Deepti wasn't happy, but there wasn't much choice.

As outlined by Deepti, the partnership with Kevin was to divide all income received from HMOs fifty-fifty; that Kevin would bring in somewhere between 1,500 and 2,000 patients to the partnership, and that any new patients would be assigned to Deepti as the primary care physician; that they would split all other revenues, half and half, with the exception of a bonus of $2,000 monthly to accrue to Kevin, for his larger patient base. All decisions would be made by both partners equally. Each partner was to contribute $17,000 to the start-up by September 10, and an additional $5,000 each on October 10 and again on November 10.

Curiously, the potential grant from St. Luke was apparently not mentioned specifically in Deepti's notes to Cooper; but Vijay—who later said that he had been fully informed by Deepti on all elements of the partnership as it was being negotiated—said that Deepti had agreed to devote the entire $10,000 grant amount to the business when it was approved. To this point, at least, no one seemed to have much doubt that Deepti would get the grant.

The week between August 12 and August 20 seems to have been a critical one as far as Deepti and Kevin were concerned.

On August 12, Kevin sent a card to Deepti. The card, with a representation of the cartoon character Tweetie on the front, was dated August 12th and labeled with the printed legend, "I tawt of you today."

Inside, Kevin wrote to Deepti:

Dear Deepti,
    I found this red pen in the bag that [Deepti's gift for Kevin's daughter] *was in, which by the way was as beautiful as it is delicate. What a day. Things were going so wrong so fast I felt it was all spinning out of control. Thank God you are around. All I could think of was calling you. Of course, hugging you and feeling you pressed up against me brings a blanket of calmness over me. That is until my respirations start quickening and, well, never mind. Just thinking of kissing you leaves a lump in my throat.*

In this note, Kevin went on to talk once more about the partnership. He was still worried about the Thatcher lease,

he said, and "now time is running out for a good alternative." But, Kevin said, he was having a hard time concen-
trating on what needed to be done. The note continued:

*Even my thoughts are scattered. While I write of this,
my mind darts back and forth to holding you; the lease;
kissing you and feeling your lips, mouth; opening in October; feeling the curves of your back, the smell of your
hair; our office and patients; of feeling your leg. See
what I mean? I'll have a letter to give you before I leave
town so stay tuned.*

Love, Kevin

The context of the note inside the card seems to indicate
that as of August 12, at least, Kevin was still committed to
going ahead with the partnership. But what is more striking
is the explicit tone. In some ways, it suggests that Kevin
and Deepti had already been intimate by then. In fact,
Kevin later gave two different answers to the question of
when he first had sex with Deepti—before August 12, as
well as after. He also said he couldn't recall exactly when
it happened the first time.

Next, it appears that at some point in that same week,
Kevin decided that the partnership with Deepti simply
wasn't going to work. He told Heidi he wasn't going to go
through with the deal with Deepti because it wasn't financially feasible. Just why it was suddenly no longer financially feasible was never made clear. At the same time,
Kevin later said, he also told Heidi that she'd been right
all along, that Deepti *did* have romantic intentions toward
him.

Heidi's reaction was predictable. "It was a classic 'I told
you so,'" Kevin recalled. "'You see? I told you. If you're
romantically involved with someone, you can't go into
business with them.' She was absolutely adamant that this
is absolute proof that I should not be going into business
with her at all. And she was upset. But she was very de-

termined on her point, that this is evidence that there was no reason to go to work with this woman."

Heidi believed that this conversation with Kevin took place on Saturday, August 14—two days after Kevin sent the card to Deepti. Then, a day or so after having this conversation with Heidi—say, Monday, August 16—Kevin met Deepti for lunch. He told her that he couldn't go into partnership with her because Heidi was against it.

"At that point I told her, 'You know, we have these personal feelings developing. It is probably not a good idea that we go into business together. My wife is against it at this point. And I don't think it is going to work out."

Deepti, according to Kevin, began to cry. "She said, 'But you said you were going to be working with me. You told me we were going to start a business together.' She said, 'We have to find a way to make this work. We can make this work somehow.'

"She said she cared about me a lot," Kevin added. "She said she felt she loved me just as much as I loved her, and she wanted—she didn't want us to—end it this way. Again I was torn."

This episode has to be taken with some skepticism, given Kevin's demonstrated tendency to blame Deepti for the affair. Again, it is one of those statements that cannot be contradicted, since the only other witness is dead. Moreover, it seems like it might be one way of putting a gloss on what the timing of the other events suggests: that Kevin had inveigled Deepti into bed, and then pulled the trapdoor on the relationship by confessing to Heidi.

A day or so after Kevin told Deepti they wouldn't be going into business together, Deepti was back at the Thatcher Building. This time the leasing agent, Tracy Thomas, showed Deepti space suitable for a single practitioner. Thomas faxed a copy of the sole practitioner proposal to Deepti on Thursday, August 19. In the light of circumstances, this was a curious action.

For one thing, even though she'd just lost her prospective rain-making partner, Kevin, here was Deepti signing a lease for herself at the expensive Thatcher doctors' digs. Where did Deepti intend to get the patients to fill her appointment books and examining rooms? The most likely answer is that at this point Deepti thought that she was going to obtain the St. Luke relocation grant of $10,000 a month. That was, after all, the true purpose of the grant—to help doctors like Deepti move into a community and establish a practice that would grow over time. One distinct possibility is that Kevin may have told Deepti that even though they wouldn't be going into business together, he would still use his influence with Rivers to make sure she got the grant.

But on the same day, or perhaps the following day, Deepti invited Kevin to have lunch at the Glendale home she shared with Vijay, who, of course, was at UCLA at the time. Apparently Kevin now told her that they might be able to work together after all. Just what had changed, if anything, wasn't made clear later, and no one ever sorted this question out.

"She was very, very happy again," Kevin said. "Because now it looked like we would be able to work together." The nanny took Deepti's daughter to the park, and she was alone with Kevin in the house. Deepti prepared a traditional Indian meal—to celebrate, it appears, Kevin's renewed agreement to the partnership.

What, if anything, is the significance of this apparent reversal by Kevin? After having told Heidi that Deepti was interested in him in a romantic way, after telling Deepti they ought to go their separate ways, suddenly Kevin wanted back in. Why? One possibility is that Deepti offered to sweeten the deal by cutting Kevin in on the action—to share some of the grant proceeds. It's worth noting that in the following week, the business planner Marvin Cooper, acting on Deepti's instructions, added clauses to the practice formation agreement, relating to the proposed grant, which awarded Kevin the equivalent of half of the grant proceeds, or $5,000 a month.

Following this celebratory meal, Deepti invited him upstairs to her bedroom "to show me a particular robe," Kevin
said later. "We started kissing and hugging, fondling, and
one thing led to the next."

Afterward, Deepti told him that she was using birth control, Kevin said later, so he didn't need to be concerned
that she would get pregnant.

And here is another conundrum: Vijay was later to say
that he and Deepti had been trying to have a child for the
four or five months prior to the month before Deepti's
death, and that they had only resumed using birth control
when the "cycle" (of auspicious fertility presumably) was
over. The cycle apparently ended around October 1, which
meant that during the period May through September, the
Guptas were not using birth control, according to Vijay.
Why, then, did Kevin say that Deepti was using birth control that day in August?

Clearly, someone was not telling the truth: either Deepti
never told Kevin she was using birth control, in which case
Kevin was being quite cavalier about the risks both were
taking, and later lying about it; or Vijay, for some reason,
was wrong; or third, Deepti wasn't telling the truth to
Kevin, and in fact, *wanted* to get pregnant.

Kevin would later say he and Deepti had sex three times
before the final, fatal encounter—once in mid-August,
likely August 20; again in mid-September, around the 15th;
and again in October, around the 14th. Each of these dates
were such that Deepti was likely to get pregnant through
having unprotected intercourse. And eventually she did.

13

On August 21, Kevin and Heidi departed to Washington, D.C., where Kevin had enrolled at a Howard University refresher course for his forthcoming new try at the certification boards for pediatrics. According to his own account of the events, Kevin did not tell Heidi about the interlude at the Gupta house the day before. Indeed, it seems as though he did not even inform her that he had told Deepti that the practice was on again.

Back in Washington, however, Heidi urged Kevin to tell several long-time Anderson friends about Deepti, and her supposed attraction to him. All these friends sided with Heidi: it would be madness to go into business with someone who was romantically attracted to you. Heidi thought Kevin was finally persuaded. He told her that when they got back, he'd make sure that Deepti understood that it was the end, really and truly.

While Kevin and Heidi were in Washington, the business planner Marvin Cooper was at work on the draft of the partnership agreement. Cooper later said that he had met with Deepti and Kevin, together, on August 23. That could not be accurate, however, since Kevin was in Washington on that date. The most likely date for this meeting at Cooper's office would have been August 20 or possibly the 21st.

In this meeting, Cooper said, he formed the impression from both Kevin and Deepti that Deepti would receive the $10,000-a-month relocation grant from St. Luke. In the agreement the three discussed that day, a paragraph was included that required Deepti to put $3,000 from the grant into the practice every month. This was to "help cover some additional monies on the practice, and the fact that Dr. Anderson had a greater proportion of the patients," Cooper

said. In addition, the same paragraph called for the first
$2,000 in anticipated monthly profit to go to Kevin in
months four through twelve of the grant period. As already
noted, this split effectively granted Kevin half of the St.
Luke grant, assuming it was awarded. For his part, Kevin
later claimed this was the first time he'd heard about the
relocation grant, which does not appear to be true, given
Ken Rivers' recollection that Kevin had first raised the issue with him while Kevin was still at Eaton Canyon.

While they were at his office, Cooper formed the impression that both Deepti and Kevin were excited about
going into business together. As they were leaving, Cooper
noticed that Kevin had left something behind. He followed
them out into the corridor leading to the elevators, and "I
saw them in an embrace. I didn't know if that was happiness over deciding to have gone into practice, but it's what
I assumed it was."

Kevin and Heidi returned from Washington on August 25,
and at this juncture, another series of events occurred that
would be shrouded in inexactitude.

Despite his apparent assurance to Heidi that he would
end the proposed partnership with Deepti, on August 26
Kevin went with Deepti back to the Thatcher Building. On
this day, real estate agent Tracy Thomas made yet another
lease proposal, this one for Deepti and Kevin together,
again. The lease was structured so that the rental costs
would be lower on the front end, higher in the final year
of the five-year agreement. The idea, Thomas said, was to
lower the partnership's start-up costs. Apparently Kevin
was still having doubts about the financial feasibility of the
deal.

Either that same day, or the next—Friday, August 27—
Kevin and Deepti met with St. Luke's Ken Rivers on the
possible relocation grant. Rivers' later recollection of the
meeting was hazy as to exactly when it took place, but
given that on Saturday, Kevin went to Lake Powell on the

Arizona–Utah border for more than a week, it could only have taken place on the 26th or the 27th.

Kevin and Deepti explained to Rivers that they intended to start a new practice, and wanted to know how to go about arranging for the relocation grant for Deepti. Rivers was cordial, and at least in Kevin and Deepti's view, encouraging. He asked a few questions about Deepti's training and qualifications, and when they would like the grant to begin. Near the end of the meeting, which Rivers thought had taken less than fifteen minutes, he brought in one of his associates, business director Linda Evans. Rivers turned Deepti over to Evans to get further details to start the grant process, and it was at this point—or perhaps later—that something went seriously awry. Just what that was, however, remains unknown to this day.

But in the wake of the meeting at Rivers' office, Kevin now signed the Thatcher lease proposal, bringing the partnership its first tangible step toward actual formation.

The following day, Kevin and Heidi left to go waterskiing for more than a week at Lake Powell, and thus, Kevin was apparently out of contact with either Deepti or Rivers for that period of time.

When he returned to La Verne on Sunday, September 5, Kevin received a call from Deepti. She was upset. She hadn't gotten the St. Luke grant.

"What happened?" Deepti asked Kevin. "What did you do? Why am I not getting the relocation allowance?"

Kevin said he had no idea why Deepti hadn't gotten the grant. He asked if Deepti had asked Ken Rivers about it.

"They said I don't qualify for it," Deepti told him.

When Kevin told Deepti that maybe she *didn't* qualify for the grant, Deepti's reply was tart: "You have to find another way to finance your practice," she said.

This was clear evidence that the grant was to be part of Kevin's contribution to the financing of the new clinic, and despite its obvious importance to the prosecution of Kevin Anderson for Deepti Gupta's murder, this facet of the events that led up to her death was never adequately investigated by the sheriff's detectives in the weeks following her death; nor was it adequately developed by Kevin's prosecutors. The issues raised by the grant would come directly to Kevin's possible motive for wanting Deepti dead. Prosecutors were to contend that they were "stonewalled" by hospital authorities on information about the grant, and so were left unable to bring it into effective play at Kevin's trial. But if Deepti had eventually threatened to sue Kevin and the hospital over the grant's denial, Kevin may have come to believe that he was in some serious legal jeopardy.

And while detectives soon interviewed Rivers, they failed to appreciate the significance of what he told them, at least at the time of their interview. Nor does it appear that anyone ever interviewed Linda Evans, the Rivers associate who was actually responsible for determining Deepti's eligibility, and who, according to Rivers, actually notified Deepti on either August 31 or September 1 that she wouldn't be getting the grant. That, of course, was when Kevin was out of town, waterskiing at Lake Powell.

In his interview with the detectives—and later at Kevin's trial—Rivers said that Deepti didn't meet the qualifications for the grant because she was already in practice in the hospital's service area.

Deepti did not qualify for the relocation assistance, Rivers said, "primarily based on the reason [that] she was already practicing in the medical office building adjacent to the hospital. So obviously she was in our primary service area." That meant she didn't need to be relocated.

But of course that wasn't true at all. Deepti hadn't been practicing at "the medical office building adjacent to the hospital," Eaton Canyon, for months—not since she had quit Dr. Ng's clinic on April 10, 1999. Nor did she have any other office in the hospital's primary service area at the time she was seeking the grant, that is, in August of 1999. On paper—and always assuming that the hospital had a need for another pediatrician, an arguable proposition— Deepti could have qualified for the grant.

Rivers later said the proposed grant was sent to the hospital's corporate parent for legal review, and that the legal people had found Deepti ineligible for the relocation assistance on the grounds that she "not only worked in the area, but lived in the area." Despite this indication that there was a paper trail on the grant request, none was ever recovered by the detectives or the prosecutors of Kevin.[6]

Deepti was convinced that Kevin had influenced Rivers *not* to give her the grant.

"You had something to do with this," she told Kevin. "You had something to do with this, didn't you?"

"What do you mean, *I* had something to do with it?" Kevin asked. "What could I do to prevent you from getting this relocation allowance? It had nothing to do with me."

At this point, Kevin now told Deepti "once and for all, finally, that I would not be going into practice with her.

"She was furious," Kevin added. "She really felt like I had been stringing her along. She felt like I had backstabbed her as far as saying I would go into practice with her and trying to be there for her and setting things up for her, then all of a sudden I back out. And she just—she was really upset.

"I told her, 'Look. We've gone back and forth through this. I told you my reasons. I don't think it is financially feasible. I don't like the options of the buildings you are trying to have us go to. And I don't think we can keep this business and personal thing separate anymore. I just think it's too much of a hassle. My wife is not in support of this and that's—that's just the end of it. We just can't do it.' "

But was this the truth—that he had nothing to do with Deepti not getting the grant? In the absence of detailed information from the hospital or its parent, that can't be

----

[6]The author contacted St. Luke Medical Center and its parent company, Tenet Healthcare Systems, Inc., to request information about the proposed grant to Deepti Gupta. A spokesman for the company, Greg Harrison, said that a check of the records had turned up no written records on the grant request.

definitively determined. One possibility is that while he was at Lake Powell, Kevin may have decided once more not to go through with the partnership. Knowing that if Deepti did not receive the grant, the partnership wouldn't be "financially feasible," Kevin may have seen denial of the grant as one way to get out of the deal with Deepti—a way in which he wouldn't have to be the bad guy.

One way to check this would have been to review Kevin's telephone records for the period he and Heidi were at Lake Powell. They returned from the resort area on Sunday, September 5. If a record of a call from Kevin to Rivers had taken place during the preceding week, it seems reasonable to suppose it might have concerned the critical grant. After all, Rivers later said that Deepti was informed by Evans that the grant had been turned down on either "the last day of August or first day of September," when Kevin was at the lake. And when Deepti informed Kevin that the grant hadn't been approved because she'd been deemed to be ineligible, Kevin had responded with the observation that perhaps she wasn't—which suggests that the decision hadn't come as much of a surprise to him.

And if, as Kevin's prosecutors were later to suggest, Kevin used his supposed influence at St. Luke to dangle the lucrative grant as a means of luring Deepti into an intimate relationship, and then later intervened to make sure she *didn't* get the grant, the issue of potential legal liability on the part of the hospital—one of Kevin's main sources of income—for being used as a cat's paw may have constituted a powerful motive for Kevin to get rid of Deepti Gupta. Permanently.

14

Two days later, Tuesday, September 7, would also remain in controversy as events later unfolded. Vijay Gupta had one version of the events, Kevin had another, and Heidi had yet a third.

This was supposed to have been the day Anderson—Gupta Pediatrics opened its doors; instead, it appeared that the whole partnership had gone up in flames of accusations and recriminations. Now there was an attempt to get the partnership back on the rails.

According to Vijay Gupta, this began either Monday evening or Tuesday morning, when Kevin called Deepti to suggest that she and Vijay make a seemingly impromptu visit to the Anderson household in La Verne as part of a campaign to convince Heidi that she had nothing to fear from Deepti working with him.

"She told me that Anderson told her," Vijay said, "that his wife was against them going into practice because she felt uncomfortable and she suspected a romantic interest between the two. So Anderson wants me, my daughter, and my housekeeper to come to his house and show them that we are one, nice family. So she [Deepti] asked me whether I'll be able to do that for her or not."

Vijay told Deepti he'd be happy to do that for her, and on Tuesday afternoon, the Guptas—Vijay, Deepti, their daughter, and the family nanny—set out for La Verne.

The plan was for Vijay to call the Andersons on his cellular telephone when they were in the neighborhood, to make it seem as though the visit was on the spur of the moment.

Kevin answered the phone.

"Oh," Kevin said. "You are in the area? You want to drop by for a few minutes?" Kevin said that was okay with him, but the visit would have to be short, because his mother and step-father were due for dinner.

Kevin greeted them as they arrived, and led them into the house, Vijay said. They all sat in the Anderson family room. Heidi had her back to them. She was cooking something in the kitchen. Vijay was aware of tension in the air. Heidi ignored them, Vijay said.

According to Vijay, Kevin and the Guptas sat in the family room making small talk while Heidi fumed in the kitchen. Suddenly, Vijay said, Heidi erupted. "She basically started shouting at us, that nothing you could say was going to change [her] mind. How can [you] go into practice with somebody you have a romantic interest in? And then she stormed out of the house."

About fifteen minutes later, Vijay said, Heidi returned and apologized for her outburst. Vijay tried to smooth things over.

"I don't know the exact words I used," he said, "but essentially, [I said] that marriage is sacred, and a lot of people find my wife beautiful. It doesn't mean she's going to leave her husband." Then Heidi went upstairs to be by herself, according to Vijay.

Heidi's version of the events was somewhat different from Vijay's, and in somewhat different order. Heidi said Kevin told her the visit from the Guptas stemmed from a call he had received from Vijay on Monday evening. Heidi said Kevin told her that Vijay was upset, and wanted Kevin to come see him right away. Kevin declined, she said, because he'd hurt his back waterskiing, and didn't want to go anywhere.

The next day, Heidi said, Vijay called and said they were coming over.

"They came to the door, and I walked with Kevin up to the door," Heidi said. "And he introduced everybody. We said hello. Dr. Gupta didn't say anything. She didn't speak the entire time she was there. Mr. Gupta spoke the entire time. He did all the talking. She [Deepti] glared at me the entire time. If looks could kill, I wouldn't be here."

As Kevin and the Guptas went into the family room, Heidi said, she went back to the kitchen to continue cooking. After a few minutes Kevin called her into the family room.

"Come on over here, Heidi," Kevin said, "and listen to what Vijay Gupta has to say."

Heidi said she didn't care what anyone had to say, she was never going to be in favor of a partnership between Kevin and Deepti. She recalled what happened next.

"Mr. Gupta went on to talk about how attractive his wife was, and how normal it is in his culture for people to have crushes on other people they work with. 'This is a very normal thing.' And, you know, that I shouldn't be concerned about it at all."

The topic made Heidi see red. She said she told the Guptas and her Kevin that she didn't care what anyone said, she was against the partnership, because it simply wouldn't work to have partners who had romantic interests in each other, besides all the other problems that the proposed partnership was having.

"I felt very harassed," she said later. "I felt like I had been polite. I had said nicely, no, I understand, but I don't agree.

"I felt like Professor Gupta was just harassing. I felt like he didn't take no for an answer. I personally felt he was trying to dump his wife on my husband, and I didn't understand that."

"I said no. And I mean no," Heidi claims to have said. Vijay continued trying to convince her, Heidi contended, but she didn't want to hear it. She told Deepti, "I don't like you. I don't like the things you do. You're just not a nice person." And with that, Heidi admitted, "I stormed out of the house."

When she came back, she apologized, Heidi said, and then went upstairs. The Guptas left shortly thereafter.

Kevin's version of these events was significantly different from either Heidi's or Vijay's. He agreed with Heidi that the visit was prompted by a call from Vijay, but very quickly his account veered off in a completely different direction.

"I guess we had just gotten back from Lake Powell. I was lying in bed. My back was sore, and I got a phone call, and it was Professor Gupta on the phone. He was extremely upset. Apparently he had just been on a trip to Japan or someplace, and had to come back early because Deepti was so upset and distraught. And he was absolutely furious on the phone.

"He said that I had upset his wife—my actions had been absolutely unacceptable. That I had done something to prevent her from getting this [grant] from St. Luke, and he was saying, you need to do something about this. You've got to do something about it. This is absolutely unacceptable.

"I just went, 'You've got to be kidding. I haven't done any of these things that you're saying. I don't know where she's getting this from. We just decided not to work together and she's probably upset about that.'

"He said, 'Well, I have a lawyer and I'm prepared to take action.'

"I said, 'Look, why don't we agree to just talk, talk as two men, and maybe we could meet and see if we could work out our differences here?' " Kevin said he then agreed to meet Vijay in Westwood, near UCLA. It was at that meeting, Kevin maintained, that the idea of the Guptas' coming to visit was first suggested by one or the other of the Guptas. He said the idea was to convince Heidi to allow him to work with Deepti, even if the partnership idea was kaput.

This recollection, however, was wrong. It later appeared that Kevin was conflating two different discussions with Vijay and Deepti. Whether this was because Kevin could no longer recall what actually happened because of the passage of time (by the time he said this, Kevin had been in jail for just over a year), or because he purposely intended to confuse the issue is unclear. But there were two indications that the events didn't happen this way.

First, as Kevin indicated, he and Heidi had just returned from Lake Powell, and he had a sore back. It wasn't very likely that he would get up from his sickbed to drive to Westwood to meet Vijay on the following day, Labor Day, and then see the Guptas again on the day after that. Second, even Kevin said that his meeting in Westwood took place after Vijay had returned from Japan. Vijay's trip to Japan didn't take place until the middle of September, and he did not return until September 22; moreover, he did not return because Deepti was "distraught" over the denial of the St. Luke grant, but because the Gupta nanny had fallen down the stairs and had dislocated her shoulder.

It *was* true that Vijay was upset, however, but for a completely different reason. By September 22, when Vijay hurried back from Japan, Deepti had discovered that Kevin had removed her from his on-call rotation at St. Luke, which had the effect of terminating her floor privileges at the hospital. The story was making the rounds of the hospital that Deepti wasn't going to practice in Pasadena anymore. That brought with it a connotation that perhaps Deepti had failed her "proctoring" by Kevin. Deepti was convinced that Kevin was involved in an attempt to ruin her reputation in the medical community.

But that didn't take place until more than a week after the blow-up at the Andersons' house in La Verne, and not until, by his own later admission, Kevin had again had sex with Deepti Gupta.

15

Based on Kevin's own handwritten notes, it appears that he was convinced that the proposed Anderson–Gupta Pediatrics was definitely a dead issue after the confrontation at the Andersons' house on September 7.

"As of La Verne," his notes read, "no partnership."

These notes would later be cited as semi-cryptic evidence that Kevin had, indeed, tried to put the kibosh on the relocation grant for Deepti. They also suggested that Kevin had made up his mind to sever all connection with his one-time protégée.

In a space next to the "no partnership" note, Kevin wrote: "3 days," accompanied by an arrow pointing to a large zero. The implication from the notes was that Kevin had decided to pull Deepti from his on-call schedule at St. Luke. And although Kevin later said he had no idea that his decision to take Deepti off his on-call contract would mean that Deepti would lose her hospital privileges, that's exactly what the contract required. Next to the zero, Kevin drew another arrow pointing to "St. Luke," an arrow pointing to "Deepti," and the words, "no money." After this there was another arrow, this one pointing to "Linda Evans."

Following that, the notes read: "Told not going to work there anymore."

The fact that these notes were made sometime after the confrontation at the Anderson home, and possibly after he had again had sex with Deepti at the Gupta house in Glendale, seems to indicate Kevin's deep conflict about the illicit relationship. It was almost as if, having partaken of the forbidden fruit [likely while Vijay was in Japan], Kevin was taking steps to prevent his future temptation by trying to make sure Deepti would no longer be around. The easiest way to do that would be to kick her out of the hospital.

Kevin had a different interpretation of his jottings, however, and this had to do with the events at the second meeting with Vijay, the one that took place in Westwood.

As indicated, that meeting took place around September 23 or 24, more than two weeks after the blow-up at the Anderson house. By that time, Kevin had already decided to go into the flourishing practice that the retiring Dr. Rodney Richard was leaving behind—in part with the encouragement of Heidi, a long-time friend of Dr. Richard. Heidi saw this as not only a great opportunity for Kevin, but a way to keep Deepti away from her husband as well.

Kevin later contended that he had been having discussions about taking over Dr. Richard's pediatric practice since sometime in August. Dr. Richard said, however, that these discussions didn't actually begin until sometime after September 7. By the middle of September, Kevin had made an informal agreement to buy Dr. Richard's practice. Kevin didn't immediately realize it, but he was buying into a business that grossed between $12,000 and $19,000 a month from January to August of 1999. If Kevin's patients at Eaton Canyon came to Dr. Richard's establishment, that figure might even double. And with his on-call income of $10,000 a month from St. Luke, as well as a $10,000 yearly retainer he had with an insurance company, Kevin suddenly was looking at the prospect of a potential gross income of over half a million dollars a year.

At this point, however, Kevin received the irate phone call from Vijay Gupta. He agreed to go to Westwood for the meeting.

Vijay met Kevin on the street near an open-air restaurant. They found a table and sat down to talk. After ten or fifteen minutes Deepti joined them.

The Guptas had several complaints. Deepti was still convinced that Kevin had influenced the hospital not to give her the relocation grant. But that wasn't the worst of it. She accused Kevin of ruining her reputation with Pasadena OB/

GYN doctors by telling them that she was no longer going to be working in the area. Those doctors, of course, were prime sources for future pediatric patients. And Kevin had removed her from his on-call rotation at St. Luke, which suggested that Deepti had somehow failed to measure up as a physician.

Kevin, according to Vijay, was apologetic. "He said, 'After how my wife treated you people at my house, I didn't think that you guys ever wanted to work with me, or in this area,' " Vijay said later. "And I just didn't see the logic in it. And I told him, 'Just because your wife is jealous about starting this practice with you doesn't mean she controls whether my wife is going to work.' "

And Deepti was upset because Kevin hadn't provided her with copies of the Eaton Canyon patient logs—the appointment lists that showed the names of all the patients Deepti had seen in her four-month stint at Dr. Ng's clinic. She wanted to notify those patients that she would be starting her own practice.

It isn't clear whether Vijay reiterated his supposed threat to sue Kevin at this meeting, but Kevin certainly believed that was the case. He seems to have been intimidated by this prospect, according to what he later told Heidi.

And here Kevin made yet another fatal mistake: rather than get up from the table and walk away from the whole mess—rather than do what he had done countless times before in other confrontational situations—Kevin made a series of concessions to the Guptas that would have the effect of tying himself even more closely to his former partner, and which would eventually lead to murder.

Later, Kevin would say he wasn't at all worried that the Guptas would have solid grounds to sue him by the time of this meeting in Westwood.

"I was initially very concerned about it," he said. "But I kind of thought about it and there was really not much to it. I didn't really feel like I had done anything wrong."

But that wasn't exactly true. Almost the first thing that

came out of Kevin's mouth after he was arrested was the fact that the Guptas had threatened to sue him; and Kevin later told Heidi that he had made the concessions to the Guptas because of Vijay's threat to sue.

So it seems clear that being the defendant in an expensive civil lawsuit was very much on Kevin's mind that day at the open-air restaurant in Westwood. Given his prior history with the nurses at St. Luke and at Huntington, Kevin may have believed he might be vulnerable to a sexual harassment lawsuit from Deepti—one that would be compounded by allegations that he had pulled strings with Rivers to get the relocation grant first dangled, then denied; that he had told Pasadena area OB/GYNs that Deepti was no longer practicing medicine in the area; that he had effectively "fired" Deepti from the on-call rotation; and that he had withheld the names of patients seen by Deepti while at Eaton Canyon in an effort to prevent her from establishing a private practice.

And if the mess ever did get to court, the chances were exactly 100 percent that at some point along the line, his intimate affair with Deepti was going to come out for the entire world, including Heidi, to know.

In the ensuing discussion, Kevin agreed to reinstate Deepti to his on-call roster, and to find the patient logs for the patients she had seen while at Eaton Canyon. These steps would help Deepti establish her patient base, both sides believed.

And that was the main thing that the Guptas wanted— patients for Deepti. In fact, the entire dance over the now-defunct partnership contained a quid pro quo: while Deepti had the money, she had very few patients; while Kevin had the patients, he had very little money. The grant, if it had been approved—and if Heidi hadn't gotten jealous—would have helped pay for Kevin's financial contribution to the partnership, even if it had to be passed through Deepti's hands first. Once the grant was turned down, Kevin couldn't afford to go into business with Deepti, even if Heidi hadn't objected.

Now here was Deepti demanding that Kevin provide her with a patient base, even though the partnership wasn't going forward, and in the background was this ominous threat of a lawsuit.

"One of the subjects that was covered," Kevin said later, "was the issue with . . . I guess . . . her desire to get her patients from me."

This was a far larger issue than just the patient logs, or the "patient list," as Kevin's prosecutors later kept referring to it. Instead it represented Deepti's determination to build a patient base out of Kevin's own list. In Deepti's mind, Kevin had promised to help her get her practice going, and he wasn't going to back out now—not after all his earlier promises, and likely, not after they had become secret lovers.

At that point, Kevin hit upon a possible solution: he was about to take over Dr. Richard's practice, Kevin pointed out. How would it be if Deepti came to work two days a week at Dr. Richard's clinic? Kevin told the Guptas he was sure he could square this with Dr. Richard, who was nearing retirement.

That way, Deepti could see her own patients at Dr. Richard's clinic while she prepared to open her own office. And, Kevin was sure, Deepti could get some additional patients while she was there.

What about the old Eaton Canyon logs? Kevin assured both Guptas that he would look for them, and as soon as he found them he'd send them over by fax.

Deepti left this meeting feeling that matters had been resolved with Kevin. Kevin had also assured her that he would contact Rivers to see if something might still be worked out with regard to a grant, and in fact, both Kevin and Rivers agreed that further discussions were held on that topic in September, but with no fruitful results.

In the meantime Deepti began writing various insurance companies and HMOs, trying to land contracts that would help her develop her patient base. On September 30, she received yet another lease proposal from the Thatcher Building, this one for a first-floor space that was much smaller than any she had looked at before. She continued pressing Kevin for the patient logs.

By this point Kevin had definitely committed to take over Dr. Richard's practice, which was located in a small clinic building near the boundary of Pasadena and the wealthy town of San Marino. Kevin seems to have been under the impression at first that Dr. Richard intended to "give" him his old practice, but Kevin soon learned that "give" meant "sell." Negotiations were opened for a purchase price based on Richard's $12,000 to $19,000 monthly gross. The price was to be calculated on the number of patients Richard actually had.

When he later was asked about his cryptic notes—"Told not going to work there anymore"—Kevin said that these jottings reflected the substance of some of Deepti's complaints while at the meeting with Vijay in Westwood. He said this was when he first learned that Deepti was angry about being taken off the on-call rotation, that she'd had her floor privileges suspended, and that the OB/GYNs had told her they'd heard she was no longer working at St. Luke. He thought Deepti had learned of these developments through Linda Evans.

But this does not seem likely, since the notes also reflect "as of La Verne, no partnership," which took place September 7, not September 23. Whether the cryptic references refer to Kevin's discussion with Linda Evans about Deepti's termination from the on-call rotation after September 7, and not the discussion in Westwood, is unclear. But since Kevin by his own admission had sex with Deepti in mid-September, it is highly unlikely that he first heard of these complaints from Deepti in Westwood. One who could have clarified the matter was Evans herself, but it appears that the police never interviewed her.

Kevin's first day at Dr. Richard's Children's Clinic was October 6. By that time Deepti had insisted that he sign a written agreement to provide the Eaton Canyon patient logs. She told associates in the Montebello clinic where she worked part-time that Kevin was dragging his feet on getting the logs to her. Kevin signed the agreement on October 8, Deepti's birthday, and told her he would fax the copies of the logs within five days. Later, when prosecutors tried to suggest that Kevin had killed Deepti because she was pressing him for these lists, Kevin told the simple truth: "I had no purpose for her lists. I didn't need her lists. If there were any lists I had of hers I would be more than happy to give them back to her."

This simple fact—that Deepti had a tiny number of patients compared to Kevin's estimated 1,500 to 2,000—seems to have eluded Kevin's prosecutors. Indeed, under the circumstances, Kevin would have been "more than happy," he would have been delighted to give Deepti any of the patient names she could claim as her own. Far from withholding patients' names from Deepti, he was anxiously searching for ways to get her *more* patients, to forestall any potential lawsuit from the Guptas. And it was here, the evidence suggests, that Kevin—and perhaps Deepti—hit on what appears to have been an ingenious, and likely fraudulent plan: to fill out Deepti's patient base from a very handy source: Dr. Richard's files.

This would solve two problems at the same time: first, it would give Deepti her long-sought patient list, while at the same time it would have the effect of lowering Kevin's cost for buying Dr. Richard's practice. Whether Deepti Gupta realized that this scheme involved cheating Dr. Richard isn't clear, but it is likely that she did—just as it also provided Kevin, in the end, a rock-solid motive for making sure she didn't live to tell anyone about it.

16

When Heidi discovered that Kevin had agreed to give Deepti two days a week at Dr. Richard's clinic, she was not happy.

"I was furious," she said later. "But Kevin said to me, 'I can't just cut her loose.' " She said Kevin told her that he hadn't wanted her to know, but that Vijay had threatened to sue him. Kevin said Vijay had accused him of stealing Deepti's patients.

It wasn't so bad, Kevin assured Heidi. It wasn't like he and Deepti would be working together. She'd be at Children's Clinic on Mondays and Tuesdays, he'd be there on Wednesdays through Fridays, so they wouldn't see one another. And anyway, Kevin assured Heidi, the arrangement was temporary. Deepti, he said, had made new arrangements at the Thatcher Building, and would be opening her own, separate office there on December 1. In the meantime, she just needed a place to see patients, and Dr. Richard had agreed to let her use space at his clinic until that happened. Richard would also be at the clinic with Deepti, since he planned to work only on Mondays and Tuesdays until he retired for good in January of 2000. Heidi said she didn't believe this; she was sure Deepti would try to find a way to stay on at the Children's Clinic even after Dr. Richard left.

On the surface of it, this deal with Deepti seemed to be a good one for Richard—Deepti agreed to pay two-fifths of the weekly rental costs at the Children's Clinic, while Kevin, as the buyer of Dr. Richard's practice, was responsible for the other three-fifths. The way Richard saw matters, it appeared that both Deepti and Kevin were energetic young practitioners eager to build their own thriving businesses. He agreed with Kevin that Deepti could see all of the clinic's Medi-Cal patients, and that she would have the right to take those patients with her when she moved on to the Thatcher Building in December.

On Monday, October 11, Deepti put a deposit on the Thatcher Building lease. It appears that she also met Richard around this time to formalize the temporary Monday—Tuesday arrangement.

Richard later admitted that he thought the situation was "a little strange." It didn't make much sense to him that Deepti would be asking her patients to leave one clinic, go to a second, and eventually wind up, less than a month later, at a third. "At the time I didn't question it," he said. "But after the fact it became more unbelievable." Richard wondered just how many patients Deepti could actually have from Eaton Canyon, and guessed that it couldn't have been so many that it was necessary for her to have the space two days a week. He wondered why Kevin was being so accommodating to Deepti.

After working out this arrangement with Richard and Deepti, Kevin said, he and Deepti decided to have another celebratory lunch at the Gupta house in Glendale. "She invited me over to her home," Kevin said, "and we had lunch there, and we had sex there."

Based on the evidence, it appears that this intimate interlude occurred around October 14 or so. And while Kevin may have believed that he was beginning to see some daylight in the labyrinth of problems created by his affair with Deepti, he was wrong—things had just become enormously more complicated, because, unknown to either Deepti or Kevin, Deepti had just gotten pregnant with Kevin's child.

It appears that once again Kevin was assaulted by guilt over his secret affair with Deepti, because shortly after this interlude, he told Heidi that she was right—it did look as if Deepti wouldn't be leaving Richard's clinic by December 1 after all.

"I was mad," Heidi said later. She told Kevin he had to

get Deepti to sign a contract agreeing to leave the Children's Clinic by January 31, 2000. And if Kevin didn't get Deepti to sign this, she said, she'd call Dr. Richard—she'd known him for many years—and complain to him about the arrangement. Kevin agreed to convince Deepti to sign a contract, and Heidi drafted one on the Andersons' home computer to present to Deepti.

In the meantime, however, Deepti had decided to spend a week in India.

Probably the first person to realize that Deepti's relationship with Kevin was taking on some unhealthy characteristics was the Hindu astrologer, Anil Sharma. After a long period of not having contact with Deepti, he began receiving calls from her again. He quickly divined that something had changed.

"In the initial stages," he said, "it was Dr. Anderson. And in October, it started becoming Kevin. Kevin, Kevin, Kevin. Kevin is pulling out. And Kevin is this, and Kevin is that. So I could sense this change in her."

Sharma thought Deepti was depressed. "And it was principally that Kevin gave her [his] word, and he pulled out."

Deepti wasn't specific about what had been going on between them, Sharma said.

"But I could sense that she was holding something back from me. And after a couple of phone calls, she started telling me that she wanted to talk to me as a friend. She wants my advice about what she should do. But she wouldn't tell me what it was."

Sharma suggested that she tell him what was wrong, but Deepti wouldn't be specific. He told her that perhaps she should just forget about going into business with Kevin. He offered to introduce her to other doctors she might work with. But Deepti was insistent on wanting to work with Kevin.

Then, Sharma said, Deepti began asking him for prayers on her behalf. Or maybe she should go to the temple, Deepti said. "Tell me what I can do, and I'll do it to make this happen, because I want to be with this person," Sharma said Deepti told him. Sharma wasn't sure if Deepti meant professionally or personally, because the two seemed to be inextricably mixed in Deepti's conversation. When Sharma asked Deepti point blank if she was intimately involved with Kevin, Deepti wouldn't say. To Sharma, if that hadn't been true, Deepti would have indignantly denied it. Her silence told him everything, Sharma said.

By October, Sharma said, he had the impression that Deepti was desperate. She began calling him with increasing frequency, sometimes two or three times a day. Although it appeared that Deepti had finally resigned herself to the idea that the partnership wasn't going to happen, she still held out hope that she would be able to work with Kevin part-time, Sharma thought. Deepti told Sharma that Kevin would be a good source of referrals for her. Whenever Sharma suggested that Deepti break off with Kevin, she wouldn't hear of it.

Whatever was going on with Deepti, it seems clear that as October unfolded, something akin to a psychological and spiritual crisis was overtaking her. Under these circumstances it isn't surprising that Deepti perhaps felt a strong need to go to India in some sort of effort to reground herself, and perhaps, come to some sort of decision about her future.

Later, at Kevin's trial, neither Vijay nor Sharma was permitted to go into detail about the events that transpired on Deepti's India trip, except to say that Deepti had gone on a religious pilgrimage—apparently to a mountain shrine that required her to walk for hours.

So what was in Deepti's mind as she made her journey? What did she hope would happen? What did she want from Sharma's prayers, and from her "homage," as Vijay later put it, to her ancestral traditions? What was her heart's desire?

Of all the things that were later said and written about

Dr. Deepti Gupta, this was by the far the hardest to fathom. Had she, as the sheriff's detectives later theorized, become "Americanized" in some fashion, enough so that she could have what Kevin at least believed was just a casual fling? In traditional Indian cultural terms, Deepti was dishonoring her "sacred" marriage, and with someone not of her "caste," to boot. Did she really believe that she and Kevin had some permanent future together, with perhaps herself as the new Mrs. Kevin Anderson? Or was she so innocent and naive that she had become the helpless prey of a heartless womanizer? Or was there something else going on inside the mind of Deepti Gupta?

What did Deepti want?

Not even Sharma, perhaps the person most familiar with Deepti's thoughts, was sure. Once, when he was asked if Deepti was thinking of leaving Vijay, Sharma said that for all her education and for all her outspokenness with her husband, Deepti was underneath still a traditional Indian woman. Even if she had had problems in her marriage, Sharma said, Deepti would not have considered a divorce.

"When I told her, time and again," he said, "[to] leave Vijay when there was [verbal] abuse, or whenever she was unhappy, she always said, 'No, in my community people will laugh at me and Vijay if I leave him. And you know, for my daughter it wouldn't be good.' "

But at the same time, Sharma had the feeling that Deepti had occasional thoughts, perhaps fantasies, that Kevin might leave Heidi—which would clear the way for the partnership to finally get off the ground. Kevin later said that Deepti had raised that possibility in her conversations with him, but that he had deflected the topic. But by the time he said this, Kevin was striving as hard as he could to portray Deepti as the one who was chasing *him*.

The unavoidable fact is, it's impossible to know what Deepti really wanted—and in truth, she herself may not have known with certainty, beyond an amorphous yearning for more of Kevin's professional and emotional support. But by the time she returned from India, on Saturday, October 30, there is reason to believe that Deepti certainly knew one thing: she was pregnant.

17

Two days after her return from India, on November 1, Deepti had her first official day of work at Richard's Children's Clinic. According to Sharma, at some point on this day, she called to tell him that she was pregnant.

"Does Vijay know?" Sharma asked.

"No," Deepti said. "I have not told him."

"Are you sure you're pregnant?" he asked.

"I'm a doctor," Deepti said. "So I know."

Deepti told Sharma that she was going to meet with Kevin "today," and tell him that she was pregnant. Sharma asked whether the child was Kevin's, and Deepti did not answer. But the way she did not respond made Sharma believe that Deepti thought the child was Vijay's. Sharma himself wasn't so sure.

Over the previous two weeks, even while she was in India, Deepti had been increasingly obsessing about Kevin, Sharma said later. She'd even called him twice from half the world away. Once she returned from her trip, the calls were to become even more frequent.

"She started calling me too often," Sharma said. "Up to the point where I told her, 'Listen, you are, you know, totally way out of control. I mean, you can forget about Dr. Anderson. And you can forget about Pasadena. Just go some other place and do something else.' " He told Deepti she was becoming "dysfunctional," Sharma said later.

"She says, 'No, I can't forget about Anderson, and I can't forget about [Pasadena].' [She was] completely obsessed with him. But you can never know whether it is obsession of a personal nature or it is [about] work."

Kevin, for his part, had been aware of a growing irritation at Deepti. He began to feel she was simply too demanding, even threatening. He was still worried about a possible lawsuit from the Guptas. He thought he'd done as much as he could for Deepti, but still she wanted more. And how much more could he give, with Heidi suspiciously looking over his shoulder all the time?

Kevin was later asked whether he had all along regarded his affair with Deepti as "just something on the side."

"I only came to that conclusion later," he said. "I thought it was a very good friendship that had turned intimate. And it was only into September and October that I felt it was something on the side. It was a passing infatuation and I hoped it would fizzle out."

Deepti worked the first two days of November at the Children's Clinic. On the first, she signed the agreement Kevin and Heidi demanded. She seemed both depressed and worried, and made several references to the "list" of patients she was supposed to receive from Kevin. At one point, Kevin came into the clinic, and Deepti asked him about "the list." Kevin made a face, as if Deepti were "bugging" him, according to a witness. He then provided her with some of the old Eaton Canyon patient logs. Deepti told him the paper represented "an old list." She wanted a newer one. Kevin said he was "still looking for it," according to the witness.

Significantly, it does not appear that she told Kevin that she was pregnant on either November 1 or 2, in spite of Sharma's recollection that she told him about the pregnancy "one or two days" after she returned from India, and that she was going to tell Kevin "today." Instead, she might not have known for sure that she was pregnant—or at least, sure enough to have discussed it with anyone, including Kevin.

In any event, Deepti telephoned Sharma again on Wednesday night, November 3, and apparently left a message on his answering machine. On Friday morning, November 5, she called Sharma yet again, and left another message. As she was driving her 1999 Mercedes SUV on the freeways and passing from relay to relay, occasionally her voice cut out.

"Good morning, Sharma," Deepti said. "It's 8 o'clock, Friday [actually it was 7:52 A.M.], and I'm only calling to apologize. I had called you Wednesday night, and I probably was troubling you a lot. And . . . I'm trying to make up my mind that I am . . . I'll try not to trouble you anymore with the phone calls, or even need you so bad. Now, once the thing is done, when everything falls into place, then I will [apparently inaudible] and then will come and meet you and thank you, because I . . . feel as if I'm troubling you too much.

"So," she continued, "if this [inaudible] worked out [inaudible], I was supposed to start working at U.S.C. and last moment, Thursday morning, my papers got stuck, and I could not work. So [inaudible] as you say, that I have to suppress my feelings for him and just pretend it is professional [inaudible] really keep troubling you for the same thing. So I want to apologize, and certainly from the depth of my heart. But I will definitely—I promise to call you whenever things fall into place and work out the way I want it to be. Bye-bye."

Later, this message would present a puzzle: what "thing" was to be done, and what was to "fall into place"?

Sharma, for one, wasn't very clear on what "the thing" might have been. He believed that Deepti was referring to her efforts to line up contracts for HMOs as support for her new, independent practice. But Sharma also suggested that it might refer to Deepti's effort to get into a more permanent business arrangement with Kevin; he also thought the reference might be to Deepti's still-flickering desire to get the St. Luke grant as a means of inducing Kevin back into the partnership with her.

Still, the choice of words—"once the thing is done"— suggests that Deepti might have had in mind some difficult or perhaps unpleasant task. One possibility that comes to mind is that Deepti may have been referring to the conversation, that, according to Sharma, she had told him she intended to have with Kevin "today." Certainly the context seems to suggest this: "suppress my feelings for him and pretend that it is just professional."

And if Sharma was right that Deepti knew about the pregnancy on October 31 or November 1, and that she intended to meet with Kevin "today," "the thing" could have referred to her decision to tell Kevin about the pregnancy. Just how being pregnant might help Deepti have "things fall into place" wasn't clear—especially if, as Sharma believed, Deepti thought the child was Vijay's.

On the other hand, there is only Sharma to suggest that Deepti believed the child was Vijay's. It seems a bit more likely that Deepti would have known who the father was than Sharma. And if that were the case, it seems possible that "the thing" was Deepti's intention to tell Kevin that *he* was the father of her child. Just how that would permit "things [to] fall into place" once again depends on just what Deepti wanted—"the way I want it to be."

There remains the possibility that Sharma was simply wrong about when he'd had the pregnancy conversation with Deepti. There is some evidence that suggests that Deepti didn't actually know she was pregnant until November 7 or 8, and so possibly she didn't tell Sharma about this until that time, rather than on the 1st or 2nd.

In that case, whatever "the thing" to be done was, and how it might cause things to "fall into place," will remain a mystery, since, if it wasn't the pregnancy, it must have been something else, at least on November 5. The lack of specificity as to the date Sharma actually had his first pregnancy conversation with Deepti eventually emerged as an important flaw in the county sheriff's investigation of the case, because it turned a potentially critical piece of evidence about Deepti's motive—and therefore, possibly Kevin's—into useless chatter.

In any event, on the following Saturday, November 6, Deepti bought two home pregnancy testing kits at a Glendale drugstore. It appears that she administered the tests to herself either the following evening or on Monday, November 8. And at that point, she called Vijay at UCLA to tell him that she was pregnant.

"She was happy," Vijay said, "and she said she was pregnant. I was—I congratulated her, and I was very happy too."

But in the back of his mind, Vijay wondered how Deepti could be pregnant, since they had been having protected sex during October. Of course, Vijay knew it was still possible to get pregnant, even with protection. He now brought this up. "We actually spoke about it," he said, "and we in fact laughed about it—that this time it was so easy. Last time we had to plan it."

After reporting her news to Vijay, Deepti went to the Children's Clinic to go to work. About noon, Kevin arrived at the clinic. He and Deepti had apparently arranged to have lunch together. Kevin asked Deepti's medical assistant, Lorena Ramirez, if she wanted to come too. But Deepti quickly interrupted him. "No," she said, "we have things to talk about."

Lorena saw Kevin and Deepti leave the clinic together. A few minutes later, she drove past a neighborhood bagel shop. She saw Kevin and Deepti seated together at a table in the window. They appeared to be engaged in conversation.

Later, prosecutors would attempt to suggest that it was at this lunch on November 8 that Deepti first told Kevin that she was pregnant.[7] Kevin was to deny that vehemently, and say that he didn't learn of this fact until two days later, November 10, and even then, he didn't believe it.

The difference was crucial, especially since the prosecution would later claim that Kevin had planned Deepti's murder. By trying to establish that Kevin had almost three full days to mull over the implications of Deepti's pregnancy, the prosecution wanted to demonstrate that the kill-

---

[7]Although, if Sharma was right, Kevin may actually have learned about this as early as November 1.

ing of Deepti was cold and calculated on Kevin's part.

There was some support for this notion, and it again came from Anil Sharma. The astrologer later said that Deepti had in fact called him after her conversation with Kevin. Sharma claimed that Deepti said she had told Kevin she was pregnant. Sharma thought that on the same day that she told Kevin she was pregnant, Kevin told her that *Heidi* was pregnant. In Sharma's mind, this talk had taken place soon after October 31 or November 1, which, if true, would have given Kevin even more time to mull over his options. But the uncertainty over when Sharma in fact first learned of Deepti's pregnancy made this impossible to establish.

"And this was told only to her [Deepti]," Sharma said. "Nobody else knew that his wife was pregnant. Nobody in the hospital knew. None of their common people knew. The [clinic?] nurses and all . . . but nobody knew this. That's what Kevin told her. And I guess he must have told her that, 'I can't leave her,' or something to that effect. Because she was very, very disturbed after telling me this."[8]

Heidi was not pregnant, so if Kevin actually made this statement to Deepti, it seems likely that it represented yet one more attempt on his part to drive Deepti away—to end the affair. According to Sharma, Deepti complained that following this conversation, Kevin refused to have any significant contact with her. "This is where the real friction started," Sharma suggested.

The day after her talk with Kevin on November 8, Deepti became embroiled in a dispute with Dr. Richard. According to Richard's understanding, Deepti, although she was paying two-fifths of the clinic rent, was only supposed to see her own patients, or Kevin's patients, and the Medi-Cal

---

[8]The failure to pin these dates down with accuracy was to severely undercut the prosecution's later attempts to establish premeditated murder on Kevin's part.

patients of both Kevin and Richard. But on November 9, at least, if not on the other days she was at Children's Clinic, Deepti also saw some private insurance patients. Richard noticed that Deepti was seeing one of these patients, and, according to Lorena Ramirez, walked into an examining room to confront Deepti while she was with a patient.

Richard opened a file and showed it to Deepti, according to Ramirez. Richard appeared to be upset that Deepti was seeing one of the private patients from his practice—the one he had agreed to sell to Kevin, based on the patient head count. Deepti looked at Richard and told him that she'd discuss the matter with him later.

It appears that this was just the sort of situation that Richard had feared when Kevin first told him that Deepti would be working on Mondays and Tuesdays at Children's Clinic. He was worried that some of his existing patients would follow Deepti to the Thatcher Building, and thereby reduce the value of what he was selling to Kevin. That was the main reason he wanted Deepti to see only the Medi-Cal patients, or patients who had originally been with either Deepti or Kevin. Kevin had agreed, at least back in October when Kevin first suggested that Deepti come to the clinic.

"I just told him I was concerned," Richard said later, "simply because patients tend to do this when a doctor's in your office, and they leave. And I was concerned because she was there to see the patients that were following him, not my patients. And I was concerned because I was trying to sell my practice, and I wanted to keep my patients. I didn't want them to go away and not have—as a result, have the value of my practice reduced."

But on November 9, Deepti was seeing one of Richard's patients. And while Richard later denied that he "burst" into the examination room to confront Deepti over this violation of the agreement, it appears that some sort of dispute did take place. That night, according to Heidi, Deepti called Kevin to complain about Richard.

Kevin told Heidi that Deepti claimed that Richard had accused her of stealing patients. Kevin spent at least an hour on the telephone with Deepti, according to Heidi, trying to "placate her."

18

Apparently Kevin's soothings had less than the desired effect, because the following day Deepti was still upset about the run-in with Richard. On the way to her part-time job at the clinic in Montebello, Deepti stopped at the Children's Clinic. Obviously angry, she removed all of her business cards from the clinic's front counter and went out to her car without a word to anyone. Between 9:18 A.M. and 9:24 A.M. she made four calls to Anil Sharma, none of which were answered. By the time she reached the Montebello clinic, she was fuming.

"She was very distraught, very disturbed," said Gloria Angelo, who worked for Deepti as a medical assistant in the Montebello clinic. "She wasn't focused on her work that day." When Angelo asked what was bothering her, Deepti said that Richard and Kevin weren't treating her fairly at the Children's Clinic. She said Richard had told her she wasn't allowed to see any of his privately insured patients. She told Angelo that she wasn't being paid appropriately for the work she was doing, and suggested that the clinic was involved in some sort of illegal billing scheme.

When she'd complained to Kevin about Richard's treatment, Kevin hadn't backed her up, Deepti said. She believed that Kevin was backing out of his promises again. What hurt almost as much was that Kevin had made her look bad in front of Dr. Richard.

Although Angelo later said that Deepti left the Montebello clinic between 4 and 4:30 P.M., the record of Deepti's cellular phone calls in the afternoon seems to indicate that she left rather earlier than that, just after noon, in fact. Where she spent the afternoon wasn't clear, later; but around 5 P.M. she was at the Children's Clinic.

Felix Ochoa, office manager at the Children's Clinic,

said he saw Deepti betwen 4:30 and 5:30 that afternoon, sitting at the clinic nurses' station, waiting, Ochoa thought, to see Kevin. Ochoa said hello and asked her how she was. Deepti said she wasn't having a good day.

Sometime around 6 P.M., Kevin saw his final patient for the day, and came out to greet Deepti. Then he and Deepti went in Kevin's car to St. Luke for Kevin to make his pediatric rounds, and to sign some medical charts. Deepti accompanied him, in part to permit Kevin to complete one of the periodic written evaluations that the hospital required Kevin to make as Deepti's "proctor." Kevin marked Deepti's work "satisfactory," the highest rating on the form.

It was obvious that Deepti wanted to clear the air with Kevin about the Richard situation. They decided to have dinner together, and went to a Mexican restaurant on Colorado Boulevard in Pasadena.

At the restaurant, according to Kevin, he asked Deepti what she wanted to talk about.

"I have some concerns," she said.

"Okay," Kevin said.

"But I don't want to talk here," Deepti said—at least, according to Kevin. Deepti said she wanted to talk in a more private place, and suggested that they go to a motel across the street. This is another instance, of course, where the only evidence of who said what comes from Kevin, so it's entirely possible that the suggestion came from him, instead. The same applies to the version of their conversation below. Taken together, the two reports depict Kevin portraying himself as largely the innocent party.

At 7:43 P.M., Kevin checked into the motel, according to the motel's records. Kevin provided his brother's Altadena address and a fake license plate for the sign-in. He didn't want Heidi to find out he'd been at the motel with Deepti, he said later.

First he and Deepti had some small talk, Kevin said. "And we hugged. And we had sex. And afterward, she began to voice her concern that I was—I was not supporting her with Dr. Richard, and that concerned her, and she didn't understand why I wasn't supporting her more.

"And I told her: 'Well, you know, you keep saying this, that I don't support you. But what do you mean, I don't support you with Dr. Richard?'

"She said, 'You took his side when there was a question of me putting my cards and flyers in different patient folders at the clinic, making it look like I was trying to steal patients from there.'

"I said, 'Well, it appeared that way. That's what I was told. That's what I was told by his medical assistants. I mean, I talked to you [the previous night on the telephone]. I thought we settled it. If you want more patients from there, if you want to be able to take some of Dr. Richard's HMO [private] patients, you have to talk to him . . . I know you can see them there, but you've got to remember, Dr. Richard and myself are in negotiations to sell his practice. It is to his advantage to have as many of his patients go to me as possible because that helps the value of his practice. So it is not a matter of not supporting you. It is a matter of doing what is right, right there.' "

If Deepti had a problem with this, Kevin said he told her, she'd have to take it up with Richard. "And she got upset about that," Kevin said. He said Deepti complained that the real reason Kevin didn't want her contacting Richard's patients was that they would go to her, not to Kevin.

According to Kevin, Deepti was growing more and more agitated as the conversation progressed.

"Her voice was raised," Kevin said. "She was shaking her fists. 'No, no. You're trying to take those patients. You're trying to make sure I don't get those patients.' "

Kevin began yelling back. "I said, 'You know, this is ridiculous! You keep saying that I'm taking all these patients from you, [that] I'm not letting you have certain patients. This is ridiculous. I don't care about all that. The number of patients you get is your business, if you want to do that.' "

Deepti brought up the agreement she'd signed with Richard and Kevin, the one that required her to pay two-fifths of the office rent. She accused Kevin of forcing her to sign the contract. Kevin denied forcing her to do anything. Deepti said the contract was all Heidi's idea.

"And then she said, 'You're choosing your wife over me. You're siding with her over me.' "

Kevin said, "Well, she's my wife." The argument grew even more heated, according to Kevin. "And she finally ended up saying, 'Well, you know, I'm going to be the number one woman, not your wife. And I'll go to her house and tell her that I'm pregnant.'

"I said, 'That's ridiculous. That's just insane. I don't want to talk about this anymore. I'm leaving.' "

Kevin said he didn't believe that Deepti was really pregnant. Deepti said that not only was she pregnant, Kevin had to be the father.

"I didn't believe it at all," he said. "I didn't believe a lot of the stuff she was saying at that time. That was just one of the other things I just attributed to a lie . . . I really felt that she was saying that as part of her way to get something from me. And I didn't really put much stock in it, to tell you the truth."

Kevin was sure Deepti wasn't telling the truth. "As far as I knew, we had been using birth control," he said. "She had stated that she did not want to get pregnant again, to me. She had too much trouble with her first pregnancy, and she did not want to go through that experience again. She was getting ready to start a new practice. She had made it very clear in the contract we were going to sign with Marvin Cooper, there was going to be no time for fun or for getting pregnant. So it didn't make sense that she would want to get pregnant. I didn't believe it for a minute, no.

"I didn't believe any of her accusations. I mean, I knew in my own heart, I didn't do anything to stop her from getting the stipend [the relocation grant]. I knew I hadn't purposely withheld her patient list. I knew I didn't backstab her with Dr. Richard. I didn't have bad [faith] as far as commitment concerning the practice over the summer, and I didn't believe she was pregnant.

"I did—I was concerned that she would go to my wife and tell her that we were having an affair and that bothered me a lot."

Just before they left the motel around 8:45 P.M., Kevin told Deepti he didn't want to argue any longer. He left the room and went to his car. Deepti followed him. She got in the passenger seat.

"We didn't really say anything for a minute," Kevin said. "I think the situation was calming down. As we drove back to [Children's Clinic], where she had parked her car, I said, 'You know, we can't leave it like this. We're going to need to talk about this some more.' And she said, 'Fine. That's a good idea.' "

Kevin suggested that they talk again on Saturday, but Deepti didn't want to wait that long. "I want to talk about it tomorrow," she said. Kevin agreed to meet her again the following day.

Later, Kevin's prosecutors were to suggest that he hadn't told the truth, the whole truth and nothing but the truth about this motel encounter with Deepti. They suspected that, having learned that Deepti was pregnant with his child, Kevin realized he was in a lot of trouble. To buy himself some time to figure out what to do, they suggested, Kevin promised Deepti that he would leave Heidi, even if he had no intention of really doing so.

As he drove home to La Verne that night, Kevin received a telephone call from Heidi, wanting to know where he'd been. Kevin lied and said he'd been at the hospital, but that he was on his way home. After the call, Kevin thought more about Deepti's threat to tell Heidi about their affair.

He didn't really believe that Deepti would tell Heidi. "Once I thought about it," he said, "I didn't really think she would do it, because, I mean, obviously if she did that, it would hurt her just as much as it would hurt me. We were both married. It was something that was going to affect both of us. So I didn't really think she would do it. But you never know."

When he got home, Kevin was depressed. He told Heidi that he'd had to tell a mother that her eleven-year-old daughter was dying of liver cancer. Then he said he hoped nothing bad ever happened to Heidi.

"I can't live without you," he told her.

19

Whatever the upshot was of the motel meeting with Kevin, something seems to have changed Deepti's unhappy outlook by the following day. In the morning, she had a telephone conversation with Lorena Ramirez, who wanted to get a check from Deepti for her work at Children's Clinic. Deepti wasn't sure she could get the check, but after a conversation with Marvin Cooper, she called Lorena back to tell her that it would be ready that afternoon. Cooper, meanwhile, confirmed that he would meet with Deepti the following Monday to introduce her to another doctor who might have referrals for her.

Around 1 P.M. Deepti went to St. Luke to check on two babies who were under Kevin's care. She seemed to be in a good mood.

"She was happy and upbeat," said Joan Hammack, who was director of the hospital's birthing center. Hammack's impression was shared by Patricia Cogger, a nurse, who said that Deepti was "talkative and upbeat . . . really bubbly."

Exactly why Deepti would have been "happy and upbeat" at this juncture wasn't clear. Kevin's prosecutors pointed to Deepti's demeanor on the afternoon of November 11 as evidence that Kevin had, in the motel meeting the night before, finally acceded to Deepti's demands to "be the number one woman," that is, he had promised her he would leave Heidi.

But the phrase "number one woman" sounds rather alien when put into Deepti's mouth by Kevin—as if he were trying to depict himself as the powerless prize between two strong-willed, competitive women. Moreover, it's difficult to envision Deepti Gupta, who seems to have been so emotionally dependent on Kevin's good feelings toward her, describing herself as intending to be "the number one woman." This smacks of aggression, rather than the supplication that marked most of Deepti's dealings with Kevin.

Was this, in fact, "the thing" that was to be done—that when it was done, "everything would fall into place"? That Deepti had informed Kevin that she was pregnant with his child, that Kevin had agreed to leave Heidi to finally support Deepti, emotionally and professionally, as she had long wanted? Was this why Deepti was "upbeat . . . really bubbly" the morning after such an intense argument with Kevin? It seems quite likely.

Just before 1 P.M., Kevin paged Deepti to remind her of their plans to meet at the Children's Clinic later that afternoon to continue their discussion. After this, Kevin went home to La Verne. At some point in the early afternoon, he stowed his stargazing telescope in his Toyota 4Runner, along with its tripod. Then he took a nap.

Heidi came home from her job at Huntington Hospital around 3 P.M. and found Kevin lying on the bed. Just before 4 P.M., Kevin received a page. He told Heidi it was St. Luke, notifying him to come to the hospital for a caesarian; in fact, he had programmed his pager to call to himself. He wanted to use the non-existent caesarian as a ruse to get out of the house to meet Deepti. Heidi offered to go with him to the hospital, but Kevin said it wasn't necessary. He claimed he left the La Verne house about 4:30 P.M., but this time was later disputed by Kevin's prosecutors.

At almost the same instant, Deepti was buying some prenatal vitamins at a drug store in Glendale. She had a short conversation with Marvin Cooper's office, then returned to her home in Glendale to meet Lorena Ramirez to give her her paycheck. Lorena arrived at about 4:45 P.M. Deepti was rushed. She told Lorena that she had to go to a meeting, and that she was having a hard time reaching the person she was supposed to see.

Kevin, meanwhile, had arrived at St. Luke, and from this point forward, his version of his movements would increasingly be at variance with other witnesses' accounts, and with the times of various telephone records, all in apparent aid of an effort on Kevin's part to push the clock ahead, in order to demonstrate that he had had no premeditated plan to kill Deepti—that in fact the crime had taken place on the spur of the moment.

Kevin later said that he had driven straight to the Children's Clinic from La Verne and waited for Deepti to arrive, but this appears to be wrong.

At some point between 5 and 6 P.M., according to Patricia Cogger, Kevin made an appearance at the hospital's birth center. Cogger recalled him asking about the caesarian. When he was informed that there was no caesarian scheduled, and that no one had called him, Kevin didn't seem very put out about it, according to Cogger. He told the nurses he was going to check some babies in the maternity ward.

At about 5:15 or 5:20 P.M., Kevin arrived at the Children's Clinic. Deepti wasn't there. Kevin waited for a few minutes, then saw Deepti in her white Mercedes SUV pull into the parking lot. She was talking on her cellphone, leaving a message for Vijay on the Gupta home answering machine. At this point, Kevin said, he asked Deepti if she was ready to go, and Deepti said yes. According to Kevin, he had asked Deepti the night before if she wanted to go up into the mountains to look at stars, and Deepti had agreed to this. But this version was somewhat contradicted by what happened next.

While Kevin was later to insist that he and Deepti had stopped at St. Luke sometime between 5:30 and 6 P.M., and that Kevin had stopped in to see the 11-year-old liver patient, what Kevin did not know was that at 5:52 P.M., Deepti was making yet another call to Anil Sharma. The context of the call makes it clear that Deepti was following Kevin into the mountains. It was physically impossible for Deepti and Kevin to have arrived in the mountains by 5:51 P.M. if they'd also stopped at St. Luke. There simply wasn't enough time. The call suggested strongly that Kevin had really made the St. Luke stop before meeting Deepti, and his remark to Patricia Cogger and the others that he was going to see babies in the maternity ward was an attempt to establish an alibi for the time of Deepti's death. Trying to arrange an alibi, of course, is evidence of premeditation.

While Deepti was following Kevin westbound on the Foothill Freeway toward La Canada between 5:30 and 5:45 P.M., a man named Richard James Burkhart was arriving at a Starbucks Coffee store in La Canada, the small town just at the foot of the San Gabriel Mountains. Burkhart got his coffee, then began driving his rental car northeast on Verdugo Road to Foothill Boulevard. At the junction of Foothill Boulevard and Angeles Crest Highway, Burkhart turned north and began driving up the mountain. At some point around 5:40 P.M., Burkhart saw two vehicles in a large turnout just north of the La Canada Country Club golf course. As he approached, the two cars pulled out onto the highway in front of him.

Past the golf course turnout, the highway began a number of twists and turns as it climbed into the mountains. Burkhart continued following the two cars. The sun had just gone down, he was to recall later. [On November 11, 1999, according to the weather bureau, sunset in the Los Angeles area was at 4:52 P.M., and full darkness descended at 5:19 P.M.]

Just ahead of him, at 5:49 P.M., as she was following Kevin's 4Runner, Deepti made a call to Anil Sharma and apparently tried to leave a message. The surrounding mountains probably blocked the call signal, so Deepti tried again, and this time was able to get through.

"Hi, Sharma," she said. "The same time as before. I'm actually in an area which is called the Crest Highway. It's near the route to Glendale. I'm going through a very winding mountain pathway. I'm following him in a car, and he said he's [unintelligible]. And so I don't know, I don't know this place, it's . . . it's in the middle of a lot of mountains, I'm going up the highway. It is very dark and I've been driving now like almost fifteen minutes. Uh . . ." At that moment the call cut off. This was the last time anyone other than Kevin heard Deepti speak.

The time of the call at 5:51, the fact that Deepti said she'd been driving almost fifteen minutes, the description of the terrain as "very dark" and "in the middle of a lot of mountains" shows that Deepti and Kevin could not have stopped at St. Luke as Kevin later insisted that they had.

Kevin, meanwhile, had called Heidi on his own cellular phone at 5:45 P.M. He told her that he was still at the hospital, and that he was "going to be a little bit late." To Heidi, Kevin seemed calm.

But Kevin later said that as he was leading Deepti up the mountain, his mind was in something of a turmoil.

"As I was going up that mountain," he said later, "all these threats, they're just bugging me. They're just getting on my nerves. I had had it, up to here, basically, with that. And I decided, you know, sure, maybe there's some threats that I can do. Maybe there's a couple of things I can do to threaten *her*."

Kevin was asked what sort of threats Deepti had made.

"She had threatened me about the patient list, first of all," he said. "Her husband had threatened to sue me if I didn't give her back some patients. She had made the accusation that I had intervened with her with the St. Luke stipend [relocation grant]. That I had intervened with her career. That I had ruined her reputation. That I had prevented her from practicing in the area. That I had stabbed her in the back with Dr. Richard. That I had abandoned her when it came to starting up the practice together. That I didn't support her with Dr. Richard. That I didn't support her when she was trying to give out cards at the Children's Clinic.

"She basically made accusations and threats, as far as what they would do legally—they being the Gupta family, her and her husband.[9] And these were all just really irri-

---

[9] "Her and her husband" and "what they could do legally" might well have included a lawsuit by Vijay against Kevin for the affair and the pregnancy, since Vijay Gupta would have standing as a wronged party.

tating. They were bugging me, and I was very frustrated that I couldn't get across to her that . . . I wasn't doing these things. And I certainly wasn't trying to do anything personally to hurt her in her practice. And it was very disconcerting."

With these thoughts in his mind as he was driving, Kevin said, he began trying to think of ways to scare Deepti.

"Maybe I could threaten her back," he said that he thought. He could tell Vijay about the affair, for instance. Or he could threaten to torch her car. "I could burn up her car, or tell her I would burn up her car." He knew that Deepti loved the white Mercedes.

At just about 6 P.M., Richard James Burkhart saw the dark Toyota 4Runner and the white Mercedes SUV pull off the highway into a turnout just in front of him. They were at the top of the mountain, at George's Gap. It looked to Burkhart as if the driver of the Mercedes was caught by surprise by the decision to turn off, because the white car's brake lights came on, then went off, as if the driver intended to go on past, before they came on again to turn off.

Burkhart drove on past the two cars in the turnout. Both were facing east, with their lights on. The white Mercedes was on the inside, closest to the roadway, and parallel to the Toyota, which was nearer the edge. Then Burkhart was past the turnout.

Burkhart kept on driving beyond the Clear Creek Ranger station—down Angeles Forest Highway, across the front side of Josephine Peak, then down to Big Tujunga Canyon Road. He got his binoculars out of the car and did some stargazing for a while. As he put it later, he liked to "kick back" in the wilderness.

Around 7:15, Burkhart got back in his rented car and started back the way he had come. About fifteen minutes later, as he passed the turnout he had gone by on the way up, he saw the same two cars, still parked in parallel in the turnout. Both still had their lights on, he noticed. Neither car was parked in such a way as to be able to see the view of the valley below from inside, Burkhart noticed. It was about 7:30 P.M.

Burkhart headed back down Angeles Crest Highway toward La Canada. A few minutes later, about 7:45 P.M., he pulled off to the side of the highway, shut off the engine and rolled a cigarette. Burkhart was listening to the car radio, his windshield facing a deep canyon.

"All of a sudden," he said, "just like a bright flashlight, [something] went over the hill."

Burkhart thought he'd heard a loud noise. He turned the radio off and listened, but whatever it was, he didn't hear it again. He turned his radio back on, and a few minutes later, put out his cigarette and finished his drive down the mountain.

Two hours later, Burkhart was in his apartment in Anaheim, watching the news.

"I saw a reporter," he said, "standing by the turnout, and she was saying they were pulling an SUV up the side of the mountain. They hadn't got it up yet. She mentioned that it was murder, and it was a doctor who killed a doctor."

20

Vijay Gupta got home from UCLA around 6 P.M. that same night. One of the first things he did was check the telephone answering system, which was run by the phone company. There were two messages on the system, both from Deepti.

"Guddu," she said, using Vijay's nickname, "I forgot my beeper, but I will keep my cell phone on, so if you need to reach me, you can call me on my cell phone."

The next message was recorded only a minute or two later. "Guddu," Deepti said, "I found my pager. It's in my coat pocket. I will keep both the pager and the phone on so you can reach me, if you need me." Deepti added that she'd found the pager in her pocket when she'd been paged by someone else.

Vijay thought Deepti had gone to St. Luke for the on-call rotation, or possibly that she was at the Montebello clinic, so her absence didn't disturb him at first; he was used to Deepti having unusual working hours.

But after some time with no further word from Deepti, Vijay began to be concerned. He checked places where Deepti might be, but couldn't locate her. Since he had erased the messages Deepti had left on the answering system, Vijay began to wonder whether she'd said something that he'd simply missed that might account for her whereabouts. He called the telephone company, but was told that once the messages had been deleted, they could no longer be retrieved.

"Then I got very worried," Vijay said. "I started calling some hospitals. Then I called, I think, some police departments, just to see if there had been an accident." But no one had any information on Dr. Deepti Gupta.

*　　*　　*

Around 10 P.M., just as Richard James Burkhart was settling back to watch the news at his Anaheim apartment, and Vijay Gupta was worrying in Glendale, Los Angeles County Sheriff's Department Sergeant Ken Gallatin was receiving a call at home from his department's dispatcher. Gallatin was the senior member of a two-person team of homicide investigators, one of six "tables" of twelve detectives each, all assigned to the sheriff's department's centralized Homicide Bureau, located in a light industrial park near Bandini Boulevard in East Los Angeles. In the L.A. County Sheriff's Department, with more than 27 stations and substations, the Homicide Bureau was a choice assignment. Gallatin had 32 years in as a deputy sheriff, and 14 in the bureau.

Because the bureau was centralized, the two-person homicide teams were available to investigate any homicide in the unincorporated area of Los Angeles County. It depended on who was "up" in the regular rotation. At a little over 4,000 square miles and populated by nearly 10 million people, L.A. County covered a lot of territory. For Gallatin and his partner, Dan McElderry, that meant they might be called out to look at murders anywhere from the Mojave Desert to Catalina Island.

After getting the basic facts while still at home—a car over the side of the Angeles Crest Highway, a dead female, a suspect in custody—Gallatin drove to the department's Crescenta Valley Regional Station, where he met McElderry. Together the two detectives drove up the mountain to Clipper Gap, accompanied by a crime scene technician, and arrived at Mile Marker 33 at 11:35 P.M. Even as they were ascending the mountain, Kevin was on his way down, handcuffed, and in the rear seat of Deputy Brandriff's patrol car, his life as a felon just begun.

At Mile Marker 33, Gallatin and McElderry were briefed by Deputy Dave Willard. A sheriff's department Search and Rescue Team of eight trained volunteers had also been called out. After Gallatin and McElderry were brought up to speed, a decision was made to retrieve the victim from the steep canyon. At about twenty minutes after midnight, on November 12, three members of the SAR team climbed down to the lifeless body of Deepti Gupta, loaded it onto a lightweight litter, and winched it back to the top of the mountain, 275 feet above.

Almost as soon as the body was examined in the portable lights, it was clear what had happened. There, across Deepti's once-beautiful neck, was a thin red line. Gallatin and McElderry had seen plenty of these. They didn't need the coroner's investigator to tell them what it was. It was the mark of a ligature, and it showed that she had been strangled to death.

A few minutes later, Gallatin and McElderry returned to their cars and drove back down the mountain to talk to Dr. Kevin Anderson. The Search and Rescue people, assisted by the Los Angeles County Fire Department, then tied their cable to Deepti's Mercedes, and winched it back to the top as well—altogether, 425 feet.

Brandriff had booked Kevin into the Crescenta Valley holding cell shortly after midnight. As standard operating procedure, Brandriff had confiscated Kevin's belt, and if he hadn't been wearing laceless boots, would have taken his shoelaces too. Under such circumstances, it wasn't unheard of for a prisoner to try to hang himself. Brandriff also took Kevin's pager; before putting it into an evidence envelope, Brandriff played back all the stored numbers of previous callers, and wrote them down. This was also standard procedure. However, Kevin's cellular telephone and his wallet were left in his Toyota 4Runner, which was towed to a garage in Crescenta Valley for later evidence processing.

The booking had gone smoothly enough. Kevin seemed remarkably calm, under the circumstances. After having told the arresting deputies, principally dog handler Wilkinson, that he was responsible for Deepti's death, and that he had "snapped," Kevin wasn't saying much else. He asked to be allowed to call Heidi. He guessed that she would be worried because she hadn't heard from him. Besides, he figured that Heidi could call to arrange a lawyer for him. But the booking deputies refused to allow him to call his wife; and indeed, it appears that they wouldn't allow Kevin to make any calls, to anyone, even a lawyer.

Gallatin and McElderry arrived at the Crescenta Valley station about 1:15 A.M. They decided to interview first the man who had been with Kevin when he was arrested—the older man Kevin had said wasn't involved. This was John David Vinson, a resident of Palmdale, who had done nothing more than try to help someone whose truck had run off the road. Gallatin and McElderry quickly determined that Vinson had nothing to do with the crime, and after providing a little information about Kevin's demeanor while they were trying to get the car freed, he was finally allowed to go home.

Next, the detectives interviewed Jay La Riviere. La Riviere told his story about passing the two end-to-end SUVs, and seeing the white car go over the cliff once more. La Riviere described his chase of Kevin's Toyota, his report at the fire station, and then finding the wreckage of Deepti's car.

After this, they interviewed Bennick and Martinez, and then at 3:30 A.M., Gallatin and McElderry began to interview Kevin.

"He was very, very calm," Gallatin recalled later. "His voice was very modulated. Our impression was, it was almost like he was relieved to tell the story. There was no emotion in his voice. He was very articulate, professional."

Like most experienced homicide detectives, Gallatin and McElderry were trained to observe human behavior when under the stress of an interrogation. That meant paying particular attention to such things as conversational false starts, in which a person starts to say something, stops, then starts again. They knew these were often examples of self-censorship, and as such, were frequently indicators of lying.

Gallatin put a portable tape recorder on the table and turned it on. The first order of business was to advise Kevin of his legal rights. McElderry read the standard Miranda warning from a card, then asked Kevin if he understood his rights. Here the detectives ran into their first snag. Kevin was later to claim that he'd already been denied the chance to make a telephone call twice before the interview started. He was to suggest that he would never have talked to the detectives if he'd had a chance to talk to Heidi, and thus to a lawyer, first. By the time of the interview, Kevin was under the impression that if he cooperated, he'd finally get his phone call.

"If—How can I get a lawyer first, though?" he asked.

"We have to do this later," one of the detectives said.

"We could do it later," the other said. "You could call an attorney . . . and he could be present while we talk to you, if that's what you want to do."

"Okay," Kevin said. "Yeah, I don't have one right now, so—"

"Do you prefer to have an attorney present while I talk to you?"

"I—I don't think so," Kevin said.

"Well," said one of the detectives, "that's your choice. I mean, we can't talk to you unless you agree to talk to us without an attorney. And that's—that's your choice."

"Uh," Kevin said, "I guess it'd be okay."

"Be okay to what?"

"To talk."

"Without an attorney?"

"Yeah," Kevin said, "without an attorney present."

The detectives now had Kevin sign a formal waiver of his rights, and then proceeded to question him. Outside of the first exchange over the right to a lawyer, Kevin was cooperative. As Gallatin put it, Kevin "got on a roll," and the detectives tried not to get in his way as he told the story. The tape recorder was rolling, and McElderry began to take written notes; but soon Kevin was talking so fast, McElderry gave up.

Kevin sketched in the basic background of his recent business relationship with Deepti, but denied that he and

Deepti had been lovers. He discussed Deepti's arrival at the Eaton Canyon clinic, the troubles she'd had with Dr. Ng, and the proposed partnership. Deepti, Kevin said, didn't get along with his wife, Heidi.

"By that time enough had happened that my wife was really against me going into practice with her," Kevin told the detectives. "And so I told Dr. Gupta that I probably wouldn't be going into practice with her . . . and she was furious. And she felt like all this stuff we had been preparing was kind of leading someone on, and she didn't really appreciate it and she said she was going to—Actually, she said that I'd ruined her career."

Kevin now brought up the relocation grant. "And she would qualify for that, just barely," he said. "They would kind of have to fudge it a little bit, but because I had worked there a long time and they knew we were going to work together, they were going to grant that, and that money would go into the practice in general. So that would pretty much float the practice for the first year."

Once they decided not to be partners, Kevin told the detectives, "they cancelled that from her. And she was really, really upset with that, and she felt like her whole chance of starting a practice in that area was gone. I said, 'Well, I'm really sorry, but I have to do this because my wife is very, very concerned about this and I think it'd be for the best.'

"And she was absolutely furious. She said, 'Look, we have to find a way to work this out. We have to find a way to make this work.' "

Kevin now told the story about the September 7 meeting at the Anderson house, the one Heidi had walked out on. After this, Kevin said, he'd decided to buy Dr. Richard's practice. After that, Kevin said, Deepti said she couldn't get her practice started because Kevin had all the patient lists from their time at Eaton Canyon. Kevin said he'd give Deepti the lists so she could contact the patients herself.

When Deepti had come to work at the Children's Clinic, Kevin continued, Heidi had objected.

"Did your wife suspect that something was going on between you and this girl?" one of the detectives asked.

"She—She—Well, nothing going on between us, but she [Heidi] felt that she [Deepti]—overliked me," Kevin said. "And I kind of argued with her on that, because I said, 'No, I think she's very professional.' "

But after they'd gone out of town, Kevin said, and Deepti had complained about his absence, he'd decided that Heidi was right—Deepti was interested in him.

"And then she hit the roof. That's when she said, 'Absolutely no way, I don't want any contact with her. She's bad karma.' "

Kevin described arranging for Deepti to work at Dr. Richard's Children's Clinic. But, he said, that too created problems. "Once she started working there, she started doing other things the retired physician didn't like, because his whole basis of selling his practice to me depended on how many patients of his actually became mine. And what she was doing was, she was taking her cards and things and passing them out to the patients so they would eventually go to her office. It wasn't such a big deal to me, because I didn't think the numbers were that big, but Dr. Richard felt it was a very big deal because, obviously, any patients that went to her and not to me, that was income lost for him, selling his practice."

Deepti had complained that he was ruining her career, Kevin said again, and so had Vijay.

"And I said, 'Well, you know, I—I—I didn't mean to ruin her career.' And then I started feeling very guilty. I started feeling like I needed to do something to kind of make it up, because I didn't want someone's career to be ruined. So I said, 'Well, look, I'll work with her at the hospital, I'll try to set up something with the patients so I can make sure she gets her patients,' that kind of thing.

"He [Vijay] says, 'Well, I mean, I've talked to a lawyer and—' You know, he was kind of making some subtle threats."

Kevin was being elliptical in his answers, approaching

the truth, then veering away with deceptions, as well as rearranging the order of events. The one thing he didn't want to admit was that he and Deepti had been lovers. But the detectives sensed his evasiveness.

"Did you and her ever become romantically involved?" one of the detectives asked.

"We—we talked about it," Kevin said. "And we talked about it to her husband and to my wife." Kevin launched into a non-responsive description of the September 7 meeting at the Anderson home, but the detectives cut him off.

"I mean," said one, "so the answer is, you did become romantically involved for a period of time? Or . . . ?"

"No," said Kevin. "We talked about it . . . but we—we chose not to act on that."

Kevin was asked if Deepti believed that the relationship could go further, and Kevin said he thought she did.

"Men being men," said one of the detectives, and Kevin now tacitly admitted that he might have encouraged Deepti to pursue him.

"I think the chum [fish bait] that I may have thrown out is that I told her on occasion sometimes my wife and I would have very big blow-ups . . ." Kevin said. The detectives asked about Deepti's relationship with her husband, and Kevin offered that Deepti and Vijay had also had problems in their marriage.

"Okay," said one of the detectives, "let's get back into leading up to tonight. What happened?"

"Okay," said Kevin. He told the detectives about the dispute over Richard's patients, and the argument over the Eaton Canyon lists. Kevin said his insurance billers discovered that Deepti was "taking some of our patients and putting them in her charts to transfer over to her office." Kevin said he talked to Deepti about this.

"And each time we talked about this issue, this is really a sore point for her," he said. "And me and Dr. Richard, especially. So that came up again. Then she said, 'You know, you've ruined so much. You know, I can ruin you too.'"

Kevin said he told Deepti that Heidi believed that he had already done a lot for Deepti by allowing her to work at Richard's clinic.

"But she said . . . she did not like my wife, she absolutely hated the woman, and she called her 'that woman.' And she said, 'You know, I'm going to get into a position where I will be the number one woman.' "

On Wednesday night, Kevin said—the night before—Deepti had come to Children's Clinic, and had confronted him. "She felt I had hung her out to dry with Dr. Richard and—she told me she was pregnant, which—which is—but that's entirely possible. I mean—I didn't—I didn't doubt that. But she implied that I was the father. And I said, 'Well, that's impossible.'

"And she said, 'Well, by the time it's known, you will be ruined.' "

"Have you ever had sex with her?" one of the detectives asked.

"No," said Kevin. "And she knew that. And I even told her, I said, 'You've said to me that you want to have another child. What's wrong—what's wrong with having it with your husband? What's wrong with doing that?' "

The detectives asked whether Deepti had threatened to tell Heidi that he had impregnated her. Kevin admitted that Deepti had.

"I thought," Kevin said, "I've got to talk to her again, I've got to do something to—to—to—to get her to not do any of these things . . . So she suggested that we talk again Thursday night."

Kevin said that he'd arranged to meet Deepti at the Children's Clinic. He'd brought his telescope, he said, because Deepti was interested in astronomy, and he thought that maybe if they looked at the stars, a positive tone might be created for their discussion. "But I didn't trust it," he said. "So I kind of thought, well, maybe if I can do something that will scare her a little bit, to have that as an ace in the hole. And I didn't really have a lot of experience with that type of thing, so I was going to tell her that I was—I could burn her car up and—because she really liked her car. But—So I—I brought the telescope."

By the time he met Deepti and they started out for Angeles Crest Highway, Kevin said, it was getting dark. McElderry reached out and picked up the tape recorder to see if it was turning. Kevin was asked what happened once he and Deepti had reached the top of the mountain. McElderry now noticed that the recorder wasn't working. He turned it on again.

"We talked," Kevin was saying. "We went and talked first. I showed her the telescope because she wanted to see it. So I showed her the telescope."

"Did she get in your car or did you get in her car, or what happened?"

"Initially, I got in her car and we talked about this issue. And—"

"The issue of her pregnancy or her alleged pregnancy?"

"Alleged pregnancy, yes," said Kevin. "And I said, 'You know, these kinds of threats, these aren't—This is not good.' She can't—can't do this. She said, 'Well, if you ruin me, I'm going to ruin you.'

"And I said, 'Well, eventually it's going to come out that this is either a hoax or this is your own child from your own family.'

"And she said, 'Yeah, but a lot of damage can be done.'

"And I said, 'Well, look, this is a very upsetting issue for me. Why don't we do something different for a few minutes and then we'll come back to this? And I—I just really think this is wrong.' "

At this point, Kevin said, Deepti threatened again to sue him over the patients. Kevin said he got out of the car to set up the telescope.

"So I went back to my car and she came around and sat in the passenger seat," he continued.

"And we kind of started talking a bit more, and—and then she—then she made a—a—another threat, I guess—I—I don't know, something in me just—just snapped. And she said that, along with the other stuff she had said before that, she said that she knows where my daughter goes to school . . . So she said . . . she could easily pick up my daughter.

"So when she said that I—I got—I just—I just lost it. And—I don't have a huge temper, but I guess when I—when I lose my temper, I—I guess it's—you know, I'm pretty su—I'm pretty angry. But I was so angry, because the first thing I thought of is that, you know, something was going to happen to my daughter. And so I—I just grabbed her and I got—I think I—I was just choking her. I—I have a—I have a tie that I wore, a Snoopy tie, that I wore to work, but I had taken it off by that time, and—but it was still in the truck and—and I grabbed it and I just started pulling it on her."

"Around her neck?"

"Around her neck. And I was—I was just really furious, but by the time I stopped, I mean, she—she looked like she was unconscious. And—and I got very scared, frankly. I—I—I got very, very scared· and I thought, 'Oh my God, what have I done here? What's going on?'

"And so I sat there for a few minutes. I started hyperventilating. And then I—"

"Did she ever regain consciousness?"

"No."

"She was dead?"

"I assume so. I—I didn't check on her—"

"Being a physician—" one of the detectives began.

"Being a physician," Kevin said, "I know, I would check her pulse or something, and I—I just didn't, I didn't even touch her, I just—just assumed that she was."

Now Gallatin and McElderry wanted to find some way to corroborate Kevin's account of what had happened on the top of the mountain. They wanted to nail down the times surrounding the deadly encounter, first to look for inconsistencies in Kevin's story, and also to see if there might be some independent witnesses.

Kevin said they'd left Children's Clinic around 5:30, and

that it took thirty to forty minutes to drive to the top. He guessed that they had reached Mile Marker 33 "somewhere between six and six-fifteen."

The detectives wanted to know how long Kevin and Deepti had talked before the murder. Kevin said he wasn't sure, but thought it might have been a hour to ninety minutes. "Yeah," he said, "probably something like that."

While he and Deepti were talking, Kevin said, he'd received a page from his ex-wife, Natalie, about arrangements for Kevin to take care of their daughter. This happened right before Deepti had "made that threat," that is, the statement that she could easily pick up Kevin's daughter. Kevin said he'd called Natalie back about fifteen minutes later. Kevin thought that his return call to Natalie had led Deepti to make the remark about his daughter.

"And when you called her [Natalie], Deepti was still alive?" one of the detectives asked.

"Yes," Kevin said. "She was sitting there listening." It was shortly after this that Deepti had made the remark he had considered a threat, Kevin said.

"Okay," said one of the detectives. "Now, Deepti is sitting there in the seat beside you, she is unconscious? Or she's not breathing, you think she's dead. What do you do next?"

"Well, it was just kind of a panic reaction at that point," Kevin said. "I mean, I didn't know what to do. So I thought, well, since we're up here, maybe—maybe I could make it look like it was an accident, like maybe she drove off the cliff or something, which was kind of inane. But, I mean, I just—in that state of mind, I didn't—I wasn't thinking, you know, logically."

Kevin was asked whether he or Deepti had been drinking or taking drugs, and Kevin said they weren't.

"And so I thought," he continued, "well, I'd better—because she was in my car. I said, well, I'd better put her back in her car. So I picked her up and put her in her car and—"

"Driver's side or passenger?"

"Driver's—driver's side. Because I wanted—you know, for this to look like an accident, she had to be on the driver's side. But I didn't really know for sure because she may—you know, she—she couldn't really fit like she was driving, or anything, so—"

At that point the recorder ran out of tape. One of the detectives stopped the machine and turned the tape over to continue the interview.

21

Kevin now gave more details of what he had done after realizing that Deepti was dead. Before moving her to her car, he said, he drove the Mercedes to the low dirt berm that marked the edge of the turnout above the ravine. He went back to his 4Runner, picked up Deepti's body, and carried it to the Mercedes. Kevin went back to his truck, removed a gasoline can that was in the truck bed, and opened the passenger door of the Mercedes. He poured gasoline on the floorboards and on the driver's seat where Deepti was sitting. Kevin said his idea was to light the gasoline and shove the car over the side to make it look as if Deepti had crashed in a fiery wreck.

Kevin said that as he was pouring the gas, however, the Mercedes began to "slowly" move forward over the edge. He "bailed out," he said, and watched it plunge into the ravine, unlit.

Kevin said he got back into his truck and started it up. He was in a panic, he said, and had no idea where he was going. He remembered his tires screeching as he rounded the curves of the mountain highway at high speed. The next thing he knew he had lost control of his truck and had run off the road.

By around 4:30 A.M., the interview was over, and Kevin was finally allowed to call Heidi.

"He was very upset," Heidi said later. "He was crying and he was just rambling and he was just—he was very upset."

Kevin explained that he had been arrested for murdering Deepti Gupta.

While Kevin was talking to Heidi, Gallatin and McElderry discussed their impressions of their interview. "We had doubts about his reason for killing her," Gallatin said later. Kevin's explanation that he and Deepti had had a falling out over business issues just didn't rise to the level of a viable motive, they thought. The supposed threat to Kevin's daughter rang particularly hollow. What did Kevin want them to think: that Deepti was an immediate threat to the daughter, miles away and enrolled in a secure private school? Even if the threat had been genuine, it wasn't as if Kevin didn't have plenty of ways of dealing with it—like calling the police, for instance.

They had also noticed Kevin's hesitations when it came to the question of whether he and Deepti had been lovers, and also over the question of who was responsible for her pregnancy. They guessed that what they really had was a lovers' quarrel—made a bit more unusual by the fact that both killer and victim were doctors, but a lovers' quarrel nevertheless.

The real question was whether Kevin had planned the murder. True, he had said that he "just snapped," implying that there was no premeditation, but Gallatin and McElderry weren't so sure about that. The location of the crime—miles away from anywhere, on a relatively isolated mountain highway—was suggestive of planning. So was Kevin's admission that he had considered "an ace in the hole," the idea of burning Deepti's Mercedes, which suggested that he had violence on his mind even before the final, fatal argument.

Kevin had been so voluble that McElderry's sketchy notes were less than complete. Both detectives believed, based on Kevin's description, that the two vehicles had been facing out toward the view when the crime occurred. If Kevin had been telling them the truth about his murderous attack, he had then moved Deepti's Mercedes to the edge of the ravine, put her body in the driver's seat, poured gasoline around the front seat, and had been surprised when the car suddenly began rolling forward, thereby preventing him from lighting it off.

There were some problems, however, with this description of what had happened. How did Kevin account for La Riviere seeing the 4Runner directly behind the Mercedes, for example? And La Riviere had said he thought he saw the 4Runner nudge the Mercedes over the side. Kevin had said he "bailed out" of the Mercedes when it started rolling, and had thus been prevented from lighting the gasoline. So this was a possible inconsistency.

There were other unanswered questions as well—questions that went to the heart of what really happened at Mile Marker 33, and whether Kevin had planned the murder. The answers to those questions would determine whether Kevin was charged with first-degree murder, and possibly be subject to the death penalty, or simply manslaughter.

Both Gallatin and McElderry knew they did not yet have enough information. And while Kevin had admitted strangling Deepti with his Snoopy tie, that raised almost as many questions as it answered. How was Kevin able to get the tie around Deepti's neck? Kevin appeared to have no defensive wounds such as scratches or bruises that might have been expected if Deepti had been conscious when Kevin first started strangling her. And: although Kevin said that he'd been pouring the gasoline over Deepti's body when the car began rolling forward, and that he'd had to "bail out," how come there wasn't any gasoline on his clothes? It didn't seem likely that if the car had been moving while Kevin was pouring that there wouldn't be a drop of the stuff on him as well. Finally, the ravine was enormously steep—at the point where the Mercedes had gone over, in fact, it was more like a cliff. It didn't seem very likely that the car had "slowly" started over the edge, as Kevin said. Instead, it was far more plausible that it had shot over the side. If Kevin had been in the car when it began to move, the chances were that he himself would have gone with it.

That same morning, while Gallatin and McElderry were conducting their interviews, two deputy sheriffs drove to the Gupta house in Glendale. About 3 A.M. they rang the doorbell. Vijay answered.

"It was two detectives at the door," he said later. "And they said I should sit down. They came in, and told me to take a seat. I knew there was something wrong."

Deepti, the detectives said, was dead.

Vijay said it was impossible. "Are you sure it's her?" he asked. The detectives assured him there was no mistake. Deepti had been identified from her driver's license, which had been found at the scene. Now the detectives asked Vijay to come to the Crescenta Valley Station so he could be interviewed.

Still in disbelief, Vijay went to the station, where he gave the detectives a lengthy account of his wife's long-running troubles with Dr. Kevin Anderson.

At 9:30 the following morning, Dr. Yulai Wang began a post-mortem examination of the body of Deepti Gupta. Wang examined the mark left by Kevin's Snoopy tie; there were distinct abrasions on the left side of Deepti's neck, as well as smaller marks on the right side. This pattern suggested that the tie had crossed on the left side of the neck, because the marks are almost always more distinct where the two ends of a ligature cross over one another, where the torque is greatest. A later dissection of the neck muscles would also show that most of the pressure from the ligature was concentrated on the left side, because that was where most of the tissue damage was.

That Deepti had died of suffocation was obvious, not only from the ligature marks but also from the tiny petechial hemorrhages in and around her eyes. Those hemorrhages, the result of the bursting of tiny blood vessels under pressure, are almost invariably the result of strangulations.

Wang formed the opinion that the bruises on the right side of Deepti's neck, which covered her carotid artery, were consistent with choking by hand. This suggested to some that Deepti had first been choked into unconsciousness, then subsequently killed with the tie.

Of even more significance were a series of bruises and scrapes on Deepti's face, the side of her head, the bridge of her nose, her back, and on her legs. Portions of her skin were beginning to slip, the result of having been soaked for some period of time in gasoline. But the bruises on her face and head were most suggestive. One, an area about six inches long by three inches wide located on the left side of the head, was accompanied by a hemorrhage beneath the scalp. Wang believed the injury came before Deepti died, that is, before the strangulation occurred, mostly because of the amount of hemorrhage—once the heart stops from strangulation, of course, blood flow ceases, ordinarily preventing extensive hemorrhage beneath the skin. He thought the large bruise was the result of blunt force trauma. That meant that she must have sustained a severe blow to the left side of the head before the strangulation.

There were a great number of other bruises and abrasions on the body. Wang decided that most of these injuries occurred after death, and were probably the result of the car going over the edge into the ravine.

Wang's examination also showed that Deepti—as she had told Sharma, Vijay and Kevin—*was* pregnant. Wang guessed that the fetus had been three to four weeks along when it died with Deepti. That would put the conception period at somewhere between October 14 and October 21, which was the day Deepti had left for her trip to India.

Taken together, Wang's findings suggested that Kevin's description of how he had killed Deepti was woefully inadequate. Instead, the evidence suggested that Deepti was first struck by a hard surface, then strangled by the Snoopy tie. And the fact that the ligature injuries were most distinct on the left side of her neck strongly suggested that the attack had come from Deepti's right. If this were true, it would be a major inconsistency with Kevin's statement, because the way Kevin described it, Deepti had been seated in the passenger seat to *his* right when he had "just snapped." That meant there wasn't any quick and easy way to get the tie around her neck to leave the marks that it did—that is, if Kevin was telling the truth. The marks showed that all the leverage had come from the other side.

This was where the lack of specificity in Kevin's statement hurt the police, and later the prosecutors. The inconsistencies between Kevin's statement to Gallatin and McElderry and Wang's physical evidence were never explained, and once Kevin had a lawyer, never would be. But Wang's evidence supported a far darker interpretation of what happened at Mile Marker 33: based on Wang's facts, it is most likely that the attack began with Kevin grabbing Deepti around the back of the neck with his right hand (thereby leaving the manual "choking" marks on the right side of her neck) when her face was momentarily turned away, then hurling Deepti's head into the dashboard of the 4Runner, stunning her while also bruising the left side of her head; then exiting the car, going around to the passenger door, looping his tie around her neck from that side, and finishing her off with the strangulation.

While the first act, thrusting Deepti's head into the dashboard, might have been because someone "just snapped," the second action of getting out of the car, moving to the passenger-side door and deliberately strangling someone would be quite a bit more intentional. The inability of the detectives and the prosecutors to arrive at a proper interpretation of the medical evidence was eventually to seriously undermine the prosecution of Kevin Anderson for first-degree murder.

On Saturday morning, November 13, Gallatin went into the office to start preparing his reports on the murder. He listened to the first side of the tape of the interview with Kevin, then turned it over.

"That's when I noticed that side B was not there," Gallatin said later. The tape recorder had malfunctioned, and neither Gallatin nor McElderry had anything like complete notes. They would have to summarize Kevin's most critical statements about exactly how he had killed Deepti from memory.[10]

---

[10]The unnoticed malfunction of the tape recorder was particularly unfortunate, in that the detectives also had access to a video camera,

22

Over the next two months, Gallatin and McElderry worked to assemble their case against Kevin. Since Kevin had readily confessed from the start that he had killed Deepti, it wasn't any kind of mystery. What was in dispute was, first, why had he done it? And second, had he intended to do it—that is, was it premeditated? Or, as the law put it, planned with "malice aforethought." The two questions were inextricably bound together.

Deepti's body was quickly prepared for a traditional Indian funeral, and brought to the Gupta home in Glendale. "In our religion we have to decorate her like a newlywed," Vijay said later. The body was then quickly cremated in accordance with the same tradition.

On Tuesday, November 16, Gallatin and McElderry inspected Kevin's car at the Crescenta Valley towing lot. There they discovered that Kevin's wallet was still in the car, as it had been since the night of his arrest. When they looked inside the wallet, the detectives discovered the receipt for a Pasadena motel dated November 10, and made out to Kevin. Since Kevin hadn't said anything about going to a motel with Deepti on the night of their big argument before the murder, Gallatin and McElderry were almost certain that Kevin had lied to them when he denied that he and Deepti had been lovers.

There is little that excites a homicide detective's attention more than the fact that the principal suspect is shown to be lying, especially about something important. The log-

---

which had earlier been used to record visuals of the crash scene. Just why the detectives failed to use the same camera for their interview of Kevin was never explained.

ical question then becomes: why? Why would Kevin lie about this? And if he lied about this, what else would he lie about?

Three days later, on November 19, Vijay found Deepti's day planner diary. He turned it over to Gallatin and Mc-Elderry without looking inside. But when the detectives opened it, they found the two cards to Deepti from Kevin, both with short notes, including the one that made it appear that Kevin and Deepti had been lovers for some time.

Gallatin and McElderry weren't the only ones who were investigating. About two days after the murder—on the same day as Deepti's funeral, in fact—Jay La Riviere, the witness who had just happened to be passing by when Deepti's car went over the side, returned to the scene of the crime. As he had the night of the murder, La Riviere hiked down the ravine to where the car had been. He explained later that the whole night seemed somehow unreal. He wanted to convince himself that it had actually happened.

The ravine was littered with car junk, La Riviere saw. "Bumpers, license plates, et cetera," he said later. "Batteries, tires."

Looking around at the place where the car had come to rest, La Riviere found "a couple of envelopes, a card, and some medicine." The medicine was pre-natal vitamins.

La Riviere looked at the greeting card. The front said "Thank you." When he opened it, it read, "Hope you know how much it's appreciated." La Riviere suddenly had the feeling that the card was directed to him personally. "It had a really warm feeling," he said later. "I felt like someone was there. It was really spiritual, weird."

As the month of November unfolded, Gallatin and Mc-Elderry conducted a number of interviews: Ken Rivers at St. Luke, a number of the nurses, office managers and medical assistants at the hospital and in the two clinics, Dr. Richard, Dr. Ng, Marvin Cooper, Kevin's tax accountant Steve Sorrell, the Thatcher Building's Tracy Thomas, and

Natalie Profant, Kevin's former wife. Witness Richard James Burkhart, who had twice passed Deepti and Kevin on the Mile Marker 33 turnout, going up the mountain around 6 P.M. and going down at about 7:45, called the detectives to report what he had seen, thus verifying Kevin's statement about of the time they had arrived at the turnout. Burkhart's eyewitness account would turn out to be very important.

Another important interview was of Anil Sharma. Sharma was excellent for helping to fill in some of the background about Deepti's state of mind, but the detectives weren't able to learn much about the critical question of when Deepti had first learned she was pregnant, since Sharma's recollection of this seemed to be at variance with Deepti's purchase of the testing kits.

Nevertheless, Sharma was of great assistance. After he learned that Deepti had been murdered, Sharma checked his answering machine. There were still three messages on the machine from Deepti, the last at 5:51 P.M. on the night she died. Sharma made a copy of his message tape and gave it to the detectives. Unfortunately, he had already erased the original.

"If I was there to pick up the phone," Sharma told the detectives, "I would have told her: 'Make a U-turn.' "

On November 30, McElderry obtained search warrants for Kevin's house in La Verne, and for his office at the Children's Clinic. The next day, the detectives, accompanied by a prosecutor and a computer expert, served the warrants.

Heidi was home at the time.

"It was like bam, bam, and the door opened," Heidi said. "I was terrified." No one had advised her that the sheriff's deputies were going to search. The detectives seized the Anderson home computer, and in the search of the bedroom, found what appeared to be a ledger Heidi had prepared, titled "Money Owed to Joint Checking Account by Kevin Anderson." It was a list of debts Heidi thought Kevin owed to their common household account. To the investigators, it looked as if Kevin was in arrears to his own wife; that in turn made him appear both greedy and unreliable. Heidi was upset that the investigators seized this document; she insisted that it had been nothing more than a joke when she toted it up.

Bit by bit, the two detectives worked to assemble thumbnail personality portraits of Kevin and Deepti. Kevin, they learned, was seen by almost everyone as calm, low-key, meticulous, unflappable in a crisis; no one could recall ever seeing him lose his temper. He was so non-confrontational, so prone to searching for compromise solutions, so fundamentally inoffensive, that some thought him almost Milquetoastish.

"He got laid a lot," said Gallatin. "He used his connections to ingratiate himself with women. And he liked to play 'Woe is me, my wife doesn't understand me,' to get women into bed with him."

Deepti, on the other hand, was portrayed as "very goal-oriented," Gallatin said, "very determined." Once Deepti had decided on something, she was difficult to sway. At first Deepti saw Kevin as someone who could help her attain her goals, but as time went by, "she became infatuated" with Kevin, Gallatin said. And where Kevin saw his romance with Deepti as a more or less casual liaison, Deepti still had enough of the traditional Indian woman in her to take the affair far more seriously than Kevin.

As November turned into December, Kevin remained in jail, despite efforts to get released on bail. To Heidi, the whole of November and December seemed like a nightmare. She'd had to find Kevin a criminal lawyer, and good ones were hardly cheap. Eventually she would have to sell their house, the ski boat, and liquidate almost all of their assets. As the New Year approached, Heidi couldn't help but feel that she'd been right all along—Deepti had been bad karma, at least for Kevin and Heidi Anderson.

And just before the turn of the year, Gallatin and McElderry found another witness: a nurse who said that

Kevin was known to proposition nurses at both Huntington and St. Luke; and that Heidi was aware of this, and was seen by some as a jealous, possibly even vindictive woman.

And while Heidi didn't immediately learn that Gallatin and McElderry were discovering these unhappy facts, she already knew enough to realize that all their private lives, whatever secrets they had, were going to be garishly splashed into the public eye—and that things were about to get a lot worse before they ever got better.

She was right.

On January 12, 2000, the Los Angeles County District Attorney's Office convened a hearing before the county grand jury on the matter of Kevin Anderson. Two days later, after hearing from La Riviere, the forest service workers, Vijay, Sharma, Lorena Ramirez, McElderry, and a number of others, the jury returned an indictment charging Kevin Paul Anderson with first-degree murder, augmented by the "special circumstance" of lying in wait; and intentionally causing the death of an unborn child, another felony. If Kevin was convicted of first-degree murder, he faced a possible death sentence.

The Trial of Kevin Paul Anderson

23

Over the nine months following Kevin's indictment, Gallatin and McElderry continued to assemble evidence on the murder of Deepti Gupta. The detectives obtained records of Kevin and Deepti's cellular telephones and pagers, which showed the numbers called and received, and the duration of each. An engineer was consulted to map the probable locations where each call was made, and the resulting chart provided a sort of visual time-and-motion study of Kevin and Deepti's movements on the last two days before the murder.

The telephone records also produced what appeared to be an anomaly in Kevin's account of the events. Kevin had said he and Deepti arrived at Mile Marker 33 around 6 P.M., and his story was backed by witness Burkhart's account. Yet Kevin's telephone records showed a voicemail page to Deepti at 6:27 P.M. that lasted for more than a minute. What was this? Why would Kevin send a voicemail page to someone who, by his own account, was sitting right next to him at the time? It didn't make sense.

The detectives checked Deepti's voicemail messages at the telephone company. Unfortunately, all had been erased automatically within forty-eight hours, so there was no way to know what message Kevin had left, or why.

But the anomalous voicemail page sparked an idea: What if the 6:27 P.M. page was an attempt by Kevin to create an alibi for the time of Deepti's death? The very fact that he'd sent a voicemail to a person sitting right next to him suggested that by the time of the message, Deepti was already dead.

If that were the case, Kevin was lying about the time that he "just snapped." Instead of killing Deepti after an hour or so of argument, he would have killed her almost immediately on arrival at Mile Marker 33. Once she was dead, Kevin would have sent the voicemail message—possibly something to the effect, "Deepti, where are you? Did you forget our meeting?" or something similar, to suggest that he was nowhere near Deepti when she died.

Then Kevin would have sat in his truck next to Deepti's body for more than an hour, waiting for the traffic to abate on Angeles Crest Highway so he could shove the Mercedes into the ravine unobserved. Later, Kevin could point to the voicemail message and say he hadn't seen Deepti that night, and perhaps even use it to suggest that Deepti had committed suicide in despair over their business difficulties or other problems.

If all this was true, it suggested that Kevin, far from "just snapping," had in fact planned a cold and calculated murder; that instead of panicking because of Deepti's death, that he'd panicked because La Riviere saw him shove the Mercedes into the ravine. In a very real sense, the voicemail was a sort of smoking gun. It was too bad the detectives weren't able to recover its contents.

This was only one of the problems faced by Kevin's criminal lawyer, Michael Abzug, as he prepared for Kevin's trial. Abzug's objective was simple, even if it would be difficult to pull off: to convince a jury that Kevin had indeed "just snapped," and that the crime was one of a spur-of-the-moment rage that would constitute voluntary manslaughter, rather than premeditated murder. To convince a jury of this, Abzug would have to show that Kevin was provoked in the course of a passionate argument, and that he had erupted without considering the consequences of his act.

The difference, to Kevin, was significant: convicted of voluntary manslaughter he might even get off with probation. Convicted of first-degree murder with special circumstances, he could get the needle.

Abzug was a Los Angeles native. He had graduated from UCLA Law School in 1974, after attending his undergrad-

uate years at the same school. He had then joined the U.S.
Attorney's Office in Manhattan, where he had worked for
Rudy Giuliani as a member of that office's Organized
Crime Strike Force. After some years in New York, Abzug
had returned to California to work in private practice, then
joined the Federal Public Defender's Office in Los Angeles
for three years. He subsequently left that office for private
defense work, and specialized mostly in federal cases. A
father of five young children, he had already tried six death
penalty cases; Kevin's would be his seventh.

Almost from the start, Abzug was struck by the unusual circumstances of the murder. Why would a respected physician, a man almost everyone agreed was
habitually non-confrontational, suddenly turn to murder?
Why would he destroy his own life, as well as that of his
victim? On the surface of things, it simply didn't make
any sense.

"This was a crime in search of a motive," Abzug said
later. And while the prosecution would offer a smorgasbord
of possibilities, none of them, in Abzug's view, were sufficient to explain just why Kevin had done what he had
done.

Motive was also on the mind of Abzug's opponent, Los
Angeles County Deputy District Attorney Marian Thompson. Thompson had been with the case almost from the
beginning. She had accompanied the detectives during their
search of the Anderson house in La Verne, and had been
involved with them in interviewing various witnesses.
Later, it had been Thompson who presented the case to the
grand jury to obtain Kevin's indictment for first-degree
murder.

In some ways, Thompson was similar to Deepti, in that
both were described by colleagues as very determined, per-
sistent, even ambitious people. She had graduated from the
University of Southern California, and then attended South-
western University Law School, graduating with a law degree in 1981. After five years in private practice, Thompson
had joined the Los Angeles County District Attorney's Of-

fice in 1987. Since that time, Thompson had prosecuted
nearly a dozen murder cases, three of them death penalty
proceedings that eventually resulted in guilty pleas when
the ultimate sanction was withdrawn. Like Abzug, she also
had five children.

To Thompson, the elements of premeditation in Kevin's
crime were obvious: Kevin's various attempts to create alibis prior to the crime showed that he had intended to kill
Deepti hours if not days before he actually did. Even the
very location of the crime, on the relatively isolated stretch
of Angeles Crest Highway, shouted out planning, at least
to Thompson.

And as for motive, Thompson could think of nearly a
half dozen.

"She was an inconvenient woman," Thompson would
claim. By this, Thompson meant that once he'd had his way
with Deepti—and once Deepti had told Kevin she was
pregnant—Deepti had become extremely troublesome to
Kevin, which was why he felt he had to dispose of her. For
other motives, Thompson would point to Heidi, and suggest
that if Heidi left Kevin because of Deepti, he would be
wiped out financially; the prospect that Kevin would have
to pay still more child support, for Deepti's unborn child;
that Kevin's reputation in the Pasadena medical community
would be destroyed if it came out that he was having an
affair; and that Kevin was somehow trying to cheat Deepti
out of her patients. As Thompson saw it, Kevin had seduced an innocent young woman with big promises, only
to get rid of her, fatally, when she became an intractable
problem.

It is, of course, the nature of the justice system's adver-
sarial process that each side moves to the extreme in the
attempt to bring the center with them. Usually, however,
the truth remains nearer the middle. And if Kevin was
something less than the paragon of inoffensiveness that Abzug tried to portray, it is likewise true that Deepti was
something less than the innocent, naive and credulous person that Thompson tried to establish.

Pasadena pediatrician Dr. Paul Kevin Anderson on the night of his arrest, November 11/12, 1999.
(Los Angeles County Sheriff's Department)

The Children's Clinic in Pasadena. Dr. Anderson had already entered negotiations to purchase the facility when Dr. Deepti Gupta was killed. *(Carlton Smith)*

The Colorado Boulevard motel where Dr. Anderson and Dr. Gupta had their next-to-last argument on the night before her death. *(Carlton Smith)*

The St. Luke Medical Center where Dr. Anderson worked and Dr. Gupta worked for him (LEFT). Dr. Anderson claimed that he and Dr. Gupta visited the hospital the evening that Deepti was killed. Prosecutors would later allege that Dr. Anderson was attempting to establish an alibi. Later, they went for a drive in the San Gabriel Mountains (BELOW LEFT). *(Both Carlton Smith)*

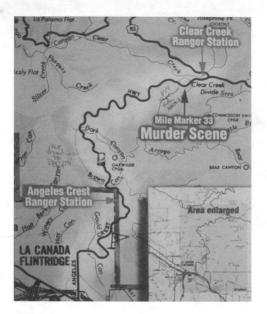

Mile Marker 33, where the doctors' remote mountain rendezvous turned deadly, as seen on the map that prosecutors used (ABOVE) ...and from the air (BELOW).
(Both Los Angeles County Sheriff's Department)

Dr. Gupta's Mercedes SUV, as it was seen by police and rescue personnel scaling down the 450-foot cliff on the night of November 12, 1999. *(Los Angeles County Sheriff's Department)*

Another shot, used in a prosecution exhibit, reveals the extent of the damage to the vehicle.
(Los Angeles County Sheriff's Department)

The turnout at Mile Marker 33, as seen in the daylight.
(Carlton Smith)

Dr. Anderson's Toyota 4Runner after he crashed it while attempting to flee the crime scene.
(Los Angeles County Sheriff's Department)

Defense Attorney Michael Abzug.
(Carlton Smith)

Heidi Anderson, Kevin Anderson's wife, at his trial for the murder of his mistress.
(Walt Mancini, Pasadena Star-News*)*

Next of kin: Dr. Vijay Gupta after Dr. Kevin Anderson was found guilty of second degree murder. Behind him is Deputy District Attorney Marian Thompson.
(Walt Mancini, Pasadena Star-News)

But each side would have its innings as the trial began in the fall of the year 2000, and by the time it was over, Kevin would be depicted by Thompson as cold, calculating, lying, and a homicidal sexual predator; while Deepti would be portrayed by Abzug as "a very aggressive, unhappy person," dissatisfied with her work and her marriage—someone who "pushed too hard" until eventually, Kevin exploded. The polarities would make both Vijay Gupta and Heidi Anderson deeply unhappy, although for different reasons.

The trial opened on the last day of October 2000—Halloween. A year before, Kevin had been grilling a hundred hot dogs at his neighborhood block party. Now he was an accused murderer facing a trial for his life.

Over the previous week a panel of seven men and five women had been culled from a list of hundreds of potential jurors summoned to the Pasadena courtroom of Superior Court Judge Teri Schwartz. Because publicity about the case had been extensive, particularly in the Pasadena area, Judge Schwartz had to call in an extra large pool of people to eliminate any with strong biases. The trial was expected to last at least a month, and 127 witnesses had been summoned to testify.

Schwartz was anxious to get the trial on its way; she had a mandatory judges' conference to attend in the last week of November, and wanted to finish the case by Thanksgiving, November 23. Throughout the trial, in fact, Schwartz continually urged the two sides to push faster, which sparked conflicts with Thompson.

Much later, Thompson would complain that Schwartz was so intent on getting the case done that the prosecution was prevented from adequately cross-examining Kevin Anderson, and was prevented from calling a rebuttal witness to demonstrate that Kevin was lying about a material fact. And when, before the trial, Thompson suggested that she was entitled to a ten-day delay because she might run into a scheduling conflict with another case, Schwartz barked at her: "Your office is on notice that we are going and we need to get this case moving and here we are . . . I know there are over one thousand deputy DAs, many of whom are certainly qualified to try something like [Thompson's other case]. I don't know why your office can't assist in accommodating the court . . . because this case is going [to trial]. I don't know how to make it any clearer."

Thompson eventually got her ten-day continuance, but the tone of conflict between the judge and the prosecutor that was to mark the trial of Kevin Anderson was thereby set, almost from the outset. By the time the trial was over, in fact, there would be three separate motions for mistrial, and a series of confrontations between Schwartz and Thompson that were astonishing for their vitriol, coming as they did in a court of law.

While normally most prospective witnesses were excluded from the courtroom to avoid their being influenced by others' testimony, Thompson and Abzug obtained permission from the judge to permit Vijay and Heidi to observe the opening statements. After each had testified, they would also be permitted to observe the remainder of the proceedings.

"I have cautioned my client's wife," Abzug said, "that even though during opening statements she may hear things that are unpleasant to hear—certainly there are going to be things in my opening statement that I don't enjoy discussing—nevertheless she should do her best to keep herself calm. I hope that the victim's husband, Professor Gupta, who will be present with my consent, will also try to exercise the same type of self-control during what must be a very painful process for him."

Just before 11 A.M., Thompson greeted the jury, and embarked on her opening statement.

"The defendant is charged with a November eleventh, 1999, first-degree, premeditated murder of his young col-

league and lover, Dr. Deepti Gupta. We will present to you
overwhelming evidence that the defendant planned her
murder.

"We will present to you overwhelming evidence that
the defendant lured Dr. Gupta to a remote location in the
Angeles National Forest with the intent to take her by
surprise, strangle her to death, killing her and their unborn child, and to destroy evidence of this crime by stag-
ing her death as a fiery traffic collision over the side of
the mountain.

"Why did Dr. Anderson kill her? The answer, ladies and
gentlemen, is almost as old as time itself. The elimination
of an inconvenient lover by a married man, a physician no
less, of position and property, to avoid the loss of his marriage, before he was ready to leave that marriage himself,
damage to his professional reputation and financial loss or
ruin.

"Why had she become inconvenient? Because she was
pregnant with his child.

"When did Dr. Anderson decide to kill Dr. Gupta? That,
ladies and gentlemen, you will find is the only real issue
in this case.

"And we will present to you overwhelming evidence that
the decision to kill her was made before the defendant
drove up that dark and winding highway known as Angeles
Crest Highway in the Angeles National Forest, armed with
a murder kit in the back of his truck, a full two-and-a-half-
gallon container of gasoline, gloves, a small length of rope,
and a tie which he had placed inside the truck."

Thompson now sketched in the events leading up to the
murder—Deepti's arrival at the Eaton Canyon clinic, the
plans for a partnership with Kevin, the developing love affair, Heidi's jealousy, the collapse of the partnership plans,
Kevin's decision to buy Dr. Richard's practice, Deepti's
complaint that Kevin was withholding the Eaton Canyon
appointment calendars, the tryst at the motel on the night
of November 10, Deepti's announcement of her pregnancy,
and Kevin's reaction to this news.

"He had just learned from her that she was pregnant with his child. If his wife ever found out, she would kick him out on the street and ruin him both professionally and financially. He might lose the opportunity to purchase Dr. Richard's practice. His reputation would be ruined at both St. Luke Hospital and Huntington Memorial Hospital, the two largest hospitals in the Pasadena area, the hospitals where he worked. His wife would make sure of that. She was a nurse in the neonatal ward at Huntington Memorial Hospital. His referral base from the local OB/GYNs would probably dry up, all in deference to his wife, who they liked and cared for."

Kevin was already paying alimony to his ex-wife Natalie, Thompson said. He was paying child support for a daughter from that marriage. "Now," Thompson continued, "he would have to pay child support for the next eighteen years for this new baby.

"Things looked bleak for Dr. Anderson. He had to figure out a way to stop Dr. Gupta from having this baby."

Kevin had admitted as much to the sheriff's detectives, Thompson said.

"He knew that once she made up her mind to have this baby, there was nothing he could do about it. His only alternative was to kill her. So he began to formulate what he thought was the perfect plan. The perfect murder. And in his arrogance, ladies and gentlemen, you'll see that he thought he could get away with it. And you will learn that he almost did."

Thompson went on to sketch in more of the evidence—Kevin's apparent attempt to set up alibis with the St. Luke nurses around 5 P.M. on November 11, the telephone call to Deepti's pager at 6:27 P.M., and a call to Natalie Profant thirteen minutes later. Kevin's intent was to light Deepti's car on fire, then send it plunging into the ravine. But, said Thompson, the plan went awry when the car moved too soon.

"Stunned by his inability to destroy evidence of his crime by lighting her body on fire, and the vehicle, the defendant returned to his vehicle and sat inside. He began to panic. Now what?

"He had the perfect plan. He thought he was going to commit the perfect murder. And now her body and her vehicle were over the side of the mountain, and he had not been able to destroy evidence of his crime."

At that point, Thompson suggested, Kevin's mind turned to thoughts of escape. He got back on the highway and headed toward Big Tujunga Canyon Road in an effort to get away. And while Kevin had told the police he had simply turned in the wrong direction in his panic, it wasn't true.

"Ladies and gentlemen, at the heart of the defendant's statement to the police, you will listen to a man who lies about everything that is important, everything that is essential in this case. He lies about the nature of his relationship with Dr. Gupta. He lies about having sex with her. He denies the child is his. You'll hear his own words. Listen to the tone of his voice. Listen to the calmness with which he speaks, as he lies about everything that is important. We will show you lie after lie."

Kevin was on the road to financial success when he committed the crime, Thompson said, and he killed Deepti because she threatened to ruin that prospect.

"He was trained to be a professional and calm in the face of overwhelming odds, in the face of life-and-death matters. He was a trained professional, ladies and gentlemen. You will be convinced beyond any doubt that this is not a man who acts on his impulses."

Kevin's patients trusted him, Thompson said, just as Deepti had trusted him—otherwise she would never have followed him up into the mountains.

"You will be convinced, ladies and gentlemen, that he violated his most sacred trust. Not only did he take the life of a fellow colleague at the beginning of her career, who was also devoted to the field of pediatrics, he also took the life of his unborn son, whose care, as a pediatrician, he took an oath to preserve. Worst of all . . . he murdered Dr. Gupta to protect himself from financial ruin."

24

Thompson finished her opening statement by showing the jury a photograph of Deepti.

"Don't forget her throughout this trial," she said. "Don't forget why you are here, to see that justice is done."

Now it was Abzug's turn. He began by taking aim at Thompson herself.

"Before Ms. Thompson started her opening statement," he said, "the judge told you two things. The first was that opening statements were not evidence, and the second was that Ms. Thompson was not supposed to argue her case to you. I heard a lot of argument from Ms. Thompson about perfect murders and murder kits and overwhelming evidence, and 'not to forget Dr. Gupta.'

"I chose to let it go. I chose to let it go for this reason . . . I'm confident that at the end of the case, those predictions that Ms. Thompson was making, those arguments she was making, you're going to find they are not supported by the evidence.

"Now, you've all heard there are two sides to every story, and that is certainly true in this case. One thing that is not going to be disputed in this case is that the homicide was totally unexpected. The people who knew Dr. Gupta and Dr. Anderson were totally astounded, surprised and shocked when they learned that Dr. Anderson killed Dr. Gupta. Nobody saw it coming, not even Dr. Anderson and Dr. Gupta.

"The evidence is going to show that this sudden act of violence, the taking of another human life, is completely inconsistent with Dr. Anderson's character, who he is, how he's lived his last forty years. You'll learn, as the testimony unfolds, that Dr. Anderson actually abhors violence; that he was exposed to violence at a very early age at the hands of an abusive stepfather, and that because of that experience as he grew up, he turned away from violence. And not being a violent person, he became the opposite. He became a mediator, a conciliator, somebody who tried to get people to get along."

Kevin, Abzug said, had dedicated his life to caring for the most vulnerable—children.

"Finally, and I think probably most important, you're going to find that this homicide was inconsistent with the feelings that Dr. Anderson and Dr. Gupta had for each other."

Contrary to Thompson's opening remarks, Abzug said, this was not a situation in which Deepti had been "somehow seduced by Dr. Anderson's charm," but a situation "where the mutual feelings of affection were reciprocal."

"The evidence is going to show that Dr. Gupta's behavior may have irritated Dr. Anderson and may have concerned him. It may have frustrated, but at no time will you hear evidence in this case that Dr. Anderson chose murder, the intentional taking of a human life, as the only solution to the problems he was having with Dr. Gupta."

There could be no dispute that Deepti had loving feelings for Kevin, Abzug continued. Why else would Deepti have kept the love notes that Kevin had written to her in the summer?

"When Dr. Gupta got these letters," Abzug said, "she didn't throw them away. She didn't turn them over to her husband. She didn't give them to a third party. The evidence will show that she kept those letters. She kept those letters in a secret place, close to her, hidden from her husband.

"The evidence is not going to show that Dr. Gupta was trying to get away from Dr. Anderson," he continued. The fact that Deepti and Kevin had had sex the night before her death showed that.

In fact, there was much more to the relationship than a mere seduction of Deepti by Kevin, Abzug said.

"Dr. Gupta looked at Dr. Anderson as a way to get out

of an unhappy marriage, and a way to advance herself professionally. That's what was going on in this case."

Now Abzug took the jury through Kevin's version of the events of 1999. But in this characterization, most of the unhappiness lay with Deepti. Deepti was unhappy with Vijay, Abzug said, and had said as much to Anil Sharma. She saw Kevin as a sort of salvation to her unhappy home life, Abzug indicated. But Deepti had a hard time being happy wherever she went, Abzug said. She didn't get along with Dr. Ng at the Eaton Canyon clinic, and later argued with Dr. Richard at Children's Clinic.

Deepti was having difficulty getting her career started, he said. "She saw Dr. Anderson as a way to jump-start her career." It was Kevin who had the patients, Kevin who had the $10,000-a-month on-call contract from St. Luke, Kevin who had the connections to Ken Rivers so that Deepti might hope to get the $10,000-a-month relocation grant.

Once both doctors decided to try to go into partnership together, Abzug said, it was Kevin who had the appointment calendars for Eaton Canyon, not Deepti.

"Now from time to time you've heard Ms. Thompson refer to this document, this list of calendar appointments as a 'patient list.' It wasn't a 'patient list,' ladies and gentlemen. The evidence is going to show that Dr. Gupta at no time had a patient list at Eaton Canyon. She didn't have one.

"But the evidence is going to show that Dr. Gupta had simply a calendar of patients she was covering for Dr. Ng. She didn't have her own patient list. Ms. Thompson claimed—argued—in her opening statement that after Dr. Gupta and Dr. Anderson decided not to go into practice, Dr. Anderson held onto the calendar of Dr. Gupta's appointments in an effort to steal her patients. Nothing is further from the truth."

Kevin had absolutely no need to "steal" Deepti's patients, Abzug said. He certainly had no reason to fear her as a competitor, as Thompson had suggested.

"He had been a practitioner for many, many years, with a successful practice. He certainly didn't need a list of her appointments for four months to build up his own practice. The evidence will also show that, indeed, Dr. Anderson did give back Dr. Gupta all of her appointment books that he could find. And finally, and probably most fundamentally, the evidence is going to show that rather than trying to hurt Dr. Gupta's practice, Dr. Anderson did everything he could . . . to help her be successful.

"He shared his appointment schedule with her. He referred patients to her over at Children's Clinic . . . right up until the end. On November tenth, one day before the homicide occurred, the evidence is going to show that Dr. Anderson actually gave Dr. Gupta the most favorable rating he could in an evaluation form provided by St. Luke Hospital. These are not the actions of somebody trying to steal another doctor's patients."

After a break for lunch, Abzug resumed.

As the partnership began to come together, Abzug told the jury, Heidi began to feel cut out. She eventually became suspicious that there were romantic feelings between Deepti and Kevin.

"The evidence is going to show Heidi was more right than she knew, because by that time, in the middle of the summer of 1999, unbeknownst to Heidi and unbeknownst to [Vijay] Gupta, the husband, Dr. Gupta and Dr. Anderson had developed a passionate love affair."

Once Heidi had voiced her suspicions to Kevin, Abzug said, and Kevin had admitted that Deepti was interested in him, Heidi "hit the roof and demanded that he pull out of the partnership . . . and [that] he just stay away from her entirely.

"So then Dr. Anderson had to turn around and tell Dr. Gupta that he was not going into private practice with her, and it was her turn to hit the roof. Privately she begged him not to abandon her, because of the strong emotional attachment they had for each other. Publicly she explained Dr. Anderson's decision not to go into practice with her by

falsely portraying herself as a victim, and, the evidence will
show, manipulating everybody around her—colleagues, her
husband, and other people."

Deepti told Vijay that Kevin had prevented her from
getting the $10,000-a-month relocation grant from St. Luke.
"That wasn't true," Abzug said.

Deepti complained that Kevin was trying to steal her
practice, he continued, and that wasn't true either. "There
was basically no practice to steal. She's a brand-new doctor. It was a charge that was ludicrous on its face, and Dr.
Anderson had no motive, as an established physician, to
take any of her patients, even if she had any."

Kevin may have been frustrated and irritated by Deepti,
but he wasn't desperate, Abzug maintained.

"He didn't feel like he was backed into a corner. He
didn't feel that the only solution for his dispute with Dr.
Gupta was to calmly decide to lure her up to the Angeles
Crest Highway and to murder her."

Then came Deepti's announcement that she was pregnant and that Kevin was the father—"not an announcement
of joy," said Abzug, "but an announcement really to try to
bludgeon him [in] to doing what she wanted. This is how
she used the pregnancy, ladies and gentlemen.

"As Dr. Anderson told the police after his arrest, 'anything is possible.' She may have been pregnant, but in his
heart, Dr. Anderson did not believe that Dr. Gupta was
pregnant." Because, Abzug added, by that point Kevin
didn't believe anything that Deepti was telling him.

On the night of Deepti's death, he continued, Kevin had
no plans to commit murder. He hadn't taken Deepti to the
top of the mountain for any sinister purpose. And while
Thompson had described the scene at Mile Marker 33 as
"remote," that was hardly the case, Abzug said.

"The evidence is going to show that Angeles Crest Highway is named Angeles Crest Highway, not the Angeles
Crest Goat Path, for a very good reason. It is a heavily
traveled highway." If Kevin had really "lured" Deepti to a

remote location to kill her, he certainly could have picked somewhere far more secluded, Abzug said.

"They sat twenty feet from the highway. They weren't behind bushes or some other obscure location. They were right next to the highway for over an hour . . . Dr. Anderson was not waiting for an opportune time to kill Dr. Gupta. The evidence will show there was no opportune time." In fact, Abzug said, the evidence would show that "roughly every sixty seconds, a car . . . is passing by this allegedly secluded spot."

There was so much traffic past the location, Abzug continued, that Kevin was easily caught. That alone showed a lack of planning and premeditation.

"Dr. Anderson was not caught in this case because of an unlucky coincidence of a Good Samaritan, who just happened, by unhappy fate, happened to be driving by. The reason he got caught, the very reason he got caught, was because the Angeles Crest Highway and that particular location is *not* secluded. The reason he got caught is precisely because he *didn't* plan to murder Dr. Gupta up at that spot. It was a sudden, quick decision, and that's why he got caught."

Nor was it true that Kevin had brought a "murder kit" with him, Abzug said.

"I assure you," he said, "there was nothing in that car that said 'murder kit.' What she was talking about was a can of gasoline that Dr. Anderson had at the rear of his SUV as they were driving up Angeles Crest Highway. The evidence will show that this can had routinely been in that SUV for about two months.

"When Dr. Anderson and Dr. Gupta started talking on November eleventh, the conversation started reasonably enough. But as the conversation went on and Dr. Anderson announced that he was not going to leave his wife, not going to be with Dr. Gupta, the evidence is going to show that she absolutely lost control of herself, and the face that Dr. Anderson saw on that night is not the same face that you see in that picture that the prosecution has hung before you.

"This woman was enraged. She was screaming accusations, the same accusations she had made against him for the last two months. She was wildly flailing her arms about. She was in his face. Then she said the one thing she had never said before to him, which was, she threatened his seven-year-old daughter . . .

"At that point, all of the two months of built-up frustration that Dr. Anderson felt with Dr. Gupta, her lies, her manipulation, her ingratitude, all boiled up, came together in one explosive instant, and he absolutely lost control of himself. He snapped. He didn't think. He acted, ladies and gentlemen. At that point, he strangled her."

This was not a crime of planning, of premeditation, Abzug said, but a classic crime of passion, of anger. "That is what happened here.

"When Dr. Gupta lay in the car, Dr. Anderson started shaking. He started hyperventilating. He was terrified and appalled at what he did. But he chose to do the exact wrong thing. He did. I suggest to you it was the very human thing, but absolute wrong thing. He didn't turn himself in. He got scared and he tried to get away.

"Premeditated? It wasn't a well-executed plan. It wasn't, as she so colorfully called it, 'a perfect murder.' It was a perfect mess. It was clumsy. It was stupid. It lasted—the cover-up lasted maybe all of a few minutes before Jay La Riviere drove up and saw him there. Dr. Anderson was so nervous and out of his mind, was so upset, he almost went over the mountain with Dr. Gupta. He didn't empty out the gas can on her. He didn't light a match. And he drove down the mountainside so quickly, in a few short minutes he crashed his own vehicle into the side of the mountain, he was so upset."

And while it was true that Kevin later lied to the police about his affair with Deepti, Abzug continued, this took place at nearly four in the morning, when Kevin was under a tremendous amount of stress.

"And under that kind of stressful situation, people aren't thinking too clearly. Dr. Anderson wasn't, of course. And frankly, neither were the police at that interview.

"Finally, the evidence is going to show that neither Dr. Anderson nor Dr. Gupta behaved very abnormally. Both individuals were married. Both individuals had small children. Both individuals lied to their respective spouses, to their colleagues about what was going on between them personally. But just as Dr. Gupta did not deserve to die because of her lying and misleading her husband, Dr. Anderson doesn't deserve to be convicted of a premeditated murder that he didn't plan, that he didn't execute, and that he didn't want, because he was deceptive to his wife and others.

"At the end of the case I'm going to ask you to render a verdict of voluntary manslaughter, not out of mercy, not out of sympathy, not because Dr. Anderson is a physician, but out of justice, and because that verdict is the only verdict I believe you will find . . . that fits the facts here."

25

With the conclusion of the two opening statements—or arguments, since both lawyers had substantially veered over the line between factual statements into pure persuasion, even though this wasn't usually permitted—the two sides settled in for the battle.

In planning her case, Thompson had two main objectives. The first was to establish all the elements of the crime of murder in the first degree, with the special circumstance of "lying in wait"; lying in wait was defined as what happened when an attacker took a victim by surprise through a ruse or concealment.

The second objective was to show Kevin's motive for murdering Deepti. While it wasn't legally required that Thompson prove the existence of a motive or motives for the murder, she was very aware that a jury was much less likely to find the element of "malice aforethought" without one. Why would Kevin have had malice if he had no motive? Certainly the notion of premeditation cried out for the establishment of a motive. So Thompson wanted to establish reasons that Kevin might have wanted to see Deepti dead.

Establishing the first elements of the crime—that a human being had been killed, and that the killing was unlawful—was simple enough. Deepti was indisputably dead, and it was quite apparent that her killing was unlawful. To prove those elements, Thompson had chosen to go with the strongest part of her case, the facts from the mountain. This was good strategy, in part because there was comparatively little dispute about the overt facts, and secondly because it was by far the most visual part of her case.

Thompson knew, as any experienced prosecutor knows, that presenting a criminal case is a bit like telling a story.

The idea is to grab the audience—in this case, the jury—
at the very beginning with a series of testimonial images
that will put the jurors in the picture. If it's done well, the
images soon form a sort of reference frame for all the more
nuanced evidence to follow. She began with Jay La Riviere.

La Riviere took the stand, and told his story once
again—how he'd locked the keys inside the rental car, how
he'd been delayed, how he had come upon the flat stretch
at George's Gap just before 8 P.M., and how he'd seen
Deepti's white Mercedes hurtling over the edge, apparently
pushed by Kevin's 4Runner. Both vehicles had their lights
off at the time, he said.

He told of passing the scene, then making his first U-
turn and going back to see what had happened. He described pulling into the turnout, shining his lights on the
4Runner, then seeing the 4Runner take off, headed north-
bound on the highway toward Palmdale. After he checked
to see if he could help anyone, he said, he got back in his
car and gave chase.

Thompson showed La Riviere a number of photographs
of the turnout. La Riviere pointed to where he'd seen the
Mercedes and the 4Runner. Then Thompson produced the
envelope Jay had used to write down Kevin's license plate
number. All of these were put into evidence for the jury to
consider.

Next La Riviere described contacting the forest service
personnel, then returning to the turnout, followed by his
trip down into the ravine to the site of the wreck. How he'd
returned to the top to meet Martinez and Bennick, then
going back down to where Bennick had discovered
Deepti's body. How the sheriff's deputies had come, how
he'd explained what he'd seen, and how, eventually, he
went to the Crescenta Valley station to be interviewed by
the detectives somewhere around 2 A.M.

La Riviere concluded his direct testimony by describing
his return to Mile Marker 33 two days after Deepti's death,
and how he'd found the greeting card.

"And is it a thank-you card?" Thompson asked.

"Yes, it is," La Riviere said, and he appeared to be prepared to describe it further when Abzug objected. He didn't want La Riviere sharing his views about supernatural greetings from Deepti with the jury.

As he rose for his cross-examination of La Riviere, Abzug had in mind his own objectives for the trial. As far as many of the fundamental facts were concerned—that Deepti was dead, for instance, and that Kevin was the one who had killed her—there wasn't much Abzug *could* do, except watch to make sure that Thompson put the evidence on fairly, and to squawk if she cut any corners.

Abzug's main objective was to undercut any evidence of premeditation, or planning, of the murder on Kevin's part. That meant any direct evidence of planning had to be directly countered with a more reasonable explanation. His secondary effort would be to take the wind out of suggestions that Kevin had motives to want to kill Deepti. And on a third level, it would be Abzug's task to try to show that Deepti had somehow provoked Kevin into an irrational, violent outburst that took place on the spur of the moment. In all of these areas, Abzug had a distinct advantage over Thompson: his principal witness could talk for himself, while Thompson's was no longer among the living.

Finally, Abzug had more than his share of the defense attorney's practiced capacity to get under a hostile witness's skin. Here the objective was simple: if a juror didn't like a witness—if he or she had a negative reaction to a personality—there was always a chance that the witness's testimony might be discounted or even ignored altogether. There was also the possibility that if he could get a witness to go too far, to be too emphatic, to appear to be too sure, that the jury might think the witness was aggrandizing himself in his testimony, and thus tend to doubt it. Abzug thought he had a candidate for this in La Riviere.

Abzug began by trying to get La Riviere to agree that there were many turnouts along Angeles Crest Highway, and that the purpose of the turnouts was to get slower traffic off the road so that fast traffic could get by. For some reason La Riviere appeared to misunderstand the question.

"I thought they were for people making out," he said, to general laughter in the courtroom.

"Do you think—this is a murder trial," Abzug said. "Do you think this is funny?"

La Riviere said no, he didn't think it was funny.

Abzug tried to get La Riviere to admit that he hadn't actually seen the 4Runner shove the Mercedes over the side, and while La Riviere admitted that he hadn't seen them touching, that was what he thought he'd seen.

Abzug tried a few more times to shake La Riviere in his testimony, without result. After a few more questions, he decided to let him go and reserve his fire for other witnesses.

The following day was November 1, 2000, exactly a year to the day when Deepti had made her first official appearance at Dr. Richard's clinic. Thompson intended to use the whole day to put on the skeletal framework of her case as established by the firefighters and sheriff's deputies who had come to the scene at Mile Marker 33.

Summoned thus to the witness stand were Bennick, who described discovering Deepti's body; Tony Martinez, who provided a similar account, and added that the ravine was well-known as a place to dump cars; Sheriff's Deputy Dave Willard, who described meeting La Riviere, Bennick and Martinez at the turnout about 8:15 P.M.; and reserve Deputy Sheriff John Camphouse, who was in charge of the sheriff's Search and Rescue unit, which recovered Deepti's body, and who was used by Thompson to authenticate a number of photographs of various turnouts along the highway.

Thompson wanted to make the point that of all the turnouts between La Canada and Mile Marker 33, the turnout used by Kevin was the only one that was not visible to cars approaching from the south. The implication was that Kevin had selected Mile Marker 33 because it was secluded from observation by oncoming cars.

There wasn't much Abzug could do with this testimony;

on the whole it was a straightforward accounting of the events of that night. About the best he could do was ask Camphouse—who had testified on direct that he'd been called to a number of suicides and murders in the Angeles National Forest over the years—whether, if he were planning a murder in the area of Mile Marker 33, he'd do it at 10:30 P.M. instead of 7:30 P.M. Camphouse said later would be better.

Following Camphouse, Thompson called Sheriff's Deputy Michael Brandriff, who had first handcuffed Kevin after his crash near Big Tujunga Canyon Road.

"As you approached the defendant," Thompson asked, "did he say anything?"

"He said, 'The guy next to me is not involved. He was just helping me out. I'm the guy you're looking for.' "

Brandriff was followed by Deputy Steve Wilkinson, the K-9 officer. Wilkinson described his conversation with Kevin, in which Kevin had rambled a bit, and had said that Deepti and Vijay had threatened to sue him, and that he "snapped."

"Deputy Wilkinson," Thompson asked, "did the defendant ever tell you that woman he talked about had ever threatened to harm him or anyone else?"

"No," Wilkinson said.

"Did he ever tell you that the woman threatened to harm his daughter?"

"No."

"The only threat he discussed with you was a lawsuit?"

"A lawsuit."

26

The next day, November 2, Thompson had reserved for some of the biggest guns in her case: Vijay Gupta, Marvin Cooper, four St. Luke nurses, Anil Sharma, Dr. Ng and Dr. Richard. Having established that Deepti was dead, and that Kevin had been arrested and had seemingly confessed to killing her, what was necessary now was to establish that it had been an "unlawful killing," as the element required, and to begin to lay the groundwork for Kevin's possible motives.

For her first witness of the day, Thompson called a deputy coroner's investigator, Tom Ratcliffe, who had come to Mile Marker 33 on the night of November 11. Ratcliffe said Deepti's body had already been brought to the top by Camphouse's SAR people when he arrived. He said he examined the body to make an initial assessment as to the manner of death.

"After you initially looked at her," Thompson asked, "did you notice anything about her body?"

"I think the thing that struck me most," Ratcliffe said, "was the odor of gasoline and the appearance of what looked like skin shearing around the hip area." The skin shearing, Ratcliffe said, was a result of the skin having been soaked for some time in gasoline.

And here Thompson missed an important opportunity. Ratcliffe had been with the county coroner's office for more than 13 years, and was obviously familiar with the effects of gasoline on human skin. Thompson might have asked Ratcliffe *how long* the skin appeared to have been subjected to gasoline soaking. If Ratcliffe had been able to offer an expert opinion that Deepti's skin had been soaking in gasoline for some substantial period of time—say, at least an hour—Kevin would have been forced to find an explanation of how this was possible, given his version of the events.

Instead, Thompson moved on to Kevin's arrest, calling Detective Gary Sica. He told about racing up Big Tujunga Canyon Road to find Kevin and the Good Samaritan John David Vinson at the 4Runner off to the side of Angeles Forest Highway.

"We proceeded to that turnout and detained both parties at gunpoint," Sica said. He identified the 4Runner as Kevin's truck.

Thompson now called Gloria Angelo from the Montebello clinic to the stand. Thompson wanted Gloria to identify a necklace Deepti nearly always wore. The necklace had never been recovered. Thompson believed that it had come off in Kevin's truck during the initial struggle, and Thompson believed that Kevin had thrown it away in the minutes following the killing. Gloria described the missing necklace, and said that Deepti always wore it. Next Thompson asked Gloria to identify an earring that had been found in Kevin's truck on the floor in front of the passenger seat. The detectives had found it during one of their searches, and believed that it also had come off in the struggle. Gloria identified the earring as one of Deepti's. Thompson now had Gloria describe Deepti's character as "very cheerful, always smiling . . . she was so innocent. There was a purity of her," and in doing so, provided an opening for Abzug.

Abzug, in his cross-examination, was now able to focus on a different aspect of Deepti's behavior. "Do you recall Dr. Gupta, after she began working at the Children's Clinic in Pasadena, telling you that she was upset because of the way that Dr. Anderson and Dr. Richard were treating her over there?"

"Yes," Gloria said.

"Did she tell you Dr. Richard and Dr. Anderson weren't compensating her properly for the patients she was seeing?"

"Yes."

"Did she tell you she didn't want to work over at Children's Clinic because of her suspicions about illegal billing practices there?"

"She wanted to get away from Dr. Anderson," Gloria offered.

"Thank you for telling me that," said Abzug, drily, "but my question to you was: did she tell you she didn't want to be part of Children's Clinic because of her suspicions about illegal billing practices over there?"

"She had mentioned that, yes."

"Did she tell you that she felt something illegal was going on over at Children's Clinic?"

"Yes."

Abzug was trying to use this testimony to portray Deepti as a person who was hard to get along with, and who wasn't above stretching the truth; he planned to put on evidence during his own case that there were no such illegal billing practices going on at Children's Clinic. This would be part of his effort to portray Deepti as a purveyor of tall tales. In turn, that would help support Kevin's assertion that he hadn't believed Deepti when she told him she was pregnant.

When she got Gloria back as a witness, Thompson asked if Deepti had ever told her that she'd asked Kevin for her patient lists, but that Kevin wouldn't give them to her.

"Yes," Gloria said.

"Patient list," Abzug asked, when it was his turn again. "It was your understanding that that was a list of patients that belonged to her over at Eaton Canyon?"

"Yes."

"That's what she told you?"

"Yes."

"And did you ever ask her why she didn't go back to Eaton Canyon and get another copy of the patient list, if it was so important to her?" Abzug asked.

Thompson objected before Gloria could answer. The question called for hearsay, she said, and at this point the trial was about to run off the rails for the first, but hardly the last time over the tricky hearsay issue; by the time the whole thing was over, virtual mountains of hearsay would be allowed in, as both sides fought a pitched battle over the true character of Deepti Gupta.

At the sidebar, next to the judge's bench, but out of hearing of the jury, Abzug struck first.

"She opened it up," he said.

"Wait. Wait," said Judge Schwartz. "Both of you have elicited testimony that calls for hearsay. I assume you have some exception in mind. Do you?"

The rule on hearsay is one of the trickier parts of the Evidence Code.[11] Basically, a statement is considered hearsay if it is a statement that was made out of court, and it is being offered as evidence for the truth of the matter asserted. When Thompson asked if Deepti had told Gloria something about what Kevin had said to her about the patient list, whatever it was that Deepti had said to Gloria was hearsay, and should have been inadmissible if offered to the jury as a representation of "the truth of the matter asserted" unless Thompson could demonstrate an exception to the hearsay rule.

Similarly, when Abzug asked Gloria what Deepti may have told her about why she hadn't gone directly to Eaton

---

[11]Section 1200 of the Evidence Code reads: "(a) 'Hearsay evidence' is evidence of a statement that was made other than by a witness while testifying at the hearing and that is offered to prove the truth of the matter stated. (b) Except as provided by law, hearsay evidence is inadmissible." Something only became hearsay, then, when it was offered to the jury as a true fact. An unproven fact could still be offered to the jury, however, not to prove the truth of something, but to explain someone's conduct; and even if that unproven fact contained "he said–she said" statements, it wasn't hearsay as defined by the Evidence Code because it wasn't offered as true. In that case, the judge was supposed to warn the jury that the statement wasn't being offered for the truth, but only to explain the subsequent conduct. This was called an "admonishment." Sometimes, however, determining whether a statement was offered for the truth or to explain subsequent conduct was difficult. Lawyers readily admit that the rules on hearsay are among the most confusing in the Rules of Evidence, and also acknowledge that many experienced lawyers get them wrong.

Canyon for the list, that also would be hearsay. The reason that hearsay wasn't supposed to be admissible as truth was that there was no way to prove that what was supposedly said, was actually said. The best evidence would be the testimony of the person who actually did the saying, under oath, not what someone said a second person said.

There were, however, a number of exceptions. One was when the person originally doing the saying—known as the *declarant*—was the accused, and the statement was against his own interests, such as an admission or confession to another person. Those *were* admissible. So were statements made by declarants that were offered as truth to show the state of mind of the declarant—that he was angry, or she was upset, or that he or she did something for some particular reason.[12]

There were numerous other exceptions to the hearsay rule, but by the time the trial of Kevin Anderson was finished, that one would be invoked over and over again; as a result, a considerable amount of such "state of mind" material came streaming in, some of it double hearsay, and some of it even triple hearsay—such as when Person A says that Person B said that Person C claimed that Person D did something for a particular reason. And some of it would come in, not because it was offered as "truth," but because it explained someone's subsequent course of conduct. It wasn't always easy to tell which was which. And so it goes.

"What's your exception?" Judge Schwartz demanded of Abzug.

"Well, my exception—" Abzug began, before Thompson interrupted.

"That you didn't object before," Thompson chided.

---

[12]Section 1250 of the Evidence Code, for example, permits admission of "evidence of a statement of the declarant's then existing state of mind, emotion, or physical sensation (including a statement of intent, plan, motive, design, mental feeling, pain or bodily health)" when it is "offered to prove the declarant's state of mind, emotion, or physical sensation" when it is at issue.

"My exception," continued Abzug, "is that it shows motive for Dr. Gupta to be involved with Dr. Anderson, that is, that she saw Dr. Anderson as . . ." Presumably Abzug was going to add "a source of patients," but was again interrupted by Thompson, who was worried that the court reporter wasn't getting their conversation. The court reporter was, however.

"It shows that she [Deepti] is not a reliable person," Abzug concluded. "The district attorney in her opening statement said that the motive for this crime was that Dr. Anderson was withholding this so-called patient list. We're going to show that no such patient list ever existed. And it is certainly relevant, as far as whether this list ever existed, as to why Dr. Gupta simply didn't go back to Eaton Canyon and get another copy. The fact is, there was no patient list. She was lying to everybody about it. She [Thompson] brought it up in her examination of this witness and I'm entitled to ask the question."

Thompson denied that she had elicited hearsay in her direct examination of Gloria, although a reading of the transcript shows she had, particularly when she asked Gloria to tell her what Deepti had said Kevin had said about the "patient list." Later, Abzug would say that he expected Thompson to ask something similar to this, and that he hadn't objected because he wanted to get his own hearsay in later. Abzug's strategy was to allow Thompson to present hearsay about Deepti, particularly testimony that appeared to show her in an innocent or at least positive light, because, he said later, he was confident he could knock this material down on his cross-examination.

All of this posed a problem for Judge Schwartz. She realized that since much of the trial was going to center around the supposed motives of both the victim and the perpetrator, it was necessary to get some common ground on the hearsay question right then.

"This is the situation," Judge Schwartz said. "If you guys only want some hearsay to come in, but not a lot of hearsay, none of it is going to come in. I can't sustain an objection and then let a whole bunch of hearsay in and then not permit further examination on it.

"I'm assuming that you are both on the same page when it comes to the hearsay of the victim coming into the trial . . . that there is a reason for it, and that it would qualify as an exception. I'm assuming the exception would be the state of mind of the victim, to explain her conduct. So that's why I haven't interposed my own objection. But if we agree that her statements are admissible under the state-of-mind exception, then they're all admissible, aren't they?"

Schwartz looked at both Thompson and Abzug, and seeing no dissent, waved them back to their places.

Now Abzug had Gloria in a difficult position. As part of his overall strategy, he intended to get from her the fact that Deepti had said things about the patient list that simply weren't true.

Gloria said that Deepti had told her that she tried to get the patient list from Eaton Canyon, but hadn't been able to. Abzug asked when. Gloria said Deepti had hired Lorena Ramirez to get the patient list from Eaton Canyon, and it then developed that Gloria had confused the Eaton Canyon clinic with Richard's Children's Clinic. Having drawn Gloria further than her own knowledge could take her, Abzug was trying to put a dent in the idea that Kevin had murdered Deepti in a dispute over the supposed list, a list that Abzug contended never actually existed.

When it was her turn again, Thompson could only try to rehabilitate Gloria as a witness by making it seem that Abzug had played a shabby trick on her.

"When the attorney asked you, 'Did you have a conversation with Dr. Gupta?' and she told you she was trying to retrieve her patient list from Eaton Canyon, you don't even know what Eaton Canyon is, right?" Thompson asked.

"No, I don't," Gloria said.

"You're just confused?"

"Yes," Gloria said, "he's confusing." She meant Abzug, but she could have been referring to the law on hearsay.

*   *   *

Now Thompson called one of her star witnesses, Vijay. Vijay was familiar with testifying, since he'd been an expert witness in court proceedings before, particularly as they related to soft-tissue injuries. Abzug wouldn't be able to trick Vijay into going too far.

Thompson took Vijay through the basic background: how he had come to the United States, become a professor of mechanical and aerospace engineering, how he'd met and married Deepti, how they had moved to southern California in 1995. Vijay described Deepti's unhappy experience at Eaton Canyon, and how she'd been furious with him when he'd tried to intervene with Dr. Ng.

Vijay next described the advent of the partnership between Kevin and his wife. In Vijay's mind, it had been Kevin who solicited Deepti, not the other way around. Deepti took the idea very seriously, Vijay indicated, and did a lot of work to prepare for the new business.

But then, said Vijay, problems began to crop up—mostly, he said, because Deepti didn't feel that Kevin was doing very much to get the business off the ground.

"She would tell me they would set up an appointment to see physical space over the weekend, and the next thing she would know, he's on a vacation, and she was extremely frustrated about that," Vijay said, in another bit of allowable hearsay.

"Did she tell you that she complained to Anderson about it?"

"Yes."

"While he was on his weekend vacations, did she tell you that she was called in for [on-call] coverage for him?"

"Yes."

"Objection. Hearsay, Your Honor," Abzug called out.

"Overruled," said Schwartz, now that she'd set the ground rules that permitted hearsay to explain state of mind, in this case Deepti's.

"Were these on days that she was not scheduled for on-call coverage?"

"Yes," said Vijay. "I was there on one of those calls,

which are made to our house. Anderson was supposed to be on-call in the hospital. They paged him. He never responded, and there was an emergency. And my wife, being the physician that she was, she immediately—we were going out. She said, 'I'll be back,' and she went out and attended this particular patient."

Eventually, said Vijay, he learned from Deepti that Heidi was opposed to her going into practice with Kevin.

"On September seventh, 1999, did your wife get a call from Anderson, first thing in the morning?"

"Yes."

"And did your wife talk to him?"

"Yes."

"And after she terminated the call, did she tell you what he talked to her about?"

"Yes."

"And what was that?"

"Objection," said Abzug. "Hearsay."

Judge Schwartz summoned the lawyers to the sidebar once more.

"What's the offer?" Judge Schwartz asked.

"It goes to the state of her mind," Thompson said. "On September seventh, Dr. Anderson contacted the victim. He suggested that she come with her husband, child, housekeeper, as a family unit, to his home, and act as if it were an impromptu visit in La Verne and—to pop over—and at that point was when the wife [Heidi] became explosive during the meeting and said, 'You're not going into this.' "

"What's the objection?" Judge Schwartz asked.

"The objection is hearsay," Abzug said. "This particular conversation is being offered for the truth of the matter asserted, 'Anderson made the suggestion.' "

Abzug was trying to make the point that the way the question was phrased assumed that Deepti had told Vijay the truth—that it was Kevin who made the suggestion that they come over, when it fact all that could be reliably testified to by Vijay was that Deepti had told him that; he had no independent knowledge of what was actually said.

"But it would also go to show or explain the subsequent conduct of the victim with respect to the negotiations with the defendant," Judge Schwartz pointed out.

"And assuming that it is true," Abzug said.

"Right," said the judge.

"Well, then," said Abzug, "if the court is inclined to let it in on that basis, I would respectfully ask you to admonish the jury as to these conversations, these hearsay conversations are being offered not to prove the truth of the matter asserted, but to prove motive and conduct of the victim." He wanted the jury to get the idea that Deepti had lied to Vijay, that it had really been her idea to visit the Andersons; an admonishment would lend credence to this notion.

"Well," Judge Schwartz said, "if it is not being offered for the truth, then it won't qualify as hearsay, and it wouldn't be necessary to find an exception. So I disagree with your requested admonishment, because it is being offered for the truth."

By now, it appears that both sides were fully intent on using the hearsay rules to maximum advantage. Part of the immediate problem was that Abzug's objection was both tendentious as well as premature: Vijay hadn't said anything yet, and if he responded by saying, "She said," or "Deepti told me," it would have qualified as hearsay, even if it hadn't been Thompson's original intent.

Schwartz tried to clarify this, but apparently only succeeded in muddying the waters further.

"My understanding of the hearsay rule," she said, "only when it is offered for the truth does it constitute hearsay. If it is not offered for the truth, it doesn't in any opinion constitute hearsay, and we don't need to discuss an exception. The fact of the matter is, all of these statements are really being offered for the truth. If the jury believes they are in fact the statements that were made, then they are coming in for the truth of what's asserted. But the hearsay exception is to demonstrate conduct, I thought, and motive. So I'll overrule the objection and deny the request." The admonishment wasn't necessary in this specific situation,

Schwartz said, because it was Deepti's state of mind that was being offered as true, and not merely Vijay's conduct in deciding to visit the Andersons.

By the time this sidebar discussion broke up, Vijay was ready. But then, he was an expert witness.

"She told me that Anderson told her," he began, "that his wife was against them going into practice because she felt uncomfortable and she suspected a romantic interest between the two. So Anderson wants me, my daughter and my housekeeper to come to his house and show them that we are one, nice family. So she asked me whether I'll be able to do that for her or not." This was hearsay, all right, and when Vijay used the words "she felt," it qualified as an exception.

Vijay said he agreed to Deepti's request, and that afternoon, he, Deepti, their daughter and the housekeeper had driven to the Andersons' house in La Verne, where the confrontation with Heidi ensued.

"Now," Thompson said, "shortly after that meeting at the defendant's house, did your wife tell you that something happened at St. Luke or Huntington?"

"Yes," Vijay said.

"What was that?"

"Objection," Abzug said. "Hearsay."

Once again at the sidebar, Thompson told Judge Schwartz that Vijay would say that Deepti had told him that she was told "by staff" that she was no longer practicing at the hospital, and that Kevin had later "admitted that he had done that."

"Three levels of hearsay," Abzug said. "His wife said that somebody else said that Anderson said. It is being offered for the truth and it shouldn't be allowed."

Schwartz said she thought the statement by Deepti was admissible, even if Deepti was simply repeating something that someone else said that Anderson had said. It tended to explain Deepti's motives, the judge said. But she also recognized that the testimony from Vijay represented multiple levels of hearsay.

"How would we get around the multiple hearsay level here?" the judge asked.

Thompson said that the supposed statement by Kevin to "the staff" would be admissible as a statement by the accused, which was allowable. Of course, it would have been better for Thompson to have called "the staff" to establish this, rather than run it through Deepti into Vijay's mouth. This is why the hearsay rule exists—to get the best evidence.

"Actually," said the judge, "I've rechecked the hearsay rule. I thought maybe I had forgotten. In this particular situation, it seems like the statement is not being offered for the truth." Instead, the statement was being offered to explain Deepti's subsequent conduct.

"I'll admonish the jury that this is not being offered for the truth, [but] just to show her state of mind." Schwartz apparently meant subsequent conduct, not state of mind. It seemed to be the third party origin of the statement—"the staff"—that troubled Schwartz on this one, although seeing how it differed from the earlier instances wasn't very clear. The fact that she'd rechecked the rule seemed to show that not even the judge was sure of the proper way to interpret it.

With that the trial reached a kind of uneasy equilibrium over the hearsay statements; the material would come in, sometimes the jurors would be warned that it wasn't necessarily true, and sometimes they wouldn't. Like everything else in the trial, it all depended on Deepti's state of mind.

Thompson's examination of Vijay continued, with Vijay describing the meeting with Kevin in Westwood, the trouble over the relocation grant, and the other developments between Deepti and Kevin through October of 1999.

When she arrived at Deepti's trip to India on October 21, she wanted Vijay to describe Deepti's religious pilgrimage. She hoped Vijay would be able to describe Deepti's conflicted state of mind regarding her relationship with Kevin. But Judge Schwartz would not permit this; she said

that, while the conflict might be relevant, what Deepti did
religiously to try to resolve it was not.

Thwarted in trying to put before the jury an important
aspect of Deepti's character, Thompson turned now to
Deepti's pregnancy. She produced the pregnancy testing
kits Deepti had used on November 7 or 8, and asked Vijay
to identify them. He did, and said he had found them in
the bathroom after Deepti's death.

Following this, Thompson took Vijay through the events
of the last two days of Deepti's life, as far as Vijay per-
ceived them, and then turned him over to Abzug for cross-
examination.

27

Abzug knew that he had to walk a fine line with Vijay. Apart from being practiced in testifying, Vijay was the surviving spouse, and a naturally sympathetic figure. Not only had he lost his wife, he had learned that he had been deceived as a husband. If Abzug put too much pressure on, it could blow up in his face.

On the other hand, Abzug wanted to use Vijay to demonstrate that Deepti was unhappy in her marriage, and certainly untruthful. The difficulty was in how to get to these areas without making it seem that he was abusing Vijay. Abzug decided that the best way to do this was to confront Vijay with the statements that the astrologer Anil Sharma had made to the police—statements that seemed to indicate that Deepti had complained to Sharma about her husband.

But first Abzug wanted to go over Deepti's tenure at Eaton Canyon, in an effort to show that Deepti was a strong, determined and often difficult-to-please person. By the time this was finished, most of the afternoon had gone, and the trial adjourned for the day.

The next morning, Abzug questioned Vijay about the September 7 confrontation with Heidi, and its aftermath. Vijay said that Kevin had admitted to him that he had told the staff that Deepti would no longer be working at the hospital. He said that Deepti had "put two and two together" and had concluded that Kevin had pulled strings to ensure the denial of the relocation grant. But Vijay admitted that he had never actually talked to Ken Rivers about the abortive grant.

When Abzug asked Vijay whether Deepti had been unhappy with her treatment by Dr. Richard at the Children's Clinic, Vijay confirmed that Deepti had told him that Richard was afraid she would steal some of his private patients, and then scored off of Abzug.

"Did you ever talk to Dr. Richard to find out if any of what your wife told you, an iota of what your wife told you, was true?" Abzug asked.

"There was no time and energy in me," Vijay said. "She worked three days. She told this to me, and then she was murdered."

Abzug asked if Vijay had ever been suspicious that Deepti was having an affair, and Vijay said no.

At this point, Abzug turned to the Guptas' relationship, at least as it had been described by Sharma to the police.

"As far as you were concerned, was your marriage a happy one during her first pregnancy?" he asked.

"Yes."

"During the first pregnancy of your wife, Professor Gupta, did you ever verbally abuse her?"

Here Vijay temporized; it is likely that he had seen a copy of Sharma's tape-recorded statement to the sheriff's detectives.

"Ladies and gentlemen," Vijay said, addressing the jury rather than Abzug, "every marriage has *discussions*. She was not a woman from a small village in India. She was a well-educated woman, a doctor. She had her own mind, and we discussed things, and arguments were there. If you call it 'verbal abuse' . . . that is *discussions* in a marriage."

"Did she ever call it 'verbal abuse' to you?"

"No."

"In those *discussions* you had during the pregnancy, were voices raised?"

"Voices were raised, yes."

"Were you yelling at her?"

"No, I never—Well, 'yelling' is a very comparative term. I was not yelling [to the degree] that the neighbors were coming to my house, but there were heated discussions."

"Did you make her cry?"

"She cried, yes."

"Did you physically abuse her during any of these discussions that we are talking about, while your wife was
pregnant with her first child?"

"Never," Vijay said. "I never touched my wife."

Abzug asked whether Deepti had confided in Sharma as
a "Hindu priest."

"He's an astrologer," Vijay said. "And she wanted to—
she believed in all this stuff." Deepti, he said, had consulted
Sharma to find the right times to do things.

"Isn't Anil Sharma an astrologer and Hindu priest?" Abzug asked.

"I don't think he was in the category of a Hindu priest,"
Vijay said.

"Were you aware, sir, that your wife's confidential ad-
visor advised her to leave you because of the verbal abuse
you were giving her during her first pregnancy?"

"No," Vijay said, "I'm not aware of that. I know one
thing for sure, that she was with me until she died. And
my daughter is two-and-a-half years old at the time. Certainly, she didn't leave me."

Vijay had effectively blunted Abzug's attempt to show
that Deepti's desire was to leave him for Kevin.

"I have no further questions," Abzug said.

On her redirect examination, Thompson scored a few
more points when Vijay testified that it was his impression,
from Deepti's remarks, that Kevin needed Deepti to open
the partnership because he didn't have enough money to
do it by himself. Deepti, Vijay said, had around $100,000
in the bank, and was board-certified, while Kevin was not.
Then Vijay got in another zinger by saying that he understood that Kevin had bad credit.

Then Thompson produced the photograph of Deepti that
had been taken in Portugal in July of 1999.

"Do you recognize the woman in this photograph?" she
asked.

"I do."

"Who is that?"

"That is my beautiful wife," Vijay said.

*   *   *

After Vijay left the stand, Thompson called Marvin Cooper, Deepti's business planner, who described all the work that had been done on the prospective partnership during the summer of 1999, as well as the way the financing would go; Cooper said he was the one who had first broached the idea of Deepti getting the relocation grant. He described how $3,000 from the aborted grant was to be put into the partnership, and how $2,000 in profit was to go to Kevin in months four through twelve after the partnership opened.

When Cooper stepped down, Thompson called a series of nurses who worked at St. Luke, who testified as to Kevin and Deepti's movements and behavior on the last two days of Deepti's life. Several of the nurses testified that Kevin had come into the hospital on the afternoon of November 11 to ask about the caesarian, and, after having been informed that there was none, then said he was going to check on some babies on another floor of the hospital. The import of this testimony was that Kevin was trying to establish an alibi for the evening, and that neither Kevin nor Deepti had stopped at the hospital on the way to Mile Marker 33, despite Kevin's insistence that they had.

Late in the afternoon, Thompson called Anil Sharma.

Sharma described meeting Vijay and Deepti for the first time in 1995, and how he had consulted with Deepti on astrological matters periodically through the years. When the idea of the partnership first arose, Sharma said, Deepti had come to see him.

"She said that there is this Dr. Kevin Anderson," Sharma said, "and he has a lot of contacts, and he's bright and intelligent and he's going to help her out." Deepti told him the private practice was Kevin's idea, Sharma said.

"Based on your conversations with her as time went on and she began calling him by the name of Kevin, did you feel that the relationship between them was progressing to something else?"

"Yes. By her actions and by a few of the comments I

got from her, I found very strong feeling, from my side, that they're emotionally attached."

Thompson asked whether Deepti had ever told him that Kevin was "pursuing" her.

"Yes. At one time she told me that 'He is after me, but I'm not interested.' And she was always looking up to him as a mentor."

"At some point in time did she tell you that he began pressuring her into a physical relationship with him?"

"Yes. She said that—something to the effect that 'He's after me, but I'm not interested.' "

Abzug now wanted the jury admonished again, that the statement wasn't being offered for the truth, but to indicate Deepti's state of mind. But Judge Schwartz refused, saying it was a hearsay exception, like all the other exceptions, and the jury didn't need to be admonished.

"My objection is respectfully denied?" Abzug asked.

"I guess so," said Schwartz.

Thompson now asked Sharma to describe Deepti, and at this point it appears that Abzug hit on another strategy to keep some of this hearsay out, or at least to blunt its impact, and this was by objecting on the grounds of relevance and foundation. Even if something did tend to show Deepti's mental state at various times, that didn't mean it was necessarily relevant to the issues. To show the relevance, Thompson would have to establish a foundation—a fundamental layer of facts that proved that not only was the testimony germane to the issues, but that the witness had a sound basis for personal knowledge about the testimony.

As the trial progressed, Abzug would repeatedly make these foundational objections to testimony, forcing Thompson to move backward in her examination to prove that the witness had the requisite personal knowledge. The tactic began to aggravate Thompson, eventually in the extreme, and before the trial was over, she and Judge Schwartz would exchange sharp words frequently, with Schwartz recurrently chastising Thompson for ignoring the rules of evidence.

Judge Schwartz now sustained Abzug's objection to Thompson's request that Sharma describe Deepti's character, and advised Thompson that she would have to "narrow it down a bit to show the relevance."

Thompson chose to go on to something else, asking Sharma whether Deepti had ever asked to confide in him as a friend. Sharma agreed that she had.

"That was at the time she started showing signs of stress," he said, "and she was distressed about something." Deepti then began talking about Dr. Anderson as "Kevin," and telling Sharma that she enjoyed being with him. Sharma said he guessed that Deepti was having an affair with Kevin by the way she talked about him.

Deepti had told him, Sharma continued, that Kevin was having trouble in his marriage to Heidi, but that he was afraid to leave Heidi because, "she's going to financially ruin him.

"That's what Deepti told me," Sharma added.

Sharma went on to describe his first pregnancy conversation with Deepti, and how Deepti had said she was going to talk to Kevin "today." Afterward, Sharma said, Deepti had told him that she thought Kevin was avoiding her.

Then Thompson had Sharma describe the last few telephone calls from Deepti, leading up to the 5:51 P.M. message she'd left on the answering machine, the one that said she was following "him" up into the mountains on the evening of her death.

But before Thompson could play this tape for the jury, the trial was adjourned for the weekend.

28

It appears that Thompson, at least, spent some part of her weekend researching the hearsay rule, because when the trial resumed on Monday, she raised the issue once more with Judge Schwartz.

"The court has ruled that a lot of the hearsay is coming in to explain the declarant's state of mind or subsequent conduct, which is at issue in this particular case," she told Schwartz before the jury was brought in. "And the court, however, has indicated it's coming in for the truth of the matter asserted as opposed to—limited for that purpose. And I'm just concerned about that, whether or not it does come in as truth of the matter asserted, or whether the court's required to give a limiting instruction."

Thompson had realized that if some of the statements were coming in without the admonishment asked for by Abzug—that the stuff wasn't necessarily true, just that it explained someone's subsequent conduct—it might be that Kevin could raise the issue on appeal. And if an appeals court found that the judge had improperly admitted the statements—that is, had taken them without the proper warning to the jury—it might provide the grounds for a reversal of the verdict if Kevin were to be convicted.

In the colloquy that followed between the judge and the lawyers, Judge Schwartz said it was up to Thompson to decide whether the testimony was being offered to the jury for the truth or some other purpose.

"I'm not deciding for you what's coming in for the truth, and what's not," the judge advised Thompson. "I'm simply ruling on objections, and there have been only a few hearsay objections . . . I think the record is quite clear that you either offered it for the truth, or you didn't. So I'm not sure what you're concerned about."

"I'm just trying to protect the record," Thompson said. "And I just want to clarify that I'm offering it under 1250 of the Government Code [Thompson meant the Evidence Code], which is a hearsay exception—"

"Exception," Judge Schwartz interrupted.

"—that it is being offered—"

"For the truth," Judge Schwartz said.

"—to prove the victim's state of mind or conduct at a particular point in time," Thompson finally concluded. But, Thompson said, even though she was offering the evidence as a state-of-mind exception to the hearsay rule, she also wanted the jury to consider the testimony for the truth of the matter asserted as well.

Schwartz said that even if an exception permitted the testimony to come in, "it does come in for the truth. I mean, that's my understanding of the first-year evidence. But it's been a long time since I've taken that."

"I just want to be clear that the hearsay that has come in so far has come in under Section 1250 of the Evidence Code," Thompson said once more.

At this point Abzug joined in.

"The record in this case speaks for itself," he said, in apparent ironic understatement. "I think, with all due respect to Ms. Thompson, I know why she's worried. And I think her comments today speak for themselves, and make the record more ambiguous and more unfavorable to the prosecution than they were earlier.

"What the record reflects is that I have consistently asked the court to give cautionary instructions, because some of these hearsay statements by Dr. Gupta which the court has—arguably, I'm not going to concede the fact—might arguably be admissible to prove her state of mind, if the jury considers them for the truth, are extremely prejudicial to my client, and I believe deny him a fair trial if they are considered for the truth of the matter asserted."

Abzug said he was convinced that Thompson was now asking the court to retroactively apply the state-of-mind exception to all the hearsay that had so far been let in, even statements not offered for truth, but to explain subsequent conduct. This was trying to reinvent history, he said.

Judge Schwartz said she was confident all the rulings on hearsay so far were correct. She noted that, few objections had been raised to the hearsay that had already been presented.

"But again," she said, "I can only rule on objections as they're made. And I would note that there has been a considerable amount of hearsay testimony presented in this trial with no objection having been made. So the record does speak for itself. I'm not concerned, and I don't know why The People[13] are concerned. But so be it. That's the way it is."

Since the central issues of the trial were the motives of both Deepti and Kevin, Abzug was right to be concerned about some of the hearsay. In effect, the jury was being asked to accept whatever Deepti had told anyone as the actual truth, even if she had a motive to lie. This was what Abzug had tried to point out to the judge almost from the beginning, and what Thompson had now realized might come back to haunt her.

Once the jury was back in the box, Thompson used Sharma to authenticate the answering machine tape, and then played the tape with its messages from Deepti.

Thompson asked Sharma if he knew what Deepti was talking about when she said "everything falls into place and works out the way I want it to be."

"She was talking about her business practice, getting all the grants she was supposed to get," Sharma said.

Abzug now pressed Sharma on this point, noting that Sharma had originally said Deepti was referring to her practice with Kevin, not her own, independent practice.

"All the way she has been talking to me about practice," Sharma said. "So I really can't pinpoint old or new. For

---

[13]In California state courts, the prosecution is referred to as "The People."

me, she wanted to get into practice, and that was not happening."

Abzug's intent was to have Sharma's testimony buttress his contention that Deepti was using her pregnancy to "bludgeon," as he had put it, Kevin into doing what she wanted him to do. That was, for Abzug, "the thing" that Deepti was talking about in the first taped message to Sharma. But Sharma wasn't going there, so Abzug had to backtrack.

After a series of other questions designed to show that Sharma had been in frequent contact with Deepti, Abzug worked back to the pregnancy from a different angle.

"Now," he said, "as time moved forward from early September to October, at some point she told you she was pregnant, correct?"

"After she came back from her trip to India, after a couple of days, she told me that she was pregnant, and she was going to see Kevin that day—evening, and tell him."

Abzug veered away again, and this time asked Sharma if Deepti was attracted to Kevin.

Sharma said Deepti told him that she wanted to be with Kevin, but Sharma wasn't sure whether she meant in business, or personally.

"So," said Abzug, "when she said that she wanted to be with him, you interpreted that she wanted to be with him professionally and not that she wanted to be with him in a romantic sense. Is that how you interpreted it?"

"I could see some kind of emotional attachment happening," Sharma said. "Because from 'Dr. Anderson,' she was referring to him as 'Kevin.' And taking liberty with a person's name is quite unusual in Indian culture."

"Did you have the feeling that—as time went on—that she was becoming obsessed with Dr. Anderson?"

"It all started with her telling that he's pressuring her to have a physical relationship and she's not interested," Sharma said. "And she mentioned that he wrote letters to her to that effect. And, all the while, she was trying to avoid it. And a certain time later on, I felt that she just broke down and gave up and might have got involved with him."

This wasn't helpful to Abzug. Sharma was making it sound like Kevin had hounded Deepti for sex.

"Did she become obsessed with Dr. Anderson, in your view?" Abzug persisted.

"She was—Every conversation that I had with her had Anderson's name in it. And Anderson was mentioned several times in every conversation. So I put it, in my way, as an obsession."

That was better, at least for Abzug's purposes. Abzug asked if it wasn't true that Deepti was obsessed to the point that Sharma recommended that she stay away from Kevin.

"I did," Sharma said. He'd offered to introduce Deepti to other doctors, but Deepti wasn't interested.

Now Abzug asked Sharma if he'd ever mentioned Deepti's obsession with Kevin to Vijay. Sharma said he had not. "Whatever my client speaks to me is private and confidential," he said. But, he said, "I did hint to Vijay Gupta when he met me later, and he took an effort to go with Deepti—" Abzug cut him off.

"This is before, or after her death?" Abzug asked.

"This was before her death, weeks before her death."

What was this? All of a sudden Sharma seemed to be suggesting that Vijay might have known something about Deepti's "obsession" with Kevin, that he had "hinted" to Vijay that something might be up, and that as a result, Vijay seems to have taken some sort of effort to—what?

Unaccountably, Abzug abandoned that line of inquiry, despite its possibilities. If, after all, Abzug's defense of Kevin was that he had somehow been entrapped into an intimate relationship with a woman who wanted to use him to further her career, evidence that Vijay might have known about the affair before the murder might be pure gold.

Abzug later said he was intent at the time on trying to depict Deepti as an untruthful person. He didn't want evidence that Deepti might have told her husband about the affair, because that would undercut his case that she was not to be trusted to tell the truth. He wanted to depict her as a person who lied. He went back to the obsession theme.

"Now," Abzug said, "how many times do you think she called you between November first and her death?"

"I will say anywhere between twenty or thirty times, I'm not sure, because I get calls from her at various times. I will say thirty or forty times."

"Thirty or forty times?"

"Yeah."

"Maybe more?"

"Maybe more," Sharma said. Abzug was trying to create a picture of a woman who was out of control.

"Was she calling you all the time, day or night?"

"Early morning, late at night," Sharma agreed.

"Early morning. Would she call you at four-thirty in the morning?"

"Yes, she did."

"Did you tell her at that point that she was becoming a dysfunctional person?"

"I hinted something to the effect that she should meditate," said Sharma, "and, you know, take it easy, and shouldn't get so stressed."

Abzug said he wasn't talking about hints, he wanted to know if that was the word Sharma had used.

"Yes," Sharma said.

Abzug now established that Sharma had told the police that Deepti had told him that she couldn't forget Kevin, and that she said this after her return from India—after she knew she was pregnant. He was trying to close the loop.

"So she wasn't saying she can't forget about him 'because I put so much energy into the practice,' at that point she was talking about the pregnancy, wasn't she?" Abzug asked.

Sharma retreated to his insistence that he could never tell when Deepti was referring to business or personal matters when she'd said that she couldn't forget about Kevin.

Abzug now turned to one more area. He wanted Sharma to confirm that Deepti had complained to him that Vijay had been verbally abusive to her during the first pregnancy.

Sharma admitted that he had told the police that.

"I did advise Deepti Gupta," Sharma said, "—which I advise all my clients—if there is abuse, Why don't you leave? I asked her: Why don't you leave? I never said: Leave your husband. I said: If you have abuse and you can't take it, why don't you leave? And she said, No, I'm not going to leave."

Now Abzug asked Sharma if it was true that Vijay had been physically abusive to Deepti on one occasion. Sharma said he wasn't sure, that he couldn't confirm it.

"You certainly saw fit to disclose this to the police, correct?" Abzug asked.

"I wanted to give whatever information I had to the best of my knowledge," Sharma said, "and be truthful."

Now Thompson wanted to try to exonerate Deepti after Abzug's questioning of Sharma.

After Deepti told him she was pregnant, Thompson asked, had she ever told him that she intended to keep the baby?

"She wanted to keep the child," Sharma said.

"Did she tell you that?"

"Yes."

"Did she tell you whether or not she was going to stay with her husband?"

"She wanted to stay with her husband."

"And she told you that as well?"

"Yes. I asked her," Sharma said.

"What did you ask her?"

"I asked her whether she's going to abort the child and whether she's going to stay with Vijay. She said she's going to keep the child, she's going to stay with Vijay."

29

When it was his turn again, Abzug asked Sharma one final question: had Deepti told him it was her idea to visit the Andersons to convince Heidi that she and Kevin could go into practice together?

"I guess, yes," Sharma said. "Because she just wanted to show that she was having a secure relationship. And [the] objective was to get into practice. So, that was her idea, to have a family visit."

Thompson went back to rehabilitating Deepti.

"Is that what she said, or was that your impression?"

"That was my impression," Sharma said.

This, of course, was a perfect illustration of the problems with taking hearsay testimony as "truth of the matter asserted." Sometimes it was just someone else's impression.

After Sharma left the stand, Thompson concentrated on getting more of her motive witnesses through the court. She called Steve Sorrell, Kevin's tax accountant, and Sorrell testified that Kevin didn't seem at all worried that he was going to invest the lion's share of the patients into the new practice. Thompson wanted to use this testimony to underscore the earlier impression left by Vijay, Cooper and Sharma that Kevin never actually intended to open a practice with Deepti, that it was just a lure to get her into bed.

Just before noon, the trial recessed for lunch. When they returned, Abzug asked Judge Schwartz for some time before the jury was brought back into the courtroom.

"Mr. Abzug," she said, "did you want to bring some matters to the court's attention?"

"Just one, Your Honor. Around the noon break, as I was coming into the court, Professor Gupta passed me and said to me, 'Sick bastard,' in a very threatening—what I thought

was a very threatening tone of voice. I then brought it to
Ms. Thompson's attention so she could talk to him, try to
calm him down. Then I spoke to Ms. Thompson about it
afterward, and her explanation of what he said to her troubled me, actually, even more, because it was clearly not
what happened." Abzug said Thompson told him that Vijay
had not been referring to him when he made the remark.

"What I understand Mr. Gupta told Ms. Thompson is,
he was advised about a newspaper article which improperly
wrote a portion of his testimony, and when he looked at
me and said 'Sick bastard,' he was talking about [the newspaper reporter], which, obviously, is not what happened."

Abzug had thought about it over the noon recess, he
said, "and this is what I've come up with.

"I'm not physically intimidated by it. But it bothered me
and it shook me up for a reason that Professor Gupta
doesn't understand at the moment, which is, none of this
is personal pleasure to me. I don't like doing what I'm
doing, in terms of causing him personal pain. It troubles
me. I've lost sleep over it. I don't enjoy any aspect of
causing him pain, who was victimized by this whole situation, or besmirching his wife's reputation. That's not what
I'm into.

"I am deeply sympathetic to him and very sad about
what's happened to his family. It shook me up because it
just makes me feel just all the worse when I think about
what I have to do as a defense counsel for Dr. Anderson.

"I'm just going to let it go. I'm reporting it to you. I
hope that Professor Gupta is listening to what I have to say,
understanding that what I'm doing is part of what I con-
ceive to be my job, certainly not motivated by any desire
to embarrass him, make him feel worse. I can't imagine
how he can feel worse than he already does by anything
I'm doing."

Judge Schwartz thanked Abzug, and said she knew that
Vijay had heard Abzug's plea for understanding.

"The obligation of the defense attorney is to put forth
the best defense that can possibly be put forth in the case,"

Schwartz said. "And I know that Professor Gupta heard
that, and understands that. And it would certainly benefit
all of us if tensions were somewhat minimized from it. I
mean, I can see the tension in the courtroom just by sitting
here." It was in everyone's best interest "not to personalize
or lash out or say anything to counsel," Schwartz said.

But the tensions would only get worse from there on in.

That afternoon, Thompson pressed on, calling Dr. Ng and
Dr. Richard. This was where Thompson first began en-
countering Abzug's foundation objections. Thompson
wanted Ng to testify that Kevin's pay at the Eaton Canyon
clinic had been drastically reduced in 1998, and that while
he had access to all the Eaton Canyon patient charts, the
patients belonged to the clinic, not to Kevin personally. Her
idea was to show that Kevin had no more right (or for that
matter, any less right) to Eaton Canyon patients than Deepti
Gupta. But Abzug kept objecting that she hadn't established
the facts sufficiently to ask the question.

"Lay a foundation, Ms. Thompson," said Judge
Schwartz. Thompson tried once more, asking Ng to describe his understanding with Kevin as to who the patients
belonged to, but was met with the same objection by Abzug. "Lay a foundation," Schwartz said again.

"Did you have an understanding between yourself and
the defendant with respect to who the patients belonged to
at Eaton Canyon?"

"Objection," Abzug said.

Thompson pointed out that it was a yes or no question,
and didn't require a foundation.

When Ng said yes, there was such an understanding,
Abzug objected once again. Another sidebar conference
was held.

"I don't see the basis of the objection," Thompson told
the judge.

"Just ask him about the conversation he had with Anderson," Abzug advised her. "You can't ask him what his
understanding is."

"You are missing a few steps here," Schwartz told her. "When I sustain it on foundation grounds, you should back up about five steps and start from the very beginning. It's real easy to get to."

"He could have had the understanding that it was based on the lunar calendar, just like the other witness," Abzug said.

Thompson suggested that she could ask if Ng had an agreement with Kevin.

"You know, 'Did you discuss it?' " said Schwartz. "Start from the beginning and we won't have these problems."

This was a weird conversation, with Abzug trying to advise Thompson on how to do her job. As the trial moved forward, however, Thompson would run into trouble again and again over this aspect of trial practice, with Abzug complaining that she was leading the witness, and as Abzug escalated his objections, she would become increasingly frustrated.

When Thompson now asked Ng if he ever talked to Kevin "about to whom the patients belonged at Eaton Canyon," Ng said he couldn't remember.

Thompson wanted Ng to establish that his agreement with Deepti provided for her to receive all the new Eaton Canyon patients as "hers," but Ng wouldn't go there. The patients were coming to the clinic, he said, not any individual doctor.

Abzug nailed this point down in his subsequent cross-examination.

"As a matter of fact," he asked, "did Dr. Gupta ever have a list of patients which belonged to her at the Eaton Canyon Medical Group?"

"We never have a list," said Ng.

"Is that because all of Dr. Gupta's patients belonged to Eaton Canyon?"

"Yes."

Ng's testimony was essentially a wash for either side. As far as Ng was concerned, the clinic's patients didn't belong to either Kevin or Deepti. They were the clinic's patients.

Thompson now called Felix Ochoa, the office manager at Dr. Richard's Children's Clinic, and asked him whether he knew if there was a problem between Richard, Kevin and Deepti over payments from HMO patients after Deepti started at the clinic on November 1.

Abzug objected again on foundational grounds.

"Lay a foundation," Schwartz said, in what was beginning to sound like a mantra.

Thompson tried again, and again Abzug objected.

"All right," said Judge Schwartz at the sidebar. "I would just indicate that we shouldn't be having these problems."

"No, we shouldn't," Thompson agreed.

"Ask a question that is not objectionable," Schwartz said. "Do you understand the foundation objection?"

"No, I don't," said Thompson. She said she'd asked whether "they" had told Ochoa that they were having problems allocating the payments between them. "What is the problem with that?"

"There is no foundation," Schwartz said again. "Who are you talking about?"

"Who am I talking about?" Thompson appeared mystified.

"You want to argue with me about Evidence One?" demanded Judge Schwartz.

"No, I don't," Thompson said.

"All right, please," said the judge. "I would indicate that just about every question you've asked throughout the beginning of this trial has been objectionable. Mr. Abzug has been selective in his objections."

The judge indicated that unless Thompson could demonstrate the basis of a witness's knowledge, she couldn't know whether the testimony was hearsay.

"How do I know the basis of a witness's knowledge?" she asked. "Did the witness see it? Did he hear it? Was he present? Was he told? And if he was told, by whom? If the answer is yes or no, if you're aware, then 'How did you know it?' You've got to lay foundations. All right? And I'm going to keep doing this and keep sustaining them. And I don't know what else to do."

Thompson's frustration with the judge was growing by the minute. She knew she would have to keep it in check, however; alienating the judge would be disastrous.

Eventually, Thompson was able to establish that Deepti had seen some HMO or private patients on behalf of Dr. Richard, and that she hadn't been paid directly for those visits. This was apparently the source of Deepti's complaint to Gloria Angelo about the "illegal billing practices" at the Children's Clinic.

When it was his turn with Ochoa, Abzug asked a simple question:

"Was the Children's Clinic engaged in illegal billing?"

"Not—No."

"You're laughing because it's ridiculous?"

"It's ridiculous," Ochoa said.

Dr. Richard now took the stand. Despite his original plan to phase out of his practice by January of 2000, he had quit for good on November 12, the day he found out that Deepti had been killed. He'd had heart pains, he said, and decided to accelerate his retirement.

Richard said he'd agreed to sell, not give, his practice to Kevin. The sale price was to be based on the number of patients whose cases Kevin would take over. Kevin had explained that he wanted Deepti to come into the clinic so she could see patients from Eaton Canyon, whom Kevin expected would follow him. He had agreed with Kevin that Deepti could see her own patients, Kevin's patients from Eaton Canyon, and all the Medi-Cal patients. He had not agreed that Deepti could see his own private insurance patients, however.

Then Deepti had begun seeing some of these patients, and he had complained, Richard said. He didn't want the value of his practice reduced, not when he and Kevin were negotiating over the final price. But Richard denied that he'd ever "burst" into an office to confront Deepti over this issue.

"Those allegations are completely false, aren't they, Dr. Richard?" Abzug asked.

"Yes," Richard said. Abzug was again trying to depict Deepti as a complainer and an exaggerator.

With that, the trial wrapped up its fifth day of testimony.

30

When the court reconvened the following morning, Thompson called two witnesses, Lorena Ramirez and the leasing agent Tracy Thomas, to fill in more of the details about Deepti's activities in the summer and fall, and on the days before her death.

Lorena testified to the lunch Kevin had with Deepti at the bagel shop on the Monday before her murder, as well as Deepti's remark to Kevin that they had things to talk about. She'd last seen Deepti alive around 4:45 P.M. at the Guptas' Glendale home, when Deepti had given her a check for her work at the Children's Clinic. Lorena said she had seen Dr. Richard enter an examination room to confront Deepti over the private patient issue. Richard appeared to have been upset with Deepti, Lorena said. She also said Deepti was upset with Kevin, because he hadn't provided her with a patient list. When Kevin finally gave her a list, Lorena said, Deepti noticed that it was from 1998. Under questioning from Abzug, Lorena said that Deepti had told her that she'd seen "hundreds and hundreds of patients" over at Eaton Canyon.

"Did she say those patients belonged to her?" Abzug asked.

"She didn't say 'belonged,' " Lorena said. "She'd seen them over there. She would like to tell them where she was, at her new office. Because she didn't have a chance to do that when she was over there."

This was a step forward to understanding Deepti's thinking about the patient list. It appeared that Deepti believed that the patients she had seen while at Eaton Canyon—whether new or old—were to be "hers." Thus, patients who had previously been seen by Dr. Ng or Kevin or any of the other doctors at the Eaton Canyon clinic and who were subsequently seen by Deepti in her four months as a contract physician for Dr. Ng, should have been on the "list," at least in Deepti's view. This seems to have been a fundamental misunderstanding between Kevin and Deepti; how much of it was due to Kevin's earlier assurances that he could get the Eaton Canyon "list" for their joint practice wasn't clear.

After Tracy Thomas testified about the comings and goings of Deepti and Kevin at the Thatcher Building—and established that Kevin had signed a lease agreement in late August of 1999, despite his promise to Heidi that he wouldn't be going into practice with Deepti—Thompson moved back to a less subjective part of her case: the scientific evidence.

She called a deputy sheriff assigned to the department's Scientific Services Bureau, Dale Falicon, who testified that he had found fingerprints from both Kevin and Deepti in Kevin's 4Runner. This definitely placed Deepti in Kevin's car, but Falicon, under questioning from Abzug, admitted that there was no way of knowing just when the print had been left there. This was a minor point, however, since even Kevin had admitted that Deepti had been in his car when he strangled her.

After Falicon, Thompson called Phil Teramoto, also a criminalist from the sheriff's Scientific Services Bureau. Teramoto testified that he'd tested items of clothing taken from Deepti's body, including a "scrunchy" used to tie up her hair; items from her car; and towels recovered from Kevin's truck. The tests showed that gasoline had been poured over Deepti's head, he said. He'd found no gasoline on Kevin's clothes or shoes, he said. Again Abzug induced an admission that no one could tell when the gasoline was poured, and again it was a minor point under the circumstances.

Thompson now called Don Johnson, also from the sheriff's Scientific Services Bureau. Johnson was responsible for collecting and analyzing biological evidence, and was an expert in DNA.

On February 1, 2000, Johnson testified, he had tested a sample of tissue from Deepti's uterus. He'd identified it as tissue from a fetus, and then subjected it to DNA testing. After comparing the results from the tissue sample to cells taken from Kevin and Vijay, Johnson had determined that Vijay could not have been the father, and that Kevin couldn't be excluded as the father.

Thompson now called Paul Colman, another DNA expert with the sheriff's department. Colman said his tests of the DNA sample, a more sophisticated type of testing called Short Tandem Repeats, was able to make a more precise calculation on the likelihood of the origin of the tissue sample. "It is a very, very discriminating system," Colman said, "and in fact, with the exception of identical twins, no two people would have the same DNA profile."

Colman said his tests showed that the particular DNA profile from the tissue sample, when matched against Kevin's control sample, showed that the father of Deepti's baby could be only one person out of 7.9 *quintillion* people of black ancestry. That would be the same as 1 in 1,000,000,000,000,000,000—one followed by 18 zeros, he said. Since the total world population was estimated at just over 6 billion, that meant the father had to be Kevin.

"We could never have this many people," Colman said. "Cumulatively, we haven't had this many people. This refers to the possible combination of those [DNA] markers that are possible. So, all the people from Adam and Eve to today and from today forward, this is the number of those combinations . . . that could exist." And only Kevin could qualify as the donor of the sperm that had made Deepti pregnant.

The baby, Colman said, would have been a boy.

The next morning, Thompson called a telephone security expert for AT&T, Brad Hooper. Thompson used Hooper to introduce the cellular telephone and pager records for Deepti, Kevin and Heidi. The records showed the numbers called, received, the duration of the call, and the "cell site" or antenna location each call used when it was made.

Next, Thompson called Philip Brown, an engineer for
AT&T wireless. Brown testified that he had tracked all the
calls made from the cellular telephones and pagers, and that
he had helped produce a map that showed the locations, by
cell site, where each call was made. The map, color-coded
to show each cell site, represented a visual representation
of where Deepti and Kevin were as they made or received
their various calls on Wednesday, November 10, and
Thursday, November 11. Using Brown's testimony,
Thompson established that Kevin's pager had received a
call from Natalie Profant at 6:13 P.M. on November 11, that
his cellular telephone was used to make a call to Deepti's
voicemail pager at 6:27 P.M., and that another call was
made by the telephone to Natalie Profant at 6:40 P.M. All
of these calls had been made or received while Kevin and
Deepti were on top of the mountain, according to Kevin's
own statement to the detectives. Thompson was laying the
groundwork for her anticipated cross-examination of Kevin,
which was still to come.

After Brown left the stand, Thompson called Yulai
Wang, the deputy medical examiner who had conducted the
autopsy of Deepti on the day after her death. Wang testified
to the injuries he had observed on Deepti's body, including
the marks and tissue damage from the strangulation. But
under questioning from Abzug, Wang admitted that he had
no way of knowing what caused the bruise to Deepti's
head, and under pressure from Abzug, acknowledged that
the bruise could have been caused about the same time that
Deepti's heart stopped from the strangling. This was important to Abzug, because he wanted to raise doubt that
there had been an extended sequence to the injuries, because that undercut the defense of explosive rage on
Kevin's part, and added weight to the argument that the
killing had been planned.

After finishing with Wang, Thompson called Detective
McElderry. McElderry's role was to testify about the investigation he and Gallatin had conducted after Kevin's ar-

rest. This allowed Thompson to introduce photos and a videotape of the crime scene at Mile Marker 33, the earring that had been discovered in Kevin's car, the letters to Deepti from Kevin, and eventually, the truncated tape-recording of Kevin's confession. But before the tape could be played, the trial recessed for the afternoon, when a juror complained of feeling sick.

When the jurors had departed, Judge Schwartz used the opportunity to update the status of the various exhibits that had been proffered; the question of which would be sent on to the jury during its deliberations still had to be decided. Abzug still wanted to keep the thank-you card found by La Riviere away from the jury. He objected to the card's admission as an exhibit on grounds of relevance.

"I don't want to speculate on what the relevance is," he told the judge. "I'll let Ms. Thompson speak for herself. It doesn't appear relevant to me. It was a thank-you card found by La Riviere in one of his numerous excursions to the crime scene. I don't know what the relevance is."

Thompson said the card had been purchased by Deepti. Judge Schwartz, looking at the receipt for the card, and the price on the back of it said it appeared that the card had been purchased on the day of the killing.

"I guess an argument could be made," said Schwartz, "that it was purchased by the victim to give to the defendant."

"I don't know," Abzug said. "I *think* I know why she's going to use it. I don't want to speculate. I would like to hear what the relevance is."

Thompson said she wanted to put the card in for what it showed about Deepti's mental state on the day she died.

"It will be our position, at least circumstantially, that the defendant had made promises to her. From the evidence, it is pretty clear she was depressed on Wednesday, had intercourse with the defendant on Wednesday night. She was giddy and happy Thursday afternoon. She went up into the mountains with him, ultimately to her death.

"Certainly," Thompson concluded, "this is not a woman who is up there making threats. In fact, she was there to thank him."

Judge Schwartz said she thought that the card was relevant, and said she would admit it as evidence.

Thompson wanted Deepti's résumé also admitted as evidence. Abzug said he thought it was hearsay, and should be kept out.

"Let me just say this," Schwartz said, "and we have discussed this before. There was a lot of hearsay evidence that was presented in this case that I felt, and I still feel, came in under an exception or two, that being the state-of-mind exception to the hearsay rule.

"And I felt, and I still feel, that a lot of statements that were elicited that were hearsay statements, specifically with reference to Dr. Gupta, were relevant and admissible to, I believe, show what the nature of the relationship was with the defendant, and it also went to explain the conduct on the night of the death, that it does tend to show there was a relationship of a romantic nature and there was a professional relationship that had gone through some ups and downs.

"And I feel that a lot of the hearsay went toward the issue of explaining just why she would go to the top of Angeles Crest Highway with the defendant. It certainly explains her conduct in doing that. That's really the issue in the case, as I understand it: was the conduct of the victim such as to provoke the defendant in committing the homicide?

"I mean, the way I see the case, the way the opening statements were phrased and presented, seems to indicate that the major issue is really the state of mind of the defendant as well as the conduct of the victim, and whether her conduct rises to the level of adequate provocation, which would warrant the response of the homicide."

The résumé, the judge said, was different. While it was hearsay, it didn't qualify as an exception to the rule as a business record, because "when one puts together a résumé, one sometimes tends to exaggerate. So the source of the information might be less than trustworthy . . ."

They continued discussing the possible exhibits. The judge excluded a bookstore record, which suggested that Kevin had once bought a book on how to reduce one's child support payments. Thompson wanted the record admitted to show that one of Kevin's motives was to eliminate child support payments for Deepti's baby.

"I think there is strong circumstantial evidence that the fact that Dr. Gupta is pregnant with his child was the factor that caused him to kill her," Thompson said. "It was going to impact him financially. It was going to impact him as far as his marriage was concerned. It was going to damage his reputation, his career, what he had worked so hard for. And, in addition, was going to be obligated to that child for the next eighteen-plus years."

Baloney, said Abzug.

"This is all simply argument," he said. "It is just an attenuated theory that the defendant would kill Dr. Gupta because of whatever problems he may have had with his ex-wife [Natalie Profant]. And who knows if she [Deepti] is going to have this baby, and who knows what his obligation to pay child support would have been to Dr. Gupta, when she was still married? None of it follows. It is too attenuated. And all we're talking about is a book that in 1998 Dr. Anderson bought himself, to inform himself about child support, and that's it."

The argument meandered on, with Thompson still trying to insist that Kevin's purchase of the book was relevant, Abzug insisting that it wasn't, and the judge suggesting that there had to be some connection with the crime for it to be relevant.

There was, Thompson insisted. "This is one continuous course of conduct. Purchasing a book—"

"Wait. Wait. Wait," said Schwartz. "What is 'one continuous course of conduct'?"

By this time of the afternoon, after more than seven days of trial, everyone was both tired and testy. Still, Thompson

hung on to her point, grimly. The bookstore record was
evidence of Kevin's motive in killing Deepti, she insisted.

It was all about Kevin not wanting to pay child support,
she said.

"Frankly, it began years earlier when he failed to pay
child support over the years, and then it continued on . . ."
In fact, Kevin had been ordered by a court to pay the back
child support to Natalie, and he was continuing to pay it
even while he was seeing Deepti. It was all "strong, circumstantial evidence of his state of mind," Thompson said.

Judge Schwartz would not be swayed, however. The
book record was refused as too remote from the crime to
be germane.

And so it went, as the lawyers argued their positions of
various bits of evidence and documents. Late in the afternoon, after considerably more discussion and dispute, the
judge made her rulings on the admissibility of the evidence.
She said she hoped to get to the defense case by Monday
afternoon. She was still pushing to get the trial over before
the mandatory judicial conference.

31

When McElderry resumed the stand the following Monday morning, it had been exactly a year and two days since Deepti Gupta's death. The wreckage that had ensued from that event had been tremendous—one doctor dead, another on trial for his life, two small children each deprived of a parent, two spouses torn from their mates, and publicly embarrassed in the news media. And there was more to come, because the defense of Kevin Anderson had not yet even begun.

McElderry was, like Gallatin, a veteran detective of the sheriff's Homicide Bureau. In his time, he had seen scores of murders, and had investigated many of them. It was doubtful, however, that he'd ever seen a case like this one.

When McElderry returned to the stand, Thompson had him identify more of the evidence recovered in the case: the now-infamous Snoopy tie, and the motel receipt from the night before the killing, as well as Kevin's notebook, in which he'd listed the various things to be done to get the partnership going, back when it still seemed like a good idea. McElderry also identified other items of evidence that had been recovered, including on-call schedules from St. Luke, the ledger of household debts seized from Heidi during the search of the Andersons' home, a number of home telephone bills of the Guptas and the Andersons and a drugstore receipt in Deepti's belongings that seemed to show that on the day of her death, she had purchased the thankyou card later found by Jay La Riviere.

By this time, it was late in the morning. Thompson now turned to the tape-recorded interview.

McElderry explained that the recorder was supposed to give an audible beep when one side of the tape ran out, to alert the user that it was time to turn the tape over. That night, McElderry said, when they noticed that one side was used up, Gallatin had turned the tape over to record on the other side. It wasn't until two days later that anyone had noticed that the machine had stopped recording. He hadn't been able to take extensive notes, McElderry said, because he didn't want to interrupt the flow of Kevin's statement. All was in place now for Thompson to play the tape of Kevin's confession. She distributed transcripts of the interview to the jury so they could follow the sound.

Just before 11 A.M., Thompson began to play the tape. McElderry identified the voices. The tape lasted for just less than 45 minutes. Afterward, Thompson wanted McElderry to describe what Kevin had talked about in the unrecorded portion of the interview.

Kevin, McElderry said, had told them he wanted to make Deepti's death look like an accident.

"Did he tell you what he did prior to putting her in the vehicle?"

"At that point—actually, Deepti was inside of his car," McElderry said. "And he moved her Mercedes to the edge of the cliff. And at that point he went back and removed Deepti from his vehicle and put her in the driver's seat of her own car."

Kevin told them he'd gone back to his truck and removed the gasoline can, then poured some of its contents over Deepti and around the front seat of the Mercedes.

"He was going to light it on fire," said McElderry, "and make it look like it had just gone over and exploded in a ball of flames . . . as he was inside the vehicle on the passenger side and he was pouring the gasoline throughout the interior, the car started slipping down the hill."

"Did he tell you what he did?"

"He jumped out of the car. And at that point the vehicle went over the edge of the cliff and careened down the cliff side."

Thompson now wanted McElderry to offer an opinion about the use of fire as a means of destroying evidence—mainly, the soft tissues of Deepti's body. After more wrangling over a proper foundation and leading questions, followed by a break for lunch, Thompson was finally able to get to the place she wanted early in the afternoon session.

"Can you explain to the jury," she asked, "why it is, in a strangulation death, [that] fire could possibly destroy evidence of the cause of death?"

"A lot of times in a strangulation death, [there is] a lot of soft tissue around the neck, either the skin or the muscle area, and if the fire consumes the skin or the muscle of the body, that evidence would be destroyed," McElderry said.

"Assuming that the defendant had been successful in lighting Dr. Gupta's body on fire, would that have made your job more difficult, to detect cause of death?"

"Yes," McElderry said.

Thompson wanted the jury to keep this matter about the destruction of soft tissue in mind when she cross-examined Kevin, if he took the stand. A doctor, she would then be able to suggest, would know better than most that a thoroughly destructive fire would make it difficult to determine how Deepti died. She had McElderry testify to the discovery of the gas can, still half full, in Kevin's truck, the gloves that he had just purchased, and several other items that she had argued constituted a "murder kit"—evidence she would say indicated that Kevin had premeditated Deepti's murder.

Thompson now moved to the letters that had been found in Deepti's day planner, and had McElderry identify them. She wanted the jury to read copies of the cards and the letters. Schwartz granted permission and Thompson passed them out to the jurors, who read them.

Abzug now asked for permission to call a witness for the defense, out of order. McElderry temporarily stepped down, and Dr. Kevin Mitchell, a long-time friend of Kevin's who had come to the trial from Missouri and had to get back to his practice that same day, took his place.

Mitchell, a surgeon, said he'd known Kevin since Howard University.

"Do you have an opinion as to whether he has a violent character?" Abzug asked.

"I would say that Kevin Anderson is an extremely good-natured, non-violent, compassionate human being," said Mitchell. "I've never seen him display any evidence of any violence, either to me or to any of my friends, or people that he has come in contact with. He has a great sense of humor and he really just goes out of his way to be a friendly person all the time."

"Do you have an opinion as to whether he is a confrontational person?"

"From the time I've known Kevin Anderson, I've never known him to be confrontational. He's always been a person who would talk things out, never was violent or angry. I've never seen him lose his temper in any way, shape or form, during the time that I've known him."

This testimony cut two ways, as would virtually all of the character testimony Abzug would bring on Kevin's behalf. On one hand, Kevin was widely regarded as a non-violent, non-confrontational person—someone hardly likely to plan a murder. But on the other hand, if he was so calm, how come he now was claiming that he'd exploded?

Thompson was determined to drive this point home.

"So when confronted with a situation where somebody would normally show anger," she asked, "he was someone who would handle the matter in a very calm fashion?"

"He was someone who pretty much avoided getting into a confrontational, angry kind of fighting situation," Mitchell said. "I've never seen him in a fight with anyone."

Abzug wanted to clarify this.

"Dr. Mitchell, do you think that Dr. Anderson would kill another human being to preserve his professional reputation?"

Thompson objected, and Schwartz ruled that the question of whether Kevin would commit murder was one for the jury to decide. But Abzug could ask whether Mitchell thought Kevin might resort to violence if his reputation or success were threatened.

"Kevin Anderson would be the last person I would think would be involved in anything such as that," Mitchell said, when Abzug asked this. "He would be someone that I would think almost incapable of doing such a thing . . . I would say it's almost inconceivable to me that Kevin Anderson would do anything to harm another human being."

McElderry resumed the witness stand after Mitchell finished, and Abzug began his cross-examination. There was really very little that Abzug could do with McElderry's testimony. His best shot was to bring out anything that Kevin had said during the unrecorded portion of the interview that tended to bolster Kevin's defense that he had acted on the spur of the moment. But since Abzug didn't know for sure what that might have been—no tape, no substantial notes having been taken by the detectives—it was a bit like shooting into the darkness.

"Was there anything he said during the unrecorded portion of his statement to you that you didn't describe to the jury during Ms. Thompson's examination of you?" Abzug asked, in sort of a legal Hail Mary.

"There may have been," McElderry said. "As a matter of fact, there was a discussion, very brief, about his relationship with his wife, her possibly having some sort of an affair with—some characterized him as a body builder, yes."

This wasn't very helpful to Abzug, so he passed on it, and eventually let McElderry go.

Just after 4 P.M. on Monday, November 13, 2000, Thompson rested her case. Abzug asked Judge Schwartz to dismiss the charges against Kevin due to lack of evidence, but it was just a formality, and everyone knew it.

"I do think," said Schwartz, "that The People's evidence and their theory, if believed by the jury, is certainly sufficient to support the charges and the special allegations."

Now the ball was in Kevin's side of the court.

32

Up to this point, Abzug's strategy had been to try to undercut whatever motive Thompson was trying to attribute to Kevin, and to similarly debunk Thompson's preferred image of Deepti as a naive innocent, corrupted in the hands of the wily predator, Kevin. This had largely been a defensive action: chivvying witnesses for going too far, and trying to damage the credibility of a dead woman. It was easy to see why Vijay was upset; it would be upsetting for anyone, as even Abzug had acknowledged.

But now, as the judge had just pointed out, the prosecutor's case was finished. Thompson had established the gruesome facts of the killing, and had left enough on the table to support the notion that Kevin had planned the murder—his statements to the nurses, implying he would still be in the hospital at the time of Deepti's death, enough smoke over the "patient list" and its possible harm to Kevin to constitute motive, Heidi's clear jealousy, and most of all Deepti's unexpected pregnancy.

Now, however, Abzug would have to go on offense. That meant relying upon his two main witnesses, first Heidi, then Kevin himself. As things stood, the only way for Kevin to beat the needle was to convince the jury that Deepti had driven Kevin into an irrational outburst of violence, and that there was utterly no reason for Kevin's actions.

For his first witness, Abzug called Natalie Profant. He wanted to wipe out Thompson's suggestion that Kevin had killed Deepti to avoid paying child support before it took root with the jury. (It may or may not have been significant, but the trial of professional football star Rae Carruth on charges of murder to avoid paying child support was in the news at the time of Kevin's own trial, and

Abzug may have wanted to limit the potential spillover if he could.)

Natalie took the stand late on the afternoon of Monday, November 13, shortly after McElderry stepped down. As a defense witness, Natalie would first be questioned by Abzug, then cross-examined by Thompson. This would be Thompson's first real chance to cross-examine a witness in the trial, and she was looking forward to it.

In the years since her 1994 divorce from Kevin, Natalie Profant had created a new life for herself. Although she remained a resident of the Pasadena area, she had remarried, and had a job as a planning executive with Los Angeles County. At the time of Kevin's trial, she had just given birth to another child.

In the spring of 1998, after Kevin's income at Eaton Canyon was sliced, Kevin went to court to ask that his child support payments for his daughter with Natalie be reduced. Eventually, the matter was settled, with Kevin agreeing to pay Natalie the outstanding balance he still owed on child support, as well as $7,500 in unpaid spousal support. Custody of the child was to be divided fifty-fifty on a trial basis. The agreement also settled a lot of child-care differences that had cropped up between Natalie and Kevin over the years.

Now Natalie was being called to testify on behalf of her former husband, the father of her first child, as he fought for his life. Certainly, in her wildest nightmares back at Pomona College, Natalie could never have foreseen such an event in her future.

Abzug's primary purpose in calling Natalie was to demonstrate that Kevin had made his child support payments in a regular fashion, which would blunt Thompson's point that Kevin had killed Deepti to avoid paying more child support.

As it turned out, however, the idea would backfire.

After taking Natalie briefly through her history with Kevin, Abzug asked her if Kevin had ever missed a monthly child support payment. Natalie said no.

"Directing your attention to November of 1999," Abzug asked, "how much child support did Dr. Anderson owe to you?"

"None," said Natalie.

"In all the time that you've known Dr. Anderson, did he ever push you around or harm you in any way?"

"No."

"Did he ever once threaten to physically harm you?"

"No," Natalie said, "never."

But Abzug's questions were artfully designed. While it was true that Kevin had never missed a payment, he hadn't always sent the full amount. And while it was true that in November of 1999, he no longer owed any child support, it was because he had paid his arrears by then.

Thompson was well aware of the facts behind Kevin's marriage to Natalie; after all, Gallatin and McElderry had interviewed her, and Thompson had a copy of the Anderson divorce file ready to enter as an exhibit.

"Now," said Thompson when she was ready, "isn't it true that the defendant was not a consistent payer of child support?"

Natalie said it was true that she wouldn't always get Kevin's check when it was due.

"And isn't it also true, not only did you not always get the check on the first, but he often paid less than what he owed?"

"Yes."

Thompson now peppered Natalie with questions about Kevin's arrearage, taking them from documents Natalie had signed under penalty of perjury in the divorce case. With the implied threat of perjury hanging over her head, Natalie admitted that at one point, Kevin was more than $17,000 behind in his payments, and that he owed Natalie another $15,000 in spousal support. Thompson also made Natalie admit that she'd contacted the district attorney's office in 1995 to get child support enforcement against Kevin, which did make it seem as though Kevin was reluctant about paying.

Thompson now wanted to go into other details of Kevin's marriage with Natalie, but Abzug wanted to cut this short. It was clear that Natalie was feeling uncomfortable on the stand.

At the sidebar, Abzug noted that Natalie had just given birth.

"How much longer do you have?" Schwartz asked Thompson.

"I don't know," she said, "maybe ten, fifteen minutes."

Abzug wanted to see if Thompson would agree to let Natalie off the hook. Thompson said she intended to ask more questions about Kevin's private life with Natalie.

"What's the relevance?" Schwartz asked. "It's all the most boring stuff and embarrassing as hell to the witness. What does it show?"

"He's a real odd character," Thompson said, referring to Kevin.

"He's a real odd character?" repeated Schwartz. "Then no further questions. The court has an obligation to protect the integrity of the proceedings including to prevent witnesses from being embarrassed. You have scored dramatically with this witness, and the rest of this stuff is just not particularly relevant to any issue."

It was nearing 5 P.M., and Schwartz wanted to let the jury go. After they trooped out of the courtroom, Schwartz chided Thompson for wanting to squeeze more out of Natalie.

"You got quite a bit of mileage with this witness," she told Thompson. "I'm going to ask you to focus, because if we're going to continue going on and on with witnesses into matters that are marginally relevant but which cause quite a bit of embarrassment to the witnesses, I have to cut it off. In this particular case, you impeached the hell of that witness, and you got from the witness everything you can get from a witness, and there is nothing more to get."

She had told the jury that it would get the case before

Thanksgiving, Schwartz said, and she wanted to keep that promise. If that meant cutting off the lawyers' questions of witnesses without prejudicing anything, that is what she would do, she said.

33

The following day was Tuesday, November 14. Thanksgiving was just nine days away, November 23, and two of those days were on a weekend. And while Abzug had significantly fewer witnesses than Thompson had, actually making the Thanksgiving deadline depended on how extended Thompson's cross-examination might be. Because the two main witnesses were expected to be Heidi and Kevin himself, Thompson was highly reluctant to confine herself to any arbitrary limit.

Abzug's next witness was Ken Rivers, the former chief executive officer at St. Luke. By the time of Kevin's trial, Rivers had moved to another Tenet Health hospital. Under questioning from Abzug, Rivers sketched in the background of the relocation grant, and said he recalled meeting "in August" with Kevin and Deepti about the grant.

"Can you be a bit more specific, late August or early August?" Abzug asked. Rivers said he thought it was in the middle of the month.

"Did Dr. Gupta eventually qualify or not qualify for the relocation assistance?"

"Did not qualify," River said, "primarily based on the reason that she was already practicing in the medical office adjacent to the hospital."

Now Abzug asked whether Kevin had done anything to either encourage or discourage the hospital from awarding the grant. "No," Rivers said.

Thompson now asked Rivers if any paperwork had been processed for Deepti's grant request.

"If we feel there's going to be a potential for the relocation assistance grant," Rivers said, "yes, there is."

Rivers said that there had been such potential, until Deepti had told the hospital that she was practicing next door, and that once that happened, it was determined that she wasn't eligible for the grant.

"Are you telling us, Mr. Rivers," Thompson asked, "that Dr. Gupta told you in this meeting of mid-August of 1999 that she was still working at [the] Eaton Canyon pediatric group?"

"She was working in the office building, yes," said Rivers. Rivers again said he believed this information had come from Deepti, not Kevin.

Since this was clearly wrong—after all, Deepti had stopped working at Eaton Canyon in April of 1999, after her blow-up with Ng—the effect of this testimony was to suggest that someone wasn't telling the truth: either Rivers, or Deepti. Why Deepti would have said something that would have prevented her from getting the grant wasn't clear, unless she had possibly been coached to say the wrong thing by Kevin. If Rivers was right, the implication was that Kevin didn't really want Deepti to get the grant at all, even if she had agreed to split the proceeds with him.

After Rivers, Abzug called Richard James Burkhart, the man who had followed Kevin and Deepti up the mountain on the night of November 11, and who had again seen their cars, in the same position in the turnout, as he went down the mountain nearly two hours later.

Burkhart told of following the 4Runner and the Mercedes up Angeles Crest Highway to the turnout, watching them pull off, then passing again on the way down. Just what Abzug hoped to gain from Burkhart's testimony wasn't at all clear, except that it seemed to confirm that Deepti's car had gone over the cliff just before 8 P.M. But this didn't help Kevin all that much.

Later, Thompson was asked why she hadn't called Burkhart as her own witness, since he was corroboration of the fact that Kevin and Deepti had left the highway at Mile Marker 33 right around 6 P.M. This was solid evidence that Kevin hadn't needed to send a voicemail page to Deepti less than a half-hour later, at 6:27 P.M., because she was sitting right next to him at the time. It strongly suggested

that Kevin was thinking in terms of an alibi, and that
therefore Deepti was already dead. And Burkhart's description of the two vehicles facing east, both with their lights
on at 7:30 P.M., meant that a few minutes later Kevin not
only had moved Deepti's car to the edge of the ravine, he'd
also moved his own truck up behind her car, if La Riviere's
7:50 P.M. account was to be believed. Kevin hadn't said
anything about moving his own truck, at least in his statement to the detectives. This was extremely damaging to
Kevin's credibility.

Thus, on balance, Burkhart was a far more effective witness for Thompson than he was for Abzug.

Thompson later said she hadn't called Burkhart because
she believed that Abzug would attack his credibility as a
witness; if Abzug called him instead, that would be much
more difficult for the defense attorney to do. Abzug said
he called Burkhart because he didn't want Thompson to be
able to produce him in rebuttal after Kevin's expected testimony; that would make it seem like the defense was trying
to hide something.

In any event, Burkhart's testimony came in, and it was
never contradicted: Kevin and Deepti had been at the turnout by 6 P.M., a fact which brought most of Kevin's story
about what happened that evening into doubt.

Abzug now called a number of character witnesses for
Kevin, in an effort to demonstrate that he was not ordinarily
a violent person, and that planning a murder would be the
last thing that anyone would have expected of him. Again,
this testimony cut two ways: while everyone agreed that
Kevin was mild-mannered and non-confrontational, the
very fact that he never seemed to lose his temper suggested
planning.

Just before 4 P.M., Abzug called Heidi to the witness
stand.

Abzug and Thompson obviously had different plans for
Heidi. The defense attorney wanted her testimony to show
that Kevin had been driven to distraction by Deepti's de-

mands through the summer and fall of 1999, that Deepti was not only "obsessed" with Kevin, but that she was untruthful. He also wanted Heidi to put the kibosh on Thompson's suggestion that Kevin feared he would have been wiped out, financially and professionally, by Heidi if she ever found out about the affair. Thompson, on the other hand, wanted to use Heidi's testimony to establish that it was Kevin who was the liar, not Deepti; that Kevin was a skirt-chaser, and that Heidi was extremely jealous—so jealous, in fact, that Kevin was prepared to commit murder to keep her from learning of his infidelity.

Abzug began by taking Heidi through the origins of her meeting Kevin in the early 1990s, their marriage in November of 1997, and their living arrangements, that is, who was responsible for what. Abzug wanted to deal with the damaging household account ledger that the detectives had taken from Heidi during their search.

"It was basically like a joke," Heidi said of the ledger page. "[Like] my dad gives my mom twenty dollars, and then he says, 'Where's the change?' And they laugh. To me it was the same thing. I really didn't—it was just something between us." The household account was more of a fun fund than anything else, she said. "If the money was there, it was there. It was our money, together. It didn't really matter."

Abzug led Heidi into a discussion of the outdoor activities she'd shared with Kevin. He wanted to give the jury the idea that the trip with Deepti to the top of the mountain to look at stars was typical of Kevin's usual leisure activity, rather than an indication that Kevin had planned to commit murder.

"Well," Heidi said, "we really liked to go waterskiing and boating. We liked to go hiking. We liked to go camping. We liked mountain-biking. We used to go snowboarding, amateur astronomy, just being outdoors. Bird watching." Abzug now introduced a number of photographs of Kevin in various places in the San Gabriel mountains during these trips.

Next, Abzug turned to the gas can that had been in Kevin's truck. He wanted to show it wasn't part of a "murder kit," but that it had been in the truck for some substantial time prior to the killing.

"When was the first time that you recall seeing this gas can?" Abzug said, pointing to the exhibit of the can that had been found in Kevin's truck.

"I think I remember seeing it sometime in the summer," Heidi said. "In the garage."

Kevin, Heidi continued, had talked on several occasions about his worry that they might run out of gas while in the boat, or while towing the boat on one of the skiing excursions. Abzug wanted to demolish Thompson's capacity to suggest that Kevin had only acquired the gas can for the purpose of burning up Deepti's Mercedes.

Now Abzug turned to the subject of Deepti. He asked Heidi when she had first met her, and Heidi told the stories of her first two encounters with Deepti, including Deepti's telling her of the arranged marriage with Vijay.

"Why would you talk to her about her arranged marriage?"

"It was interesting," Heidi said. "We were both kind of newly married and it was interesting."

"What did she say to you about it?"

"She said that she was unhappy."

Thompson objected on hearsay grounds, but Schwartz denied the objection, and Thompson didn't squawk, since the testimony was offered as proof of Deepti's state of mind.

Abzug turned to the proposed partnership between Deepti and Kevin, and the fact that Heidi was soon cut out of the planning.

"I said, 'I don't understand,' " Heidi said she'd told Kevin. "I mean, I was supporting this, and initially we had gone together. I just wanted to know why. He said it seemed like every time he would suggest something I had suggested, and he told her, Dr. Gupta, that it was my suggestion, she got very upset and didn't like it."

Deepti, Heidi now said, began calling the Anderson residence ever more frequently as the summer of 1999 unfolded, and soon she was sick of hearing from Dr. Gupta. That was when Heidi had chided Kevin about Deepti's neediness, she said, and she'd wondered why Vijay wasn't doing more of the moral support. She said Deepti had treated her shabbily and glared at her when she tried to get involved in the partnership discussions.

During their trip to Washington, Heidi said, she and others had talked to Kevin about the proposed partnership. By that time, Kevin had admitted to her that there were romantic feelings in the air. But that was hardly the only reason Kevin was advised against the partnership, Heidi said.

"There were just basic philosophical differences. Control of the vacation time. Him leaving town. The [Colorado River] trip was just a huge thing. She was so upset because we [were] going to be leaving town."

Heidi said that she'd urged Kevin not to go into the partnership because he would be giving up control over his life to Deepti; after all, she said, the whole point of starting his own practice was to be able to have time to do the things he liked doing.

At the September 7 confrontation at the Andersons' house, Heidi said, it was true that she'd lost her temper after Vijay's remarks. After she'd left the house, Heidi said, she'd gone to a neighbor's to calm down.

"And she said, 'You know, you just need to stand firm. When you say no, stand firm. Don't lose your temper. Just keep telling them no, and mean it when you say no. Go back and apologize.'

"I said, 'You're right.' I went back in the house, and it killed me, but I did it. I said, 'I apologize, I'm sorry I stormed out of here.' And then I said, 'I said no, and I mean no.' "

After this, Heidi said, she'd encouraged Kevin to buy Dr. Richard's practice. When she learned that Deepti was going to be working at Richard's clinic, however, she had insisted that Kevin make Deepti sign the agreement to leave by January.

The courtroom clock was now pushing 5 P.M., but Schwartz was determined to have Abzug finish his direct examination of Heidi by the end of the day, so Abzug pressed on. He asked Heidi if she'd ever had arguments with Kevin.

Yes, Heidi said. Sometimes the arguments were so bad that Kevin would stay away from home overnight.

"Did the arguments involve you raising your voice and trying to provoke Dr. Anderson?"

"Yes."

"Is there one argument that you had with Dr. Anderson that you remember especially?"

"Yes," Heidi said, and recalled that one such fight had occurred in 1996 or 1997. "We had been arguing. I don't even remember what we were arguing about. It had been one of those arguments that had been going on for quite some time. I tend to be the more verbal person, very emotional, and I was yelling and shouting, and saying just about everything I could to him. We were downstairs, and I was pushing him, trying to get a reaction out of him. And I kept pushing him and pushing him."

"What tone of voice were you using at this point?" Abzug asked.

"Oh, I was screaming," Heidi said. "I was screaming. I was screaming. I was screaming. Yelling. I use many choice curse words. I know it isn't right, but I do it. And I was just yelling. I was trying to get a reaction out of him. I was very upset.

"He actually pushed me back, and then I—I got really mad, because he pushed me back, so I pushed him back. He pushed me back, and then I said, 'You know what? You're just like your dad.' He just kind of got this weird, glazed look in his eye. He grabbed me and he dragged me. He's like, 'You're out of here.' He was going to throw me out the door." Heidi said it was only when she yelled at him that he was going to break her arm that Kevin regained his self-control. Afterward, Kevin was worried about his behavior, and left the house to calm down.

With this, Abzug finally had some character testimony that he could use. It appeared from Heidi's story that Kevin, while usually calm and non-confrontational, could in fact erupt in rage if he was sufficiently provoked. Abzug was trying to set the stage for Kevin's own coming testimony, when he would have to describe just how Deepti had provoked him to kill.

Abzug now closed in on his ending; he wanted the jury to leave that day with something to think about.

"Now, Ms. Anderson," Abzug said, "you know that Dr. Anderson has cheated on you, do you not?"

"Yes."

"You know that Dr. Anderson killed another human being, correct?"

"Yes."

"You now know that that human being was pregnant, do you not?"

"Yes."

"You now know that that pregnancy belonged to your husband, that is, he was the father. You know that, do you not?"

"Yes."

"Ms. Anderson, have you filed for divorce?"

"No."

"Have you undertaken any action, Ms. Anderson, after knowing all these things, to financially ruin your husband?"

"No."

"Are you supportive of your husband to this day?"

"Yes," Heidi said.

With that, the trial recessed for the day; Thompson would have her chance to cross-examine Heidi the following morning.

34

Thompson began her attack on Heidi's testimony almost as soon as she resumed the witness stand the following morning. She asked Heidi if it wasn't true that Kevin had flirted with her in 1992, when she was a nurse at Huntington Hospital, and Kevin was still married to Natalie. Thompson wanted to show that Kevin was always on the prowl, married or not, and that Heidi herself had reason to know this.

Heidi said Kevin hadn't flirted in 1992, "not really, in my opinion."

Thompson asked Heidi if when she first began dating Kevin, they were each also dating others. Abzug objected on relevance grounds.

"I think it goes to this witness's credibility," Thompson told Schwartz. "I think what I'm going to establish is that she's an extremely jealous person, and very insecure in her relationship with the defendant. That he did in fact see other women while he was dating her. And it goes to this woman's credibility, as far as all her testimony yesterday that, you know, the victim was the one who glared at her and was nasty to her, when it is clear this woman is the insecure individual. She was jealous of the victim's connection to the defendant, and the time the defendant spent with the victim. It think it *is* relevant."

It wasn't, Abzug said. Whatever happened back in 1992 had nothing to do with the case in 1999.

"I think it demonstrates their entire, tumultuous relationship," Thompson persisted.

"There is no question that this was a tumultuous relationship," Schwartz said. But it wasn't that probative of the issues in the trial, the judge added, so she sustained Abzug's objection.

Thompson resumed her pecking at Heidi's previous testimony, trying to open a vein that might lead to damaging admissions. She tried the ledger, but Heidi didn't crack:

"You're telling us you spent time in gathering all this information about the money he owed you and the money he paid you, but this was merely a joke between the two of you?"

"It was a reminder to him," Heidi said. " 'Hey, let's put some money into our joint checking account.' "

Thompson next tried Heidi's black belt; she told Schwartz, when Abzug objected, that it was to demonstrate that Heidi expected Kevin to become violent with her. But when Heidi testified that Kevin had no skills in martial arts, Thompson abandoned that line.

Soon Thompson arrived at the gas can. The best she could do with this was to get Heidi to admit that although she and Kevin had had the boat since 1994, it wasn't until the summer of 1999 that the can had been purchased. That didn't help very much, because it certainly didn't suggest that Kevin bought the can for the sole purpose of threatening to burn Deepti's car.

At length, Thompson turned to the partnership. Heidi admitted that Kevin had told her one reason he wanted to go into business with Deepti was that she had a substantial sum of money to invest. But it wasn't the only reason, Heidi indicated: Kevin thought Deepti was a very good doctor.

Now Thompson turned back to the theme of Heidi's supposed jealousy.

"Now, during the course of your relationship with the defendant," she asked Heidi, "did you ever become jealous?"

"No."

"Did you ever become distrustful of him?"

"Distrustful of him?"

"Yes," Thompson said.

"Not really."

"Did you ever feel he was being unfaithful to you?"

"No."

"You always trusted him, is that your testimony?"

"Yes."

"Did you ever have a conversation with [another nurse], where you told her that you believed your husband was having an affair with one of the nurses at St. Luke, and that you would kick their ass if you found out?"

"Absolutely not," Heidi said.

As the morning progressed, Thompson took Heidi through the events of the summer, leading up to the trip she and Kevin had made to Washington for Kevin's board certification refresher course. Heidi said at first she was for the partnership, then against it, when she realized there were so many differences between Kevin and Deepti. When she began to suspect that Deepti was interested in Kevin, she became adamantly opposed, Heidi said. Kevin had told her the interest was all on Deepti's part, Heidi said.

"When you learned from the defendant that he was not interested in Dr. Gupta, but she was interested in him, did you ever have a discussion with your husband *after* that about whether or not he was interested in her?"

"I don't remember," Heidi said.

"So you had no suspicions at all about any romantic relationship between the two of them, up through and including the time of the murder—is that your testimony?"

"Yes."

"And your husband gave you no reason to even think that there was anything romantic between him and Dr. Gupta, is that your testimony?"

"Yes."

"But you never feared that he was interested in her, is that your testimony?"

"Yes," Heidi said. "No, I didn't. Yes."

"Because as far as you knew, your husband had always been faithful to you, is that right?"

"Yes."

"And you don't consider yourself an insecure woman, is that your testimony?"

"No."

After another break, Thompson resumed her mining of Heidi's testimony.

"Now, when did you first learn that your husband had had an affair with Dr. Gupta?" she asked.

"Probably after he was arrested," Heidi said.

"How long after?"

"I don't remember. I mean, I can't tell you. The whole first month of this was just horrible. I was like living in a daze."

"His disgrace is your disgrace, is that it?"

Heidi said she didn't understand the question, Abzug objected, and Schwartz sustained the objection. Thompson moved on to the night of Kevin's arrest, and the phone call that Kevin had made to Heidi that night, when he'd lied about having to be at the hospital.

"How was he in that phone conversation?" Thompson asked. "Did he appear to be very calm?"

"He seemed like Kevin to me," Heidi said.

"Nothing out of the ordinary?"

"Not really, no."

"Now, do you love your husband very much?"

"Yes."

"You loved him in 1998?"

"Yes."

"Loved him in 1997?"

"Yes."

"Loved him in 1999?"

"Yes."

"During the course of your marriage to your husband, were you unfaithful to him?"

"Yes."

"And how many times?"

"Once."

"And was that with a body builder?"

"That was with a friend of mine."

"Did you at one point arrive home with this friend of yours and your husband saw you together?"

"Yes."

"And how did he handle that situation?"

"He broke down. He was tearful."

"In front of this other man, he was tearful?"

"It was very quick. When I talked to him, he was broken down. He was very tearful. He was crying. He was devastated. He was devastated."

"Let me ask you this," said Thompson. "When he saw you together, isn't it true that he walked out and shook the man's hand and said: 'Thank you for taking care of my wife'?"

"No," Heidi said.

"That is not true?"

"No."

Abzug kept silent throughout this exchange. It appears he could have stopped it on grounds of relevancy, although Thompson was trying to show that Kevin was extraordinarily difficult to provoke. It was humiliating for Heidi, and tinged with mean spirit on Thompson's part. But it only helped Kevin in another way, because it made his affair with Deepti seem all the more human, even as it made no friends for Thompson among the jurors.

But then, neither Abzug nor Thompson were playing beanbag, not with a possible death penalty in the balance.

Schwartz now recessed the trial for the day.

35

Before the jury was brought in the following morning, Thompson raised an issue that had been lurking around the trial almost from the beginning. She wanted to get a new ruling from Schwartz on whether she would be permitted to ask Heidi about the sexual harassment complaints that had previously been voiced against Kevin.

This issue, which was potentially devastating to Kevin's defense, had first been raised before the trial, when Abzug convinced Schwartz to keep all references to the complaints out of the trial on the grounds that they were more prejudicial than probative in the matter of whether Kevin had premeditated Deepti's killing. Thompson hadn't agreed with the judge's decision, and wanted to raise the issue again, now that Heidi was on the stand.

"Why?" Schwartz asked.

"Because," Thompson told her, "she's indicated she's never been jealous, her husband was not a womanizer, she never suspected that he was involved with any other woman. We have information that shortly after she claimed she had the affair in 1998 . . . the sexual harassment complaints had been made against the defendant . . . it is my belief that he discussed it with her and she retaliated against the nurses."

"Retaliated? How?" asked Schwartz.

"By being rude and nasty and controlling, trying to control schedules."

Schwartz mulled this over and agreed that Thompson could ask, although "I don't know how far we're going to get."

This Abzug absolutely did not want.

There now ensued a discussion of these complaints, which Abzug said were never verified. It appeared that

Kevin had been accused of rubbing against women from the back at Huntington Hospital, and that a supervising physician had warned him that there had been a complaint.

After more discussion, Schwartz eventually said she would allow Thompson to ask Heidi if she'd ever been aware of the complaints, but that was as far as she would permit the topic to be pursued. But, said Schwartz, Thompson should not use the words "sexual harassment" or refer to the fact that there had been complaints. That would be prejudicial.

"If I may briefly respond," said Thompson.

"I don't want to hear any more," Schwartz said.

"Okay," Thompson said.

"I hate to say it," Schwartz said, "but we're beating a dead horse here."

When Heidi resumed the witness stand, Thompson brought up her "body builder" affair, and asked whether she was trying to get even with Kevin "for having slept with someone else."

Heidi said no.

"Were you aware of any complaints by nurses or other female employees at Huntington Memorial Hospital that the defendant had made sexual advances or sexual overtures?"

"Objection," said Abzug.

"Rephrase the question," Schwartz ordered Thompson.

"Move for a mistrial, Your Honor," Abzug said.

"Rephrase the question," Schwartz ordered Thompson once more.

"My motion," Abzug persisted.

"Your motion is taken under submission," Schwartz said. "We'll discuss it later at sidebar. Go ahead." This, to Thompson.

"Were you aware of any nurses or other female employees at Huntington Memorial Hospital who were concerned about Anderson's conduct toward them?"

"Objection, same objection," said Abzug.

Schwartz sighed. "Let's go to the sidebar," she said.

*   *   *

This was serious. Abzug's motion for a mistrial could wipe out the entire trial so far; theoretically, under certain circumstances, it might even require dismissal of the charges against Kevin. Abzug was furious with Thompson for using the word "complaint."

"I cannot believe she did that," he told Schwartz. "I cannot believe she did that after you had—"

"What did I do?" Thompson asked.

"You used the word 'complaint,' and then you used the word 'concern,' " Schwartz told her. "I'm going to admonish you once again. Ask your questions succinctly, to the point, without characterizing the nature of the complaints, Ms. Thompson."

"My understanding [is], I couldn't say 'sexual harassment,' " Thompson said.

"You can't characterize," said Schwartz. "You can say, 'Are you aware of overtures.' "

"All right," Thompson said.

"It was very simple," Abzug said. "Move for a mistrial."

"The motion for a mistrial is denied. I certainly don't think the conduct involved was that which would rise to the level of willful prosecutorial misconduct. It is certainly a violation of my [pre-trial] order."

"What type of overtures?" Thompson asked.

"Don't put a spin on it," Schwartz said.

"All right," Thompson said.

Back before the jury, Thompson tried again, and this time simply asked if Heidi was aware of any "overtures" by Kevin to any nurses. By then, however, it was quite clear that Thompson wasn't talking about symphonies.

Heidi said no, she hadn't been aware of any overtures.

Now Thompson asked a series of questions about Heidi's movements on the day of the killing, and then moved on to the contents of Kevin's truck. This was not particularly productive, however, and eventually Thompson turned to an exhibit she had prepared, a large poster board with Kevin's four-page "determined" letter to Deepti in blown-up writing. She intended to question Heidi about this letter.

Almost as soon as the board went up, however, Heidi blanched. She wanted to talk to Schwartz—privately.

At the sidebar, Heidi told the judge, "Mr. Gupta just got up in his seat and he went like this at me." Heidi demonstrated by making a face.

"Mr. Gupta?" asked Schwartz.

"He scared me," Heidi said. "I'm sorry, I'm sorry. I'm trying to hold it together, but—"

"Hang on one second," said Schwartz. She called a brief recess, and sent the jury out of the courtroom.

When the jury had left, Schwartz said she wanted the record to be clear: "Ms. Anderson," said the judge, "you said that yesterday [Professor] Gupta made some gestures, said something to you. I want the record to be clear as to what is causing you to shake right now."

"My friend is here," Heidi said, "and my brother-in-law, who was here, had sat in front and this is what he told me. They wouldn't tell me all the comments, but just some, like, 'That little shit,' "Bitch," just making—they didn't want to tell me everything. That's kind of scary. He hates me."

"What happened when you were testifying, when Ms. Thompson was showing you [the poster board]? Did something happen that got you upset?" the judge asked.

"He was sitting in his seat. He keeps staring at me, making me uncomfortable. I can live with that. That's fine. But he got up in his seat and went—"

"Got up in his seat and—?"

"Made this terrible face at me and opened his eyes really wide like he was going to pounce on me or something," Heidi finished.

This was why Schwartz had sent the jury out of the room: Heidi was shook up over Vijay's behavior.

"It scared me," Heidi said. "I didn't know what he was going to do. I kind of fear for my safety, too. But I didn't do anything. He's always grinning at me and stuff."

Schwartz told Heidi to step into an anteroom. She wanted to talk to Vijay.

After Heidi left, Schwartz spoke again. "For the record, [Professor] Gupta is present in the courtroom. He's seated in the front row, which is close to the witness. I've got to tell you, I've never seen a witness become so unglued as I just saw this witness here, Ms. Thompson."

"I've witnessed her react the same way, when we executed the search warrant at the defendant's house," Thompson shot back.

"That's interesting," said Schwartz, "but it doesn't help me."

Schwartz wanted to know how much more cross-examination Thompson had of Heidi.

"I have a few questions," Thompson said.

"I'm going to call Professor Gupta up to the sidebar," Schwartz said, "and strongly admonish him. This is not the first time he has done something that has upset somebody. The last time it was Mr. Abzug."

"I have to tell you," Abzug said, "I'm getting a little nervous. I'm getting a little concerned myself, and I'm a big boy. I can take care of myself. I don't know what is going on."

Vijay came to the sidebar.

Schwartz told Vijay that Heidi had accused him of doing something, which had caused a disruption in the trial.

"I don't want to have any further disruptions," she added. "So—you may not have done anything. I wasn't watching you. All I know is, she's visibly shaken, and she's shaking right now, and we had to take a break."

"Thank you, Your Honor," Vijay said, "and I'd like to be heard as well."

Schwartz said she wasn't accusing Vijay of anything. But she wanted him to move to another seat in the courtroom.

Thompson had a different take on what was going on. She thought Heidi's reaction was to the poster board. "It's the letters the defendant wrote," Thompson said.

Abzug chimed in, saying he thought his own reaction to Vijay's earlier remark about the "sick bastard," whoever Vijay meant, was quite moderate, under the circumstances.

"I didn't say anything to you," Vijay interrupted. "I explained that through Ms. Thompson. I've done absolutely nothing. I won't have that accusation right now in the presence of—" Vijay wanted to make clear he'd done nothing to unnerve Heidi.

Things were getting out of control. Schwartz moved to cut it all off.

"Professor Gupta," she said, "this is a courtroom I have to run. I'm doing my best to get through this proceeding. I know this is painful to you." She suggested again that Vijay move his seat, and to try to keep from saying things people might overhear.

"I'm not asking her [Heidi] to look at me," Vijay said. "There is nothing in the world that I can [do to] control her eyes . . . maybe she doesn't want to be in this courtroom, just because she's saying lie after lie."

Vijay left the sidebar, and Abzug suggested that he be excluded for the remainder of Heidi's testimony. Schwartz said she couldn't do that.

"I'm not saying permanently," Abzug said.

"Just an observation," Schwartz said. "This is an extremely painful proceeding for all of the parties, including Ms. Anderson, including Professor Gupta. My heart goes out to these people. That's why I'm pushing you guys along." She turned to Thompson. "How much more do you have?"

"I have a few questions," Thompson said again.

Now Abzug raised the objection he had intended to make even before the "disruption."

"It is improper," he said, "to cross-examine Ms. Anderson on the contents of a letter that she never saw."

"Where are we going with this," Schwartz asked Thompson, "except to embarrass and humiliate her?"

Thompson said she intended to ask Heidi whether she'd

ever told Kevin that caring for his daughter from the marriage to Natalie was a burden.

This sent Abzug over the top.

"You can't use the letter," he said, heatedly. "You can't
use the letter, which she has never seen, and put it up in
front of the jury like that, number one. Number two, you
already went through this yesterday [with McElderry]."

"Let's settle down," said Schwartz. "I'm not—"

"I'm perfectly calm," said Abzug.

Schwartz said she wouldn't permit Thompson to question Heidi about a letter she'd never seen. "You can question the defendant about that when he testifies," she told
Thompson. "Let's just move forward."

Thompson made one more attempt to ask Heidi questions from Kevin's letter to Deepti, and when this was rebuffed by the judge, ended her cross-examination.

36

Just before noon, Abzug reclaimed Heidi as a witness. He asked several questions about Kevin's reaction to her November 1998 affair, and Heidi said again that Kevin was very hurt and tearful. Abzug asked her what the cause of some of their arguments was, and Heidi said most of their fights were caused by miscommunications.

"I would say one thing and he would interpret it as another," she said. "We had a lot of fights over sports, World Cup soccer. A lot of times family, in-law issues. Also, sometimes just basic issues regarding prejudice and race, and his perceptions versus my perceptions."

Kevin would sometimes tell her that she just couldn't know what it was like to be the minority in a mixed-race couple, and Heidi would argue with him about that.

Abzug now asked Heidi what Kevin had told her about arranging for Deepti to work at Richard's Children's Clinic.

"Well, the basic reason was that she and her husband were very upset," Heidi said, referring to Deepti and Vijay, "because he really didn't any longer want to go into business with them. And he felt it would be a good way to help her get started, by letting her start seeing some patients, and letting her take some of the patients from Dr. Richard's practice . . . and that way she could start building a practice so she could go off on her own. He was trying to help her."

Abzug did some more cleanup work on the contents of Kevin's truck, and then produced a home video of Kevin, Heidi and another couple waterskiing. On the tape Kevin was heard to say something about the need to have extra gasoline for the boat, which Abzug wanted to use to demonstrate that Kevin had always been concerned about possibly running out of gas—to account for the gas being in the back of the 4Runner on the night of the murder, not as a "murder kit," but as a normal occurrence.

After having Heidi tell about talking to Kevin on the night he was arrested, and the subsequent search of their house, Abzug finished by asking why she seemed so shook up when Thompson had put up the poster board with Kevin's letter. As he had explained to Schwartz earlier, he didn't want the jury to think it was the board that had spooked Heidi, even though Thompson said that's what it was.

Heidi said Vijay had scared her by gritting his teeth at her. "I thought he was going to jump over the railing," she said. "It really, really scared me. I didn't know what else to do."

"I have nothing further," Abzug said.

Thompson now asked Heidi whether Abzug had told her the questions that he had intended to ask her. She wanted the jury to be left with the impression that Heidi was rehearsed in her testimony. Abzug objected to this, and Schwartz ordered both lawyers to the sidebar again.

Schwartz wanted to know why Thompson had asked this question.

"As is typical—" Thompson began, but Schwartz stopped her.

"Wait," Schwartz said sharply, "let's knock that off."

"That's not called for," Abzug seconded.

"I don't believe I finished," Thompson said.

Schwartz thought Thompson was going to make a nasty crack about defense lawyers putting words in witnesses' mouths.

"You know 'As is typical' is something that is objectionable, and I don't want you to talk like that," Schwartz told her.

Thompson said she didn't mean any disrespect, only that it was common for lawyers to discuss expected testimony with witnesses. Schwartz said it sounded to her like Thompson was fishing for an answer that might involve privileged communications between Heidi and Abzug.

Thus rebuked, Thompson asked a few more questions of Heidi, and then let her go.

When the afternoon session began, Thompson returned to the chastisement she had received from Schwartz before the noon break. She said that people in the courtroom had heard her dressing-down by the judge.

"I'm concerned about the jury being influenced by any comments the court makes to me in a negative fashion," Thompson said. "And I know the court doesn't mean anything you do or say to influence the jury, but I think that jurors are only human, and I'm concerned about any influence that may have on The People's case.

"And then, secondly, the court had asked Mr. Gupta if he would be kind enough to move to the other side of the room, and not be in direct sight of Ms. Anderson, to avoid upsetting Ms. Anderson . . ."

This, Thompson suggested, could be taken as an inference by the jury that Heidi's reaction was valid—that Vijay *had* done something to scare her. Thompson wanted Schwartz to admonish the jury that just because Vijay had changed his seat, that didn't mean that he had behaved badly, whatever Heidi had said.

Schwartz said she wasn't going to do that. Thompson was free to call Vijay to let the jury hear his side of the story, Schwartz said, but she wasn't going to take sides in the matter, because she hadn't seen what actually happened.

As for her "negative" comment to Thompson, the judge said she thought she'd been "remarkably restrained.

"I am not normally so restrained," Schwartz added. "What you saw this morning may not be terribly restrained, coming off several well-taken objections by Mr. Abzug, a motion for mistrial, which causes me grave concern. I want to point out, this is a capital prosecution. And everyone's conduct comes under scrutiny, if this should result in such a penalty being imposed, not just by the [state] courts but, as you know, the federal courts.

"And in particular, prosecutorial conduct is a subject

that many federal justices look very carefully at. And in this case there have been some things that have transpired, although Mr. Abzug has not raised an objection, I have got to tell you that if he did, I would be sustaining objections."

Having gotten started about Thompson's conduct of the case so far, Schwartz went on: "And I think this might be an appropriate time to go into some of those things, just so the record is clear.

"Number one, you keep referring to this as 'a murder,' 'the day of the murder,' 'the day of the murder.' Had Mr. Abzug objected to that, I would have sustained it."

Schwartz was quite correct in pointing this out to Thompson, since the issue before the jury was whether a "murder" had been committed, or whether it was actually manslaughter. By using the word "murder" in her questions, an argument could be made that Thompson was improperly trying to influence the jury.

"It is disturbing to the court," Schwartz went on, "that the questions are being phrased that way, in all candor, Ms. Thompson. I'm trying not to interject my opinions or feelings about these things . . . But I have to say, this being a capital case, if I were sitting in your chair, I would want to be very careful about everything I say and do, whether objected to or not.

"What happened this morning with me raising my voice at sidebar, I think, was something that occurred simply because of the reference you made . . . It is a culmination of what I believe to be somewhat of a reaction to some of the things that have gone on in this court."

It bothered her, Schwartz said, when Thompson had seemed to ignore her instructions on the sexual harassment issue.

"I tell you at sidebar specifically not to editorialize or categorize, or say anything with reference to sexual harassment, sexual misconduct, so on and so forth, and then right out of the box the questions are objectionable. It is disturbing to me. It's disturbing." It had gotten to the point, she said, that she would "strongly admonish" Thompson at the sidebar if she persisted in asking objectionable questions.

Thompson now said she didn't think she'd actually violated the judge's order with her questions. "The court didn't want me to talk about sexual harassment. I stayed away from that."

"I am urging you to tone it down a bit," Schwartz said. When Thompson had prefaced her recent remark with "As is typical," that was too much, the judge said, and she had decided to put a stop to it.

"We had a heck of a morning here with the witnesses and the motions for mistrial," Schwartz continued. And if the jury came back with a conviction and a death penalty, she said, everything would be looked at, including Thompson's presentation. "I'm just cautioning you in that regard," Schwartz said.

But this wouldn't be the last clash between Thompson and the judge.

Abzug spent the early part of the afternoon with witnesses who had driven over Angeles Crest Highway, trying to establish that the highway was well-traveled, and that the turnout at Mile Marker 33 wasn't the most secluded one along the road—there were others even more hidden on the way to Mt. Wilson. He called another friend of Kevin's to corroborate that Kevin had worried before about not having enough gasoline. He called McElderry, and forced the detective to admit that he had made a mistake when he had said in a report that Vijay had told him that Kevin's $10,000-a-month stipend from St. Luke was going to be invested into the practice. He played a tape of Gallatin and McElderry's interview with Jay La Riviere, in part to show that La Riviere's glimpse of Deepti's car going over the cliff was a fragmentary one, one that took only a split second as La Riviere drove by.

Then he called his main witness—Kevin himself.

By this time it was obvious to everyone that Kevin's

fate would rise or fall on his own testimony. Although
Kevin did not have to testify on his own behalf, as the
only living witness to much of what motivated him as
well as Deepti, Kevin's credibility in the witness chair
would be crucial to whether the jury believed him, or
Thompson.

In this, Abzug was focused on the instructions that he
knew the judge would eventually give to the jury:

> To constitute a deliberate and premeditated killing, the
> slayer must weigh and consider the question of killing,
> and the reasons for and against such choice, and having
> in mind the consequences, he decides and does kill . . .
> to reduce an unlawful killing from the offense of murder
> to manslaughter upon the ground of sudden quarrel or
> heat of passion, the provocation must be of the character
> and degree as naturally would excite and arouse the pas-
> sion, and the assailant must act under the influence of
> that sudden quarrel or heat of passion . . .

Abzug's objectives in putting Kevin on as his own witness were clear: he wanted to show first that Kevin had no
strong motive to murder Deepti Gupta—the "reasons"; that
he did not plan it—the "consequences"; and that Deepti had
provoked him into an irrational act—the "passion." Simultaneously, Abzug wanted to use Kevin's testimony to help
paint the picture of Deepti as "dysfunctional" and "out of
control," as Sharma had described her. If Abzug could help
Kevin humanize himself to the members of the jury, that
was all to the good.

Abzug began easily, leading Kevin through a series of
questions about his background, establishing his considerable accomplishments, and the fact that he had been a life-
long resident of the area. The testimony moved to Deepti's
arrival at the Eaton Canyon clinic, her troubles with Ng,
and the plans Kevin and Deepti had made for their ill-fated
partnership. Thompson sat quietly, making notes to herself
as Kevin talked, but never intervening with any objections.

The more Kevin talked, the better Thompson liked it. At length, the afternoon session came to a close. Very little had happened, but everyone in the courtroom knew it was just the calm before the hurricane.

37

Kevin was transported from his jail holding cell the following morning, as he had been every day of the trial so far, looking for all the world as though he were the successful young professional he had been. Clad in a conservative suit, with a tasteful tie, Kevin appeared to be the incarnation of reasoned calm. It was almost impossible to believe that he was on trial for murder.

Today was Friday, and if Abzug did his job right, he would be able to stretch Kevin's direct testimony for the whole day, leaving the jurors the whole weekend to think it over. Abzug hoped it would sink in deep enough for some of it to remain once Thompson started in on Kevin with her cross-examination on the following Monday morning.

As Kevin settled into the witness chair, Abzug returned to the partnership. He wanted to try to dispose of the business about the patient list once and for all. Kevin said he'd arranged with his billers to begin calling patients who were on his Eaton Canyon logs to let them know that he and Deepti would be going into practice together. He gave the billers a stack of logs that were about an inch-and-a-half or perhaps two inches thick. The billers were supposed to find telephone numbers for the patients, and call them individually to let them know that the partnership would be starting up soon. When he explained his plan to Deepti, he said, she decided to obtain her patient logs so that Kevin's billers could do the same with those records.

"Did you do anything at all, Dr. Anderson, to prevent Dr. Gupta from either retaining a copy of what she gave you, or contacting the patients herself?" Abzug asked. Kevin said he hadn't.

"Did you pay a great deal of attention to the amount of

so-called patient lists that she gave you, at the time she
gave them to you?"

"No," Kevin said. "I just kind of grabbed them, threw
them in the stack. I didn't really pay that much attention."

Under questioning from Abzug, Kevin continued to describe the events of 1999—Heidi's unhappiness with being
kept out of the planning for the clinic, her resentment of
Deepti's telephone calls, and especially Deepti's insistence
that Kevin not take so much time off for "fun."

Eventually, as the summer wore on, his relationship with
Deepti began to change, Kevin said. It began with shared
confidences, usually complaints about their spouses, and by
August it had developed into a love affair. Kevin said it
was Deepti who had been pressing him for intimacy, not
the other way around.

After he told Heidi that Deepti was romantically interested in him, Kevin said, he began to see that the business
relationship wasn't going to work. But still, he said, he felt
torn: one part of him felt very attracted to Deepti, and
wanted to continue, while the other part kept pulling away.
It was after he'd told Deepti that the partnership wouldn't
work that they first had sex together, Kevin said.

"I was emotionally torn," Kevin said. "I mean, on the
one hand I wanted to—I was attracted to Deepti. I wanted
to work with her. I wanted to see how we could make this
work. On the other hand, I felt like I wasn't doing the right
thing. I felt a little guilty, and I didn't really know how to
handle this situation that well. So I just kind of plodded
along at that point, thinking that somehow it will all work
out."

Abzug asked Kevin about the letters he wrote to Deepti,
particularly the first letter, the one about commitment.
"What did you mean by that?" he asked.

"I was trying to give her reassurances throughout the
letter," Kevin said. "I felt like I was committed. I felt like
I was doing my part for this whole endeavor . . . I wanted
to tell her that I respect that decision in her, but I personally
was going to continue to try to open up an office."

"Even without her?"

"Yeah, even without her."

Abzug asked Kevin about the relocation grant. Kevin said the first he'd heard of it was in Marvin Cooper's office in August of 1999. After this, Deepti had asked him to try to lobby Ken Rivers so she could get the grant, Kevin indicated. When the grant wasn't approved, Deepti blamed him, he said.

Even before this happened, Kevin said, he'd been thinking of going over to join Dr. Richard's clinic. After he and Heidi had returned from Washington, he made up his mind once and for all not to go into practice with Deepti. He then began negotiations with Richard instead.

It was after he and Heidi had returned from Lake Powell that Vijay had called him and insisted on meeting in Westwood, Kevin said. That was where he had first learned that Deepti had lost her hospital privileges. The next day, the Guptas came to visit.

"To me," said Kevin, "the meeting was a disaster. There was really no way that I saw that my wife was convinced about anything as far as me working with Deepti.

"From a personal point of view it was terrible, because my wife was upset. She didn't like what was being said. She apparently didn't like what Dr. Gupta was non-verbally communicating to her. She left the house very upset. She later came back and apologized."

But while she was out of the house, Kevin said, he told Vijay that maybe he could talk Heidi into not objecting if Deepti came to work at the Children's Clinic. Eventually, that was what happened, Kevin said. Heidi then wrote the agreement calling for Deepti to be out of the clinic by January, and Deepti signed it.

Abzug now took Kevin through all the events of October 1999—the sporadic arguments over the "patient list," Richard's agreement to let Deepti work two days a week there, the sex at the Gupta house in October. Deepti kept coming to the clinic to see him in October, Kevin said.

"What was going through your mind as to why you were

having sexual relations with Dr. Gupta at this point?"

"Well, I was still somewhat emotionally attached to her," Kevin said. "I still felt close to her. I knew she was very happy that she was going to see the patients at Children's Clinic until her offices were opened. I think she was appreciative, at least then, that I was trying to help her out with that." Kevin thought it made Deepti happy to know she would be able to see him during the week.

"On the other hand," he said, "I was trying to make sure that she went off on her own, and I went off on my own. I was trying to keep the home front happy and still trying to focus on getting a business started."

He had never dreamed Deepti would get pregnant, Kevin said, because she had assured him that she was using birth control. And, Kevin said, he had been there the day Deepti had told the Thatcher leasing manager that she had no immediate intention of having children.

"When Dr. Gupta started working at Dr. Richard's office, were you concerned that your marriage or career might be in jeopardy?"

"No. No. Not at all," Kevin said. "Actually, by the time she started, I felt pretty good. I felt like: Okay, I was working now at a clinic that I liked. I liked the people there. They were very good. They were very nice. She was pacified because now she wouldn't have to be pestering me about getting into practice with her."

After Deepti started at the clinic, Kevin said, he even referred some of his patients to her. He believed things were going well.

Then, on November 10, Kevin continued, he'd met her as he finished at the clinic, and she wanted to talk to him. Kevin said they went to the restaurant, and Deepti indicated that she had "some concerns." They then went across the street to the motel and had their argument, Kevin said, in which Deepti had complained that Richard had accused her of stealing patients. That was when Deepti told him that she was pregnant, and that she would tell Heidi, Kevin said.

"What was your state of mind as to whether you actually

thought that she would follow through with that threat, to tell Heidi that you were having an affair?"

"Well, once I thought about it, I didn't really think she would do it, because obviously if she did that, it would hurt her as much as it would hurt me."

"On November tenth, did you see murder as the only alternative to preserving your marriage?" Abzug asked.

"No, absolutely not," Kevin said. "I mean, murder? Murder wasn't even in my mind. It was not something that was even in the realm of possibility. I felt she was blowing off a lot of steam. I felt she was making accusations against me for her own reasons. A lot of it had to do with the fact that we weren't going to be practicing together. I did not want her telling my wife about this affair. I was hoping it would not come to that. But no, that [murder] was not even a consideration."

"Were you concerned, on November tenth, that Dr. Gupta might destroy your professional reputation, your ability to make a livelihood, if she publicly disclosed she was having an affair with you, and carrying your child?"

"No. Not at all. I mean, I think my reputation had been established for a long time. Whether or not I had an affair with someone, it may not look so good morally, but I don't think it would affect whether or not someone decided to come see me [as a doctor]. It might affect some, but I don't think it would have done much to me financially, no."

38

Before the trial resumed for the afternoon session, there was another minor flap that Schwartz had to sort through. This time, one of the jurors had seen Heidi in the hall talking to some of Kevin's relatives during the morning recess. One of them, a man, had hugged Heidi and thanked her for her testimony. The man told Heidi that Kevin also wanted to thank her. Then, according to the juror, Kevin's relative said something to the effect that no matter what had happened between Kevin and Heidi, Heidi's testimony was "pleasing to God," and that her testimony was bringing everyone together, to be "reconciled."

The juror told the judge that she thought that she'd heard something she wasn't supposed to hear.

Schwartz had an idea of what this meant, but kept it to herself. Whether it meant that Heidi had tailored her testimony to help Kevin was immaterial. The real question was whether the juror had been affected by it. The juror said she hadn't. Schwartz asked Thompson and Abzug if they wanted to challenge the juror at this point, and neither said they did. It wasn't really Heidi's fault; the corridor outside the courtroom was so crowded with witnesses, jurors and spectators that it was difficult to keep everyone separated.

Kevin resumed the stand for the afternoon session. Abzug was trying to deal with all the supposed motives Kevin might have had for murdering Deepti. He believed he had disposed of the patient list problem, the divorce problem, and the professional ruination problem. Now he wanted to get rid of the child support motive.

After Deepti had told him she was pregnant, Abzug asked, was Kevin worried about paying child support?

"No, I wasn't worried about child support," Kevin replied. "I didn't think there was a child. I didn't think she was pregnant. That was not of concern."

But, said Abzug, what did Kevin mean when he'd told the sheriff's detectives that he had to get Deepti "not to do this thing"? Abzug misstated what Kevin had told the detectives: what he actually said was "not to do any of these things," apparently referring to the threat to tell Heidi about the affair, and that she was pregnant.

Kevin now returned a long convoluted, narrative that didn't answer the question. Kevin said that he used that expression a lot, and that what he'd been referring to was helping Deepti get set up at the Children's Clinic.

This wasn't helpful, so Abzug tried another way.

"So from the time, roughly, that Dr. Gupta alleged that she was pregnant, to her death, what was it you were planning on doing?" Abzug hoped that Kevin would get the question and jump on it, smack it out of the park with some sort of answer that would explain that seemingly incriminating remark.

"I was fairly hopeful," Kevin said. "I thought we would be able to work out a lot of these issues. I thought, with talking, we would be able to come to some kind of agreement, what our conduct was going to be for the remaining two months at Children's Clinic." He hoped they would be able to work out some sort of compromise, Kevin said.

This still wasn't it. But then, Kevin had just said that he didn't believe that Deepti really was pregnant, so why wouldn't his thoughts naturally be on trying to work out their other difficulties? It was subtle, but Abzug hoped that the jury would get what Kevin meant.

He also hoped that the jury wouldn't pay too much attention to the fact that Kevin's actual worry, that Deepti would tell Heidi about the affair, "to do this thing," hadn't seemed to enter into Kevin's mind at all, at least to hear Kevin tell it. In one way, that was a bad sign: if the jury didn't think Kevin was worried about the most immediate threat, the threat to tell Heidi, would it be because they believed that Kevin in fact had begun to plan the murder?

Abzug asked Kevin about the pre-natal vitamins, and Kevin said he hadn't known anything about these until the trial.

Abzug was now up to the day of the murder in his examination. He asked Kevin what had happened. Kevin said he arranged to meet Deepti at the clinic to go stargazing. He got there about 5 P.M., he said, and waited about fifteen or twenty minutes for Deepti to arrive. Once Deepti came, he said, he told her he had to make a stop.

"We stopped at St. Luke Hospital," he said.

"And how long were you there?"

"Fifteen or twenty minutes at the most."

Thompson was writing this all down. She was sure she could prove Kevin was wrong about these times, and thereby destroy his credibility with the jury.

Abzug veered away from the events leading to the murder to establish the contents of Kevin's truck. He wanted the jury to understand that Kevin hadn't had anything like a "murder kit" in the truck on the night that Deepti died. Then Abzug came back to the point: "Did you, Dr. Anderson, pick the San Gabriel Mountains to see Dr. Gupta because it was a secluded place where you could ambush her?"

"No," Kevin said, "absolutely not."

If he'd wanted to do that, Kevin now said, there were plenty of places farther up the highway that were far more isolated. He'd selected Mile Marker 33 because it was simply the first turnout to give an unobstructed view of the city to the south, and the stars to the north. On the way up to the turnout, Kevin said, he'd twice communicated with Deepti to pull over, to let faster traffic behind them pass. Once, he said, he sent a voicemail page to Deepti "to let her know I was going to be pulling off at some point." This happened, he said, "about halfway to the turnout."

"Now, what were you thinking about as you were driving up the Angeles Crest Highway, proceeding on to Mile Marker 33?"

"The whole reason for going there," Kevin said, "was

to try to work through all these problems we were having. So I was frustrated. I was a little agitated, I admit, because it seemed like these things wouldn't go away . . . there had been so many threats and accusations, everything from Dr. Richard to the practice over the summer, to this stipend [relocation grant], or now this alleged pregnancy or affair she was going to talk about. She even had her husband threaten me on the phone."

As he was driving up the highway, Kevin said, he thought about threatening to burn the Mercedes. "But I didn't really seriously think we were going to act on any of these threats," he said. "I figured we were going to be able to come to some sort of agreement. I was pretty hopeful."

"What did you do when you reached the turnout?"

Kevin said they both pulled in parallel to each other, with Deepti's Mercedes slightly ahead. He got out of his car and sat in the passenger seat of the Mercedes.

"I got in and sat down," he said. "I closed the door. And the first thing I asked her, I said, 'How do you like the view?' And she had never been up there before, and she really liked it. And so we started talking, small talk at first.

"And I said at some point, 'You know, we really need to—We really need to hammer all this stuff out and talk about it.'

"And she said, 'Well, I'm firm in my belief that what I told you before is the way I feel now.' "

Kevin said he told Deepti that he was upset at what she'd been saying.

"She said, 'Well, it is very clear to me what's been going on. You've done what you could to ruin my career, and you started out in the summer saying you were going to work with me. Then you bailed out of that. You said you were going to help me get this stipend, and then you turned around and you sabotaged it.' "

Kevin said he denied sabotaging the relocation grant.

"She said, 'I know you did. It wasn't a coincidence when

we decided not to work together, suddenly this stipend wasn't coming my way.' "

Kevin said he began to grow more irritated as the discussion progressed.

"She was getting more agitated because I was denying all this stuff. And I was getting very angry."

Kevin said he got out of the Mercedes, telling Deepti he couldn't talk any more. He said by the end of the argument, Deepti was yelling at him and pointing her finger.

Kevin said this first argument lasted about fifteen or twenty minutes, he wasn't sure.

"While you were arguing back and forth, were you waiting for an opportune time to strangle Dr. Gupta?"

"No. No," Kevin said.

After he got out of Deepti's car, Kevin said, he began setting up the telescope. While they'd been arguing, he said, he'd gotten a page, which he'd ignored.

Deepti got out of the Mercedes, and they looked through the telescope for a while, Kevin said.

"I showed her the moon. I showed her a couple of things down in the city. I showed her Jupiter. You could also see the moons of Jupiter," Kevin said.

"We got back in my car," he said. Kevin said he returned the page he'd received, which was from Natalie.

Then, he said, he and Deepti returned to their argument.

"We went back over this stipend [the relocation allowance]. This whole idea of the stipend was really bugging me at this point. It wasn't even an issue to me anymore." Kevin said he felt bad that Deepti thought he had had something to do with the fact that she hadn't gotten the grant.

"She basically didn't believe a word I said. It was my fault. I did it somehow. I rigged it with the CEO at St. Luke, and that's just the way it is. She started talking about Dr. Richard again. And we went on and talked about this lawsuit threat, about these 'patient lists.' And as soon as I mentioned the words 'patient lists' she started yelling.

"She was shaking her hands like this," Kevin said, making fists, "and at the same time she was yelling at me. I was yelling back. 'I don't have your lists. I've given you everything that you gave to me, and I resent the fact that you continuously, in front of my staff, in front of the office, you come barging in there. You're calling me all the time. You're always asking about these lists. There are no more lists, and you don't need the lists anyway. You can start getting your own practice. You don't even need these lists.'

"She started yelling more. She said that I favored my wife in any discussion that we had. I said: 'She's my wife.' And she said I was putting my wife before her.

"And you know, at this point I was yelling at her. I was telling her that my wife is who she is. She has her own personality. She's not going to change. She likes to get involved in things and that's the way it is.

" 'I see your wife go to work all the time,' " Kevin said Deepti now said.

"And it just kind of struck me, what do you mean by that? What's that supposed to mean? The first thing I thought of, she's in the parking lot and she sees my wife going to work. What is she implying by this? She said— then she mentioned my daughter: 'I know where your daughter goes to school.'

"And at this point we were—I—everything just snapped. I mean, I started yelling at her to shut up, shut up. I reached down. I guess I must have reached down and grabbed this tie. I looped it around her neck, and I started pulling, yelling, 'Shut up! Shut up! Not my daughter! Shut up!'

"And I guess, at some point, I mean, I stopped. And she—it was just real quiet. We had gone from yelling and screaming and all of a sudden it was just real quiet. And I started getting scared.

"I let go of the tie and she just kind of slumped forward and . . . I pulled her back off the dashboard. And she . . . her eyes were open and there was like a gasp or something, like you would take a breath, that came out. And I thought to myself—'Oh my God, she's dead.' "

"How long did the struggle last, Dr. Anderson? How long did you have the tie around her neck?"

"I don't know. I can't remember. I don't know. I was just so angry. I was so enraged at that point, I wasn't thinking about the tie."

"What did you do once Dr. Gupta slumped over?"

"I pulled her back, and she wasn't breathing. I mean, she wasn't moving. Her eyes were open. I think I even said, 'Deepti.' I mean, I knew she was dead right then."

He was overcome with fear, Kevin said.

"My legs were shaking. My own breathing was deep, and I couldn't control it. I couldn't stop it, and I was just sitting there, thinking, 'She's gone, she's gone.'

"The next thing that I can remember was, I was very terrified of what could happen, what was going to happen to me. And I did the absolute wrong thing at that point. It was very stupid. I thought maybe I could make this look like a traffic accident. The car goes over the cliff, you know, bursts into flames.

"And I got out of my car. I moved her car over to the edge, and I got out of the driver's seat of her car and picked her up out of mine and put her over there. I grabbed the gas can in my car, some matches, and I got in the passenger side of her car. I just sprayed some gas on her and on the floorboard at her feet. While I had the match, my hands were shaking. Then, I guess I didn't put the car in park, and while we were sitting there at the edge, I felt the car starting to tip, and we started going down the incline, and I panicked again. The gas can was on my right leg next to the car door. I just turned and opened the car door and jumped out at that point. I ran up the hillside and got in my car."

Kevin said he saw a car pull into the turnout, then drove off. "I felt terrified. I wanted to get away from that, and get somewhere, maybe, to collect my thoughts. I was hitting my hands on the steering wheel, saying to myself, 'What have I done?' "

Kevin said as his truck raced down the mountain, he

could hear the tires screeching as he took the curves. He was going too fast, he said, and missed a turn. "I just held onto the steering wheel and slammed the brakes and just closed my eyes. The truck just skidded and kept skidding and kind of stopped with a thud."

He got out of the 4Runner and saw that he had barely missed going into a deep ravine. "If I had gone over that, I probably would have been killed myself," he said.

Abzug asked Kevin about his arrest. Kevin said at first no one had asked him what had happened, so he didn't give a complete statement to the arresting deputies. When he got to the station, he wasn't allowed to call anyone, he said. Later, when he was interviewed by Gallatin and McElderry, he lied about having an affair with Deepti. "I was still trying to conceal that from my wife," he explained.

"When you went up the mountainside on November eleventh with Dr. Gupta, were you planning to kill her?"

"No," Kevin said. "I did not want this to be the way it ended up, for either one of us."

39

Over the weekend, Thompson pored over the transcript of Kevin's testimony, and examined her notes. She believed that she had Kevin right where she wanted him. Kevin was lying, Thompson was convinced, and she was sure she could prove it. There were simply too many inconsistencies in his story. The question was, could she expose these holes so that the jury would be as convinced as she was?

By this point, Thompson had a near encyclopedic grasp of the details of the case. Because this was the first death penalty proceeding she had taken to trial, she wanted to make certain that she covered everything. If Kevin avoided conviction, Thompson didn't want it to be because she had inadvertently left something on the cutting room floor. But as Thompson strove to get every detail in, she soon ran into impatience from Judge Schwartz, who was feeling an increased urgency to speed things along. Thanksgiving, after all, was only three days away. And Thompson's desire to be all-inclusive soon ran into a storm of objections from Abzug on grounds of relevancy and foundation. Schwartz sustained many of these objections, increasing Thompson's frustration and adding to Schwartz's own rising anxiety about the looming deadline. As the trial pushed on in what would be a marathon session lasting until past 6 P.M., these conflicts would boil over.

Thompson began by asking Kevin about his medical training. She wanted to establish that Kevin was experienced in dealing with stressful situations, and so, would be unlikely to react to an intense argument with violence. When Thompson tried to get Kevin to admit that he knew how to resuscitate someone who couldn't breathe, Kevin said he'd never had "adult" CPR training.

"Do you think, sir," Thompson asked, "as a competent

physician, you could tell the difference between whether anyone is unconscious or dead?"

Kevin said he thought that would be easy.

"If someone is strangled, sir, is there any hope that re-suscitation could revive that person?" Thompson asked. It would depend on how long the person had been strangled, Kevin replied.

"Why don't you tell us the situation with Dr. Gupta? Was it long, was it medium, was it short when you strangled her to death?" Thompson asked.

"With Dr. Gupta I really wasn't thinking about resuscitation," Kevin said.

"Did it take you seconds to kill her, sir?"

"I wouldn't be able to give a number on that. I don't know."

"Minutes?"

"I don't know."

"Well, you strangled Dr. Gupta to death, did you not?"

"That's correct."

"And did you take any steps to resuscitate or revive her in any fashion?"

"You know, I was in a rage, and I didn't."

"The truth is, you took no steps to revive Dr. Gupta, is that correct?"

"I don't recall doing anything that would revive her," Kevin said. "I did check, just looked at her. She wasn't breathing, and her eyes were open and . . ."

Thompson had begun with one of her most potent points: the fact that Kevin had no interest in seeing that Deepti come back to life, even after he saw her lying unresponsive right next to him, appeared to show that this was no spur-of-the-moment violence, but rather an intentional act.

Thompson now backed away from the events at Mile Marker 33 for the time being. She wanted to show that Kevin had a long pattern of deceitfulness that was evident well before the fatal encounter. She used Kevin's July "commitment" letter to Deepti to show that he was capable of lying.

Thompson established that Kevin had tried six times to get board certification as a pediatrician, not once as he had implied in the letter. When Thompson asked him about Heidi's affair with the "body builder" in November of 1998, which Kevin had blamed for his failure to pass the test, Kevin said he hadn't known at the time that it was a sexual relationship. He had felt it was still a betrayal of trust by Heidi, Kevin said.

"Did you trust Dr. Gupta?" Thompson asked.

"Initially I trusted her, yes," Kevin said. It was only when Deepti accused him of trying to steal her patients, and sabotaging the relocation grant that he began to think Deepti was not to be trusted.

Thompson asked Kevin if he didn't think it was reasonable for Deepti to suspect that he had interfered with the grant process. Kevin insisted again that he'd had nothing to do with it.

After inducing Kevin to admit that Deepti was a highly qualified doctor, certainly not someone likely to engage in emotional histrionics, Thompson turned to Kevin's history with Natalie. She wanted to show that Kevin had tried to have his child support payments reduced in 1998, even when he was earning a substantial income from Eaton Canyon. She asked him whether he'd bought books on how to reduce his child support; that way, Thompson was able to introduce those books that Schwartz had previously ruled inadmissible. Thompson's intent was to show that Kevin had, at least in the past, been motivated to reduce or even eliminate his child support payments.

Now Thompson tried to get into the question of Kevin's reputed womanizing.

"Did you ever give Heidi any reason to be insecure about her relationship with you, sir?"

Abzug objected, saying it was irrelevant, and Schwartz sustained the objection.

"Were you unfaithful at all in your relationship with Heidi?"

"With Gupta, I was."

Thompson asked if he'd been unfaithful to Heidi before they were married, with others, and again Abzug objected on relevancy grounds.

"Is it fair to say, sir, that you were pretty good at pulling the wool over your wife's eyes?"

"Objection."

Schwartz sustained again.

As the noon hour approached, Thompson tried to get Kevin to admit that money was very important to him. She made Kevin list a number of things that he and Heidi had acquired; Thompson wanted to suggest to the jury that Deepti's pregnancy threatened Kevin and Heidi's comfortable lifestyle.

When the noon break came, Abzug told Schwartz that he was disturbed by the way Thompson had been questioning his client.

"The record reflects that there's been what I would characterize as an unrelenting pattern of argumentative questions," he said, "which the court has repeatedly sustained. I believe we're getting to the point where this examination is being turned into an opportunity for another closing argument. I simply want to alert my opposing counsel, in the most respectful way possible, that if it continues on, I'll move for a mistrial."

Thompson didn't say anything, but Schwartz warned her to be careful.

40

The questioning resumed in the afternoon, with Thompson boring in on point after point in an effort to show that Kevin was lying—that he'd lied repeatedly to Deepti, to Heidi, to the detectives, to the jury—and that as a liar, he couldn't be trusted to be telling the truth when he said that strangling Deepti had been an unplanned, explosive act.

At one point, Thompson brought out the fact that Natalie had briefly had a relationship with one of Kevin's brothers, after they had separated. Abzug objected, saying it was irrelevant to the issues at trial.

Once again at the sidebar, Thompson argued that since the defense had originally brought the issue up during the testimony of one of Kevin's character witnesses, the prosecution was entitled to use it to show that Kevin had never lost his temper before, even under the most extreme provocation.

Schwartz said she wasn't sure that it was necessary to show this.

"It tends to show this man does not become enraged," Thompson argued. "Here his wife is having an affair with his brother and he handles it with the utmost calm."

"You have that evidence ten times over," Schwartz said. Schwartz said that was abundantly clear to everyone, and told Thompson to ask another question.

Thompson now moved to the days when the partnership idea was first broached. She used Kevin's own handwritten notes, and asked him questions designed to pin him down on just when the partnership idea fell apart. It was Thompson's contention that Kevin had never really intended to go into partnership with Deepti, and that the whole thing had been a ruse from the very beginning to get Deepti into bed. If she could get Kevin to acknowledge that he actually did very little to get the partnership into existence, her case would be bolstered. Along the way, however, Thompson also established that Deepti had been dependent on Kevin's good will.

This led once again to the grant proposal, and eventually the September 7 meeting at the Andersons' house. Kevin insisted that by the time of the meeting, he'd already told Deepti he wouldn't be going into partnership with her, and that she had by then learned she wasn't getting the grant. Those two problems were why Vijay had insisted on meeting him in Westwood, Kevin said. By then he had decided to try to get Deepti space at Richard's clinic, Kevin insisted, in order to help her out.

But Thompson knew Kevin was wrong about this. The Westwood meeting hadn't happened until late September, not the day before the meeting at the Anderson house. Thompson, in her questions, made it clear she thought Kevin was lying about the purpose of the meeting, as well as the date. By establishing that Kevin was lying, Thompson hoped to convince the jury that even after the partnership idea had come apart, Kevin was still dangling the prospect of prosperity in front of Deepti, in a continuing effort to have sex with her.

"When did you become attracted to Dr. Gupta?" Thompson asked.

"Probably in the summer," Kevin said.

"And how did you handle those feelings of attraction?"

"Not very well," Kevin said. "I didn't do what I probably should have done. I tended to act."

"Isn't it true that you pursued her?"

"I think it was mutual, that we both pursued each other."

Thompson again tried to establish that Kevin had pursued other women, as well as Deepti, in 1999, and again Abzug objected. Schwartz ruled once more that the topic was irrelevant.

Next Thompson tried to establish that Kevin had first told Deepti that there would be no partnership, then there would be, and then had sex with her in August of 1999. It was a pattern that had occurred again in September, and a third time in October, Thompson pointed out with her questions—on each occasion Kevin had pulled back, then given in, then had sex. Kevin said he couldn't remember the exact sequence of the events in August.

"And when," said Thompson, "in relation to having sex with her, did you tell her that it was over, that you were no longer going into practice with her?"

"I told her that after we had sex, but the exact day I don't know."

"Now, why is it that you told her that *after* you had sex?"

"It had nothing to do with having sex," Kevin said. The partnership had come apart over finding a place to lease, he insisted.

By the middle of the afternoon, Thompson had reached the events of November. She asked Kevin if it wasn't true that Deepti had told him on either November 1 or 2 that she was pregnant, and that Kevin thereafter tried to avoid her. Kevin denied that Deepti had told him she was pregnant, but admitted that he'd been trying to avoid her during the first week of November.

Thompson asked Kevin if Deepti had told him she was pregnant during their lunch at the bagel shop on Monday, November 8, and Kevin denied this, as well. He insisted Deepti hadn't told him about the pregnancy until the Wednesday night in the motel across the street from the restaurant.

"Now," said Thompson, "when you were with her in that [motel] room, did you tell her that you loved her?"

"I don't think so, no."

"Did you tell her, sir, that the timing wasn't right for a baby?"

"No."

"Did you make any promises to her, sir?"

"Not that I know of, no."

"Did you tell her that you would leave your wife if she had an abortion?"

"No."

"Did you tell her to have an abortion?"

"No."

"She's implying, sir, that this is your child, according to your own testimony, is that right?"

"That's correct."

"And she's a physician, isn't she?"

"Yes, she is."

"And she would know, would she not, if she was pregnant with a child, wouldn't she?"

"I would assume so, unless she was lying."

"Didn't she tell you that she had confirmed it by taking some pregnancy tests that previous Sunday?"

"No, she never told me that," Kevin said.

"She never told you that?"

"No."

"She didn't need to convince you because the fact is, sir, she told you that she was pregnant, and you believed her, isn't that right?"

Kevin said he thought Deepti was lying.

Hadn't the reason Kevin had agreed to meet with Deepti on the next night, November 11, been that he intended to convince her to have an abortion?

"No, that wasn't part of what we were going to discuss," Kevin said.

"Now, isn't it true, sir, that if you couldn't convince her not to have this baby, the only way to stop her was to kill her?"

"First of all," Kevin said, "I hadn't thought of convincing her not to have a baby. I never believed there *was* a baby. As far as killing somebody because they're going to have a baby, that's—that doesn't even make sense. I would never even think of doing something like that."

41

Now Thompson was closing in on Kevin. She was nearing the events at Mile Marker 33, and she had something she thought would blow Kevin's story to smithereens.

Schwartz was still pressing Thompson to hurry up. "We need to move a bit faster," she said, "and we need to stay focused on the issues. And Ms. Thompson, there's such a thing as beating a dead horse."

"I agree," Thompson said.

"The evidence is pretty substantial at this point," Schwartz said. "We've had four hours of cross-examination . . . so ask the questions succinctly. And when you ask the question and get an answer, don't ask the question three more times. Let's move on, all right?"

Thompson now established that Kevin's daughter attended a school with some significant security measures, including a wall and locked gates. For a stranger to pick up a student, Kevin admitted, there would have to be written authorization from a parent.

"Dr. Gupta knew that you loved your daughter, isn't that right?" she asked Kevin.

Kevin said that was true.

"And Dr. Gupta wouldn't do anything to hurt your daughter, would she, sir?"

"I didn't think so," Kevin said. "Not up until the night of her death."

"Sir, did Dr. Gupta have anything to gain by making threats about your daughter?"

"I don't know what she had to gain, to tell you the truth," Kevin said.

"Absolutely zero, isn't that right?"

"No," Kevin said. "I'm saying, I don't know what she had to gain."

"Wouldn't those threats just alienate you further?"

"When I first heard the threat against my daughter, I mean, we were at the point in time of yelling and screaming back and forth to each other. And she had just threatened my wife. And I heard that, and I just—you know, that was it. I had just really had it at that point." He wasn't really thinking about Deepti's motives, he said.

Thompson switched topics to ask about the gas can. Wasn't it true that Kevin had put gas in the can on November 10? "No," Kevin said.

"Isn't it true you told the detectives that you had the gas container with you on November eleventh for the purpose of threatening to burn Dr. Gupta's car?"

Kevin said he didn't recall saying that to Gallatin and McElderry.

Now Thompson began to focus in on Kevin's November 11 time line.

Kevin said he'd gone directly from his house in La Verne to the Children's Clinic to meet Deepti. He said he made no stops.

This, of course, was different from what Thompson believed. She had already established that Kevin had been at St. Luke between 5 and 6 P.M. from the testimony of the nurses. The fact that he'd been to the hospital *before* meeting Deepti at the Children's Clinic was evidence that Kevin was trying to establish his alibi, Thompson thought.

Later, Thompson would say that she believed that Kevin needed to lie about the timing of his movements because otherwise he couldn't account for the 6:27 voicemail page he'd made to Deepti—which, by his original story, she would have received while she was sitting in the car right next to him. Her earlier call to Vijay had already established that the pager was on: "Guddu—I will keep both the pager and the phone on so you can reach me, if you need me," Deepti had said.

That meant Kevin had to shove back his estimates of

when he and Deepti had arrived at Mile Marker 33, from the original, 6 P.M. to 6:15 P.M., to after 6:30. He'd already suggested, under questioning from Abzug, that the 6:27 voicemail to Deepti was to alert her to turn off at Mile Marker 33. Claiming they'd stopped at the hospital first was one way to push the time line back fifteen or twenty minutes.

The trouble with this was, of course, the testimony of Richard James Burkhart, who had testified that he'd seen the Mercedes and the 4-Runner turn off at Mile Marker 33 right around 6 P.M. Thompson thus knew she had Kevin in a box. She intended to close it up on him.

She asked what time Kevin had arrived at the Children's Clinic to meet Deepti. Kevin said he had gotten there around 5 P.M. and waited. After Deepti arrived, he said, they both went to St. Luke.

"What time is it that you left the Children's Clinic, sir?" Thompson asked.

"I don't remember exactly—exactly what time we left," Kevin said. "She arrived there, maybe between five P.M., five-fifteen, five-thirty. So we left not too long after she arrived, so somewhere between five-fifteen and a quarter to six."

This covered a multitude of possibilities. Thompson tried to pin Kevin down. She showed him a list of the cellphone calls made by Deepti, and pointed out the one that had been picked up by the antenna serving the Children's Clinic area. That call had been made at 5:26, and was one of the two made to Vijay by Deepti—the ones about her beeper.

Kevin now admitted that when Deepti arrived at the clinic, she had been on her cellphone. They had stayed less than five minutes there, he said.

"So is it fair to say, then," Thompson asked, "that you left the Children's Clinic right around five-thirty P.M.?"

"Yeah," Kevin said. "That would probably be close to when we left."

Thompson now asked Kevin how long it normally took

to get from the clinic to St. Luke. Kevin said it usually took seven to ten minutes. By Kevin's clock, that meant they were entering the hospital between 5:37 P.M. and 5:40 P.M. The time before Deepti's cellphone call to Anil Sharma at 5:51 P.M.—when she'd said they were "in the mountains"— was growing perilously short for Kevin. In fact, if Deepti had been right about them driving for fifteen minutes "in the mountains," the visit at St. Luke had to have taken place in minus time, another dimension.

Thompson now asked what he and Deepti had done at the hospital—since she believed that they never in truth went to the hospital at all, she wanted to pin Kevin down on this point to contradict him with the other testimony she'd already established from the nurses. Besides, every minute Kevin said he and Deepti spent in the hospital was one less minute they had to drive before the call to Sharma could be made.

Kevin said he and Deepti both went into the hospital separately.

"We need to pick up the pace," Schwartz warned. Thompson said she would try to go faster if Kevin would only give yes or no answers. Abzug objected. "That will be stricken," Schwartz ordered, meaning Thompson's comment.

Abzug's objection and Schwartz's admonishment may have rattled Thompson briefly. She now failed to ask how long Kevin had been in the hospital on this putative side-trip, but instead went directly to the trip up the mountain.

"How long did it take you," she asked, "to get from Angeles Crest Highway to Mile Marker Thirty-three?"

"I don't know," Kevin said. "I would say that the total time from St. Luke to that turnout was probably about thirty minutes—possibly up to forty minutes." Now by Kevin's clock—if one assumed that he and Deepti had actually been in the hospital, that this wasn't a lie—that would mean they would arrive at Mile Marker 33 between 6:30 and 6:40 P.M. Of course, that left Deepti's 5:51 P.M. "we're in the mountains" call to Sharma, along with Burkhart's eyewitness account, to be somehow explained.

Now Thompson asked if it wasn't true that Kevin had originally told Gallatin and McElderry that he'd gone directly to Mile Marker 33 from the clinic, without stopping at St. Luke.

"Yes," Kevin said. "I had forgotten to mention that we did stop at St. Luke. That's true."

"And isn't it true, sir," asked Thompson, "that you also told them that you left Children's Clinic at about five-thirty and arrived somewhere between six and six-fifteen at Mile Marker Thirty-three?"

He'd made a mistake, Kevin said. When he'd forgotten that they'd stopped at the hospital on the way, his time estimate was thrown off. "So my initial estimate of arrival time at the turnout was probably off by about ten to fifteen minutes."

Thompson sprung the trap she had been trying to set up.

"Now, sir," she began, "you testified on Friday that you paged Dr. Gupta as you were going up the mountain. Do you recall that?"

"Yeah," Kevin said. "I left the voice message for her."

"And what message did you tell her on that voicemail message?"

"I told her that cars were starting to pile up behind us, and we probably needed to pull over pretty soon just to let some cars go by."

Thompson asked Kevin to put a mark on the map to show his location when he sent the voicemail.

"I couldn't tell," Kevin said. "I have no idea." Kevin thought this over, then offered the notion that it was someplace above the La Canada Golf Course, but before the Mile Marker 33 turnout. "It's an approximation," he said.

Kevin ended up waving Deepti over at Mile Marker 33, he admitted. They sat there looking at the view for a while, he said, and then he received a page from Natalie.

"And where were you, sir, when you got the call from Natalie Profant?"

"Where was I?"

"Yes," Thompson said.

"Where was I when she paged me? I was in the passenger seat of Deepti's car."

"At Mile Marker Thirty-three?"

"We were at Mile Marker Thirty-three at that point."

Thompson now showed Kevin the records from his cellphone. Didn't the records show that he'd sent the voicemail page to Deepti at 6:27 P.M.?

"Yes, it does," Kevin admitted. "Wait a minute. This is the voicemail page to Dr. Gupta? Okay. Okay."

"So it was at 6:27 P.M. when you were halfway up Angeles Crest Highway, is that your testimony?"

"Uh huh."

"Is that a yes?"

"Yes."

"Isn't it true that Natalie Profant paged you at six-eleven P.M. that evening?"

"I don't know what time exactly she paged me," Kevin said. "I just remember I was in Deepti's car."

Kevin was caught in the trap. He'd just said he was sitting next to Deepti in her car when he received Natalie's page at 6:11 P.M. But he'd also said he was still leading Deepti up the mountain in *his* car when he'd sent the voicemail page sixteen minutes later at 6:27 P.M. He couldn't have it both ways. He had to be lying.

42

Thompson was nearing the end. She decided to step up the pressure on Kevin.

"Sir, was [Deepti] kind and loving with children?"

"From my experience, she had been," Kevin said.

"Are you telling us, sir, that in a flash of a second you disregarded it all, and [that] on the basis of some ambiguous, some veiled threat, you choked her to death?"

"Objection, Your Honor," Abzug called out. "I move for a mistrial."

At the sidebar, Abzug complained that Thompson was again asking "argumentative and suggestive" questions.

"And I voiced my objection at the last break, and she ignored it," Abzug added. "Apparently it doesn't mean anything to her. She keeps doing it and doing it. I don't know what you can do to get her to stop."

Furthermore, Abzug added, Thompson had suggested by her questions that Kevin had told the detectives that he'd put the gas can in the 4Runner "for the purpose of" scaring Deepti. That was completely improper, Abzug said. "I couldn't believe my ears when I heard it." He'd double-checked the police report and all the other documents the case had spawned, and "at no time did he ever say that."

Thompson said Kevin *had* said that.

Schwartz said they were running out of time, and the issue of the gas can was too far afield. She denied Abzug's motion for a mistrial, his second of the trial, and told Thompson her question was inappropriate.

Following this, Schwartz told the jury that she'd "admonished" Thompson for her last question, and that they were to disregard her question as argumentative. "Closing argument will come soon enough, and she'll be given an opportunity to argue the case at that time."

Thompson went back to pounding on Kevin.

When Deepti had supposedly made the statements threatening Heidi and Kevin's daughter, had Kevin bothered to ask her what she meant?

Kevin said he hadn't asked her anything. "I was so angry at that point," he said, "when I heard that, I immediately feared for the safety of my wife and daughter. And I—I lost it."

Couldn't Kevin have contacted the police? Thompson asked. Couldn't he have contacted the school? Couldn't he have called Vijay? Couldn't he have had Deepti committed for 72 hours of psychiatric observation?

Kevin said he hadn't thought of any of those alternatives.

Kevin denied choking Deepti with his hands before strangling her with his tie. He denied hitting her.

"Did she try to fight you off?" Thompson asked.

"I—I don't remember," Kevin said. "She was angry. I seem to remember her hands being up."

"When you were choking her to death?"

"Her hands were up like this—" Kevin demonstrated "—when she was screaming and yelling before we actually—before I actually started choking her."

"Was she angry while you were strangling her, or was she frightened?"

"We were both very angry at that point. And I didn't assess whether there was fear going on. We were both very angry."

"How much force did you have to exert, sir?"

"I don't know how much force."

"Were you pulling very hard, sir?"

"I was pulling. I was pulling."

"And how long did it take before she stopped struggling?"

"I don't know. I don't know."

"Did she struggle, sir?"

"Like I said, I don't recall that particular part of it."

"Was she kicking her feet?"

"I don't seem to remember her kicking her legs."

"What caused you to stop pulling on that tie?"

"I don't remember if there was any one thing."

"Now, once you stopped pulling on the tie, you noticed that Dr. Gupta was not moving, is that right?"

"Among other things I noticed that she was not moving."

"Did you do anything at all to check if she was still alive?"

"I didn't purposely, like, check a pulse or check her heart. She appeared dead to me. Her eyes were open. She wasn't breathing and she wasn't moving."

"So you took no steps whatsoever to revive her, isn't that true?"

"No. If I had to do it over again, looking at it now, I probably should have, but I didn't."

Thompson asked Kevin if he'd cried after strangling Deepti, or while he was arranging the Mercedes to make the death look like a traffic accident. Kevin said he was first too angry, and then too scared. The first time he cried he said, he was in custody at the sheriff's station.

"Did you ever tell the homicide detectives that you were sorry for killing Dr. Gupta?" Thompson asked.

Kevin said he hadn't said that, exactly, only that he felt terrible about what had happened.

"Did you think about Dr. Gupta's two-year-old daughter as you strangled her to death?"

Abzug objected and was sustained.

"Did you ever tell the detectives that you felt bad about leaving Dr. Gupta's small daughter motherless?"

"Objection, Your Honor," Abzug said. "I move for a mistrial."

"We'll ask Ms. Thompson right now to finish," said Schwartz.

"That is my last question," Thompson said.

*　　*　　*

"As you know," said Abzug, after the jury had left for the night, "the jury is supposed to base its verdict on the evidence, and not because of any kind of passion, prejudice or sympathy. The absolute, only reason that Ms. Thompson would have asked that question is to try to inflame the jury against my client by throwing up this picture of this motherless child as a reason to convict. There is no other reason."

Schwartz said she would take the motion for mistrial under submission.

"I am concerned," Schwartz said. "I am concerned about the cross-examination and references to matters that were clearly inflammatory and inappropriate, as I previously admonished Ms. Thompson."

A lot of the cross-examination had been troubling, Schwartz said.

"And the court takes exception," she added, "to Ms. Thompson laughing when I sustain an objection. That occurred within the last hour or so, and I'm not real happy about that, and the jury saw that as well."

Schwartz said she would rule on the mistrial motion the following morning.

43

But the next morning Abzug told Schwartz that, after thinking it over, he didn't want a mistrial after all.

"Did you say you *don't*?" Schwartz asked.

Abzug said a mistrial would require them to try the case again, and the case so far had already imposed an enormous toll on Kevin and Heidi, both emotionally and financially. Instead, said Abzug, he wanted Schwartz to dismiss the case on the basis of prosecutorial misconduct.

"The improper conduct in this case," he said, "really started at the opening statement . . . Ms. Thompson argued throughout the opening statement. The record is very, very clear."

Throughout the trial, Abzug continued, Thompson had continually tried to put before the jury matters that were prejudicial—the sex harassment complaints, for example, "which [are] very, very damaging to Dr. Anderson, and factually not true."

Even when the court had admonished Thompson, Abzug said, she had persisted. Later, he said, Thompson asked questions about Kevin's conversations with Deepti about having an abortion, which implied to the jury that Thompson had inside information about that topic.

"Again we had a hearing outside the presence of the jury," Abzug said. "I gave her every opportunity to modify her behavior. I warned her not to do it again, in essence beseeched her not to do it again, and told her if she did it again, I was going to move for a mistrial."

And then came the questions about Deepti's daughter at the close of the cross-examination, Abzug said, which prompted his last motion for a mistrial.

"The court made an observation early on in this trial that I was being subdued . . . but God forbid, [that] this guy gets convicted of the death penalty in this case. This record will be examined with a fine-tooth comb. He's here when you made that comment. His family is here when you made that comment. They're looking at me, why am I letting this go on?"

He didn't want a mistrial, Abzug said again, but Schwartz's options were limited.

"You've admonished her [Thompson] repeatedly. Repeatedly, repeatedly. It just doesn't do any good. Something has to be done to protect this man."

Abzug said as far as he could see, the court only had two choices. "You can find, I think, there's been prosecutorial misconduct and just dismiss the case. I well understand how reluctant you would be to do that. As far as I'm concerned you've been pushed to the last nerve. *I* have. I'm really starting to lose my ability to deal with this in a composed and professional way. So my first request is the court dismiss this case for prosecutorial misconduct."

If Schwartz wasn't willing to do that, Abzug said, he wanted to at least discuss the ramifications of a mistrial with Kevin and Heidi.

And there was also an insidious problem the court should consider, Abzug said. It was possible that, because he'd made so many objections that had been sustained by the court, the jury might get the idea that he and Schwartz were "ganging up on Ms. Thompson, that you and I are being unfair to her. That I'm objecting because I have something to hide." That could be prejudicial as well, he said.

"So I don't know what to say," he concluded. "I'm really depressed and discouraged. I've tried this case in a way that I thought would maximize the chance for a good, clean trial. I think the court has done its best to do that. We have a good jury here. And here we are, one day before the closing argument, and this happens, so that's it."

Schwartz now asked Thompson what she had to say.

Thompson said she thought her questions to Kevin were appropriate—especially when she had asked him if he had simply disregarded all his prior experience with Deepti when she supposedly made her threats against Heidi and his daughter.

"How could you feel that *that* question was an appropriate question?" Schwartz asked. "That is argument, and maybe that's the problem. For the life of me I can't understand why a DA with as much experience as you have would come into this court with the amount of evidence that you have, and present this case the way it's been presented. I don't understand. I just don't understand.

"Maybe that is Ms. Thompson's style, and it is certainly not willful and prejudicial—willful misconduct. But I've got to tell you, it's walking a fine line and pushing an envelope where the envelope doesn't even need to be sealed. This is a tremendously strong case. I just don't understand why one needs to resort to this type of presentation.

"I'm not asking you to defend or disagree with anything I've said," Schwartz told Thompson. "I'm not making an expressed finding of intentional misconduct. But there certainly is a lot in this record that can be construed as a deliberate attempt to inflame the passions of the jury as a way to disregard the court's orders."

The way Thompson had presented her case was "just senseless to me," Schwartz said once more.

Now Schwartz said she'd read the law on both prosecutorial misconduct and mistrial scenarios. "I think I have been able to cure whatever prejudice has flowed from Ms. Thompson's conduct," she said. She'd let the jury know she was displeased with Thompson, but she didn't think the jury would believe that she and Abzug were "ganging up" against the deputy district attorney. "I think Ms. Thompson damaged her own case, to be quite candid with you," Schwartz told Abzug.

A mistrial would be inappropriate, Schwartz concluded. She would instead warn the jury that Thompson's last few questions were improper, and that they were to disregard any thoughts they might have as a result of the questions.

Which, of course, was far easier to say, than do.

The trial now entered its final hours, with Thompson calling a few rebuttal witnesses—first, Vijay to testify that the Westwood meeting with Kevin had occurred in late September, not September 6, as Kevin had wrongly testified, and that it had occurred upon his return from Japan. Vijay's passport showing his reentry into the U.S. on September 22 was offered as evidence. Next Thompson called Gallatin, who testified that Kevin had told him he had put gasoline in the can for the specific purpose of threatening to burn Deepti's car. But Gallatin was forced to admit that his notes didn't show anything like that, and that this had just been his "impression."

At 3 P.M. on November 21, after a little more than three weeks of testimony from scores of witnesses, after well over 200 exhibits, after hours of wrangling between Thompson, Abzug and Schwartz, over the hearsay rule, over proper foundation, over prejudicial questions, the case was almost ready for closing arguments by Thompson and Abzug, and then it would go the jury.

But first Schwartz had one more task: she had to instruct the jurors on the law.

Was the killing of Deepti Gupta the intention of Kevin Anderson as he led her up Angeles Crest Highway to Mile Marker 33? Or was it something that simply occurred, without "malice aforethought," an eruption of violence that took place in the heat of passion? This is what all the testimony, all the exhibits, all of the hearsay evidence, finally came down to: was there proof that Kevin had deliberately come to the conclusion that Deepti Gupta must die?

Or was this just what Kevin had all along insisted: a horrible tragedy that had erupted without warning, an explosion of rage that had been building for months, or even, if all of Kevin's friends and relatives were right, for years?

On Wednesday, November 22, the day before Thanksgiving, Thompson and Abzug delivered their parting shots to the jury.

Thompson had stayed up most of the night on her computer, sharpening her argument, composing a chronological chart of the events of 1999 broken into two columns: "undisputed" and "disputed." Her intention was to winnow the kernels of contention from the chaff of the interminable testimony about patient lists, relocation grants, lease agreements and contracts. Then Thompson intended to zero in on those points to destroy Kevin's defense. She would have the chart blown up and put onto poster boards for the jury to follow while she gave her summation.

As she worked away at her computer at 2 in the morning, the power suddenly went out. The city's utility had forewarned the public that an outage in Thompson's neighborhood was scheduled between 2 and 5 A.M., but Thompson had thought they were talking about 2 to 5 P.M. The fact that Thompson actually believed that the utility would shut off power on the afternoon of the day before Thanksgiving shows how completely consumed she was about her case.

Thompson got on the telephone in the middle of the night and pleaded with the city's power authority to turn the lights back on. They assured her they would do everything they could to get her the juice. At 5 A.M., just as originally scheduled, the lights came back on. Thompson rushed to finish her charts, and by the time she staggered into court that morning, she was exhausted. Her voice was going, as well.

As she began, Thompson arranged her poster boards on an easel for the jury to see.

Why had Kevin killed Deepti Gupta? Thompson asked. That was one of the questions the jury had to think about, just as she had said at the beginning of the trial.

"And I told you . . . the answer is as old as time itself," Thompson said. "The elimination of an inconvenient lover by a married man, a physician, and [a man of] property, to avoid damage to his marriage—the last of his marriages—a marriage he wasn't ready to leave, damage to his professional reputation, and possible financial loss or ruin." Deepti had become "inconvenient" to Kevin because she had gotten pregnant.

"So, *when* did Dr. Anderson decide to kill her? That is the only real issue in this case."

Now Thompson apologized if she had offended anyone in her presentation over the previous weeks. Despite the contentious days with Abzug, she said, she and the defense lawyer "actually like each other very much. If I've done anything in this case to offend anybody, I want to apologize now. That has not been my intent."

Thompson now discussed the law of homicide. There were two different kinds of unlawful homicide, she said: murder and manslaughter. Murder was when a homicide was committed with "malice aforethought." Manslaughter was when homicide was committed without malice aforethought. And each kind of homicide had two different degrees: first- and second-degree murder, and voluntary and involuntary manslaughter.

"Malice aforethought," she continued, meant "deliberate intent."

"What does 'deliberate' mean? It means weighing the pros and cons," she said. An example of weighing the pros and cons might be when a driver approaches a yellow light. All the members of the jury, she said, had probably had that experience. As the light nears, a driver would think of the pros and cons: Can I make it? Will I get hit by another car? Is there a policeman around? That was deliberation, or "premeditation."

And it didn't mean that the deliberation had to take place

hours or days beforehand. "In other words, you can commit a premeditated murder in a very quick period of time." Thompson snapped her fingers. "If you weigh the pros and cons and you considered it beforehand, that is a premeditated murder.

"In our case, ladies and gentlemen, this is a first-degree murder. There is an absolute intent to kill. When the defendant took that tie, grabbed it, and put it around her neck, he wasn't intending to hurt her. He intended to kill her. There is no question about that—he intended to kill her."

When he strangled Deepti, Kevin had considered the pros and cons of doing so, and formed the intent to kill, Thompson continued. Thus, Kevin had committed murder, not manslaughter, Thompson said. "When he put that tie around her neck and began pulling as hard as he could, that was an intentional act.

"Clearly, there is no way that that is not an intentional act. And if you find that putting the tie around someone's neck and pulling as hard as you can is dangerous to human life, which it clearly is, and if you find that [it] was deliberately performed with knowledge of the danger to and conscious disregard for human life, then it is [at least] second-degree murder."

Of the two degrees of murder, Thompson said, first-degree required evidence of either planning or lying in wait. Second-degree murder meant that Kevin intended to kill when he put the tie around Deepti's neck, but that he hadn't thought it through beforehand. That meant that the least Kevin was guilty of was second-degree murder, she said once more. But Thompson said the evidence showed that Kevin *did* think of the killing beforehand, that he in fact planned it, and that he had "lured" Deepti up to Mile Marker 33 with the idea of killing her clearly in mind.

Now Thompson turned to her charts. She intended to show how the evidence proved that Kevin had consciously and deliberately planned the murder hours, if not days, before it took place.

Thompson used her charts to trace the flow of the events

of the summer of 1999: the beginning of the partnership, the jealousy of Heidi, the love affair between Deepti and Kevin, Kevin's vacillation on going into business with Deepti. "All undisputed," Thompson said.

True, there was a dispute over when Kevin and Vijay had their meeting in Westwood, but Kevin's own testimony, supplemented by Vijay's passport, showed that Kevin hadn't told the truth about that pivotal event, when Vijay had first threatened to sue Kevin for damaging Deepti's reputation at the hospital.

"Why is it that the defendant had to lie about that?" Thompson asked. "Because he wants to create this picture that the victim had been so irrational and unreasonable, when that was not the case."

It was undisputed that, rather than being irrational and unreasonable, Deepti had decided not to practice with Kevin at all by the end of September—that she had in fact decided to open her own practice, without him. And it was clear from Kevin's own notes that Deepti was upset, not because the joint practice had fallen through, but because Deepti had had her hospital privileges suspended—because Kevin had dropped her from his on-call rotation. There was no "obsessive" behavior at all—only Kevin's actions, calculated to drive away a woman he felt guilty for having taken advantage of.

Thompson turned to the patient lists. It was undisputed that Deepti had given him a list of patients she had seen, back in the days when the partnership was still in the works. And it was undisputed that Kevin had signed an agreement to return that list to her, on October 8. It didn't matter how many names were on Deepti's list, Thompson stated. "Whether there were ten pages of patients or twenty pages of patients or whatever, the fact is, they were a list of her patients. She was entitled to contact them and let them know she was opening her own practice." It was not an "unreasonable," "obsessive" request, Thompson said.

It was undisputed that Deepti came to work at Richard's clinic after the Westwood meeting, Thompson continued.

Kevin, she said, "was feeling guilty." He also wanted to make sure the Guptas didn't sue him. That was why he arranged for Deepti to come to the clinic, not because Deepti was "obsessive" about him.

And, Thompson added, when Heidi learned that Deepti would be at the clinic two days a week, she threatened to complain to Dr. Richard. "And what does that tell you? Guess who else knows what Heidi is capable of? Her husband, the defendant." Kevin was afraid that if she found out that he'd been having an affair with Deepti, Heidi would cause Richard to pull out of the deal to sell the clinic, and would destroy his reputation among the OB/GYNs in the Pasadena area, so that Kevin's source of pediatric referrals would dry up. Heidi, Thompson suggested, had the capacity to ruin Kevin professionally and financially—or at least, Kevin thought she did.

Kevin's defense rested almost entirely on the bogus notion that Deepti was acting irrationally in the weeks just before the murder, Thompson declared. The defense wanted to use the patient list question to make it seem like Deepti was out-of-control crazy. Nothing could be further from the truth, Thompson said.

"Were these *demands*?" Thompson asked. "Was she stamping her foot like my four-year-old daughter does when she wants something, like little kids do? 'Where are my patient lists?' Was she doing that? No. The testimony you heard was that this was not an irrational woman. She politely, cordially, professionally asked: 'Where are my patient lists that you promised me? Where are they?'

" 'I thought I gave them to you.' 'No, you didn't. I don't have all my patient lists.' 'Well, I'm looking for them.'

"Where is the hostility? Where is the anger? Where are these repeated demands that are causing him so much frustration and aggravation? They are not there, ladies and gentlemen. It simply didn't exist. He's trying to create a picture of Dr. Gupta that did not exist."

The whole patient list issue was simply Kevin's attempt

to justify his crime, she said. It had never been a real problem at all—at least not to Kevin.

Thompson urged the jurors to listen to the tapes of Deepti talking to Sharma in the days before her death. This was not the voice of someone who was "obsessive" or out of control, she said. "Listen to her voice. Hear her soft-spoken quality—not some raving maniac the defendant is trying to paint for you."

Thompson turned to the Monday lunch meeting at the bagel shop. It was undisputed that Deepti had wanted to talk to Kevin that day.

"What was she going to talk to him about? What was most pressing on her mind at the time? I don't know how the men here feel, but the women, when you're pregnant, that is the most pressing thing on your mind, and you want to tell the father. And you don't know how he's going to react.

"Whether you're married to him, whether he's your lover, whether it was the guy you've slept with one night, whatever, this is something that is going to be most pressing on your mind.

"And it is even more pressing, ladies and gentlemen. Why? Dr. Gupta is married to Professor Gupta. She does not believe he is the father of this child. She has had unprotected sex with the defendant. She knows when. She's a physician. She's a woman. She knows who the father is.

"This is a very, very difficult situation. There's going to be pain and hurt on both sides of the family. And when she's calling her spiritual guide, she wants peace. She wants resolution of conflict.

"She meets with him. On the disputed side of the ledger, ladies and gentlemen, is whether the victim told the defendant she was pregnant with his child at this meeting, and to suggest that she didn't mention anything, that she engaged in small talk, on the Monday after she purchased the pregnancy testing kit, I think is absolutely absurd."

Why had Kevin told the jury they had only engaged in "small talk"? Thompson asked.

"Because he doesn't want you to know. He doesn't want you to use that against him, that he knew from earlier on in the week that she was pregnant with his child."

It was undisputed that after this meeting at the bagel shop, Kevin had tried to avoid Deepti. "He didn't want to deal with the situation," Thompson said. "He didn't know what he was going to do . . . if his wife ever found out, that would be the end of their relationship, that would mean alimony again, possible child support for the next eighteen years for Dr. Gupta."

Then came the meeting in the motel room on November 10, Thompson said.

"He said he walked out on her when she told him that she was pregnant. All right. That is the defendant's typical M.O. He walks out when he's upset."

But the point was, Thompson suggested, that Wednesday night was the very latest time Kevin could have learned that Deepti was pregnant. "Whether he learned it on Monday, which is our position, or whether he learned it for the first time on Wednesday, really doesn't matter in the big scheme of things, as to whether this [killing] was planned."

After leaving the motel, Thompson pointed out, Deepti made calls to Anil Sharma. Meanwhile, Kevin returned to Heidi and "told his wife he couldn't live without her. That's undisputed."

"Is he really thinking about a patient, a girl who had a life-threatening tumor? Or is he thinking about the fact of what is going to happen to his marriage with Heidi?

"Despite all their problems, despite all their conflicts, this is the woman he is married to. This is a tumultuous relationship, between the two of them. And whether or not there is unhappiness in that relationship, he is not prepared to end that relationship right then.

"This man wants to be blameless. He wants to be absolutely harmless, and here, what did he do? He got his lover pregnant. My God! For men, I'm sorry. I can't imagine the lack of control that you will feel—you have felt. I don't know of any experience like this. Even to contemplate the lack of control that you might feel when you impregnate a woman. If she chooses to have that child, you have no control over that. Absolutely none.

"Ladies and gentlemen, none of you—none of you—will go back into that jury room and will say, because a man got a woman pregnant, it justifies killing her. An ordinary, reasonable person would never react to that situation in that way, no matter how distressed the defendant was, [how] very concerned his wife would [be, to] learn of his affair with the victim."

When Kevin said he hadn't believed Deepti, it was ridiculous, Thompson said. It was undisputed that Kevin had had unprotected sex with Deepti. He had to have known it was a possibility.

"The defendant had to figure out a way of stopping Dr. Gupta from telling his wife. You hear his own words on tape: 'I had to figure out a way to get her not to do these things.' "

Had Deepti really threatened to tell, that night in the motel? Maybe, maybe not, Thompson said. "Only the defendant was there. We may never know for sure whether she actually threatened to tell his wife.

"But that's not important. Because—guess what? We know that he knew she was claiming to be pregnant. And we know she was. And he is so concerned about this situation that he starts coming up with ideas on how to scare her."

When Kevin told the detectives that he thought of threatening to burn Deepti's car, it was a thought that showed where his mind was, Thompson said. "Where the heck did that come up? Threaten to burn her car up? Is that the first thing you think of when you are in a situation?" He had to tell the detectives that, Thompson said, because "he had the gas can in his car because he planned to murder her."

It was ridiculous for Kevin to claim that he'd had the half-full can in the back of his car for two months, Thompson said. It was dangerous, and Kevin knew it. He'd put it in the truck for the purpose of covering up his planned murder of Deepti. "Who in God's green earth carries a can with gas in their car for two months straight in a row? Nobody."

And there was evidence that despite Kevin's assertion that he had previously arranged to go stargazing with Deepti, the trip had come as a surprise to her, Thompson said. The evidence was in what Deepti was wearing–high-heeled shoes, no stockings, a dress. "This woman was not prepared to go into the mountains to go stargaze with the defendant."

Thompson came to the events of November 11, and Kevin's differing time line.

"It is very important, because the defendant wants to push it back. He wants you to believe he went to St. Luke after he met with Dr. Gupta at the Children's Clinic."

The times of the cellular telephone calls and pages, along with the antennas they used, made it clear that Kevin and Deepti had reached Mile Marker 33 just after 6 P.M., not after 6:30 P.M. as Kevin later insisted. The defense's own witness, Richard James Burkhart, proved that. "And he followed them all the way up to Mile Marker Thirty-three."

Kevin's page to Deepti's voicemail at 6:27 P.M. meant that he'd had to lie about when they arrived at the turnout, Thompson said.

"Why in God's name is he paging the victim's pager if she's with him? Is she already dead? Is she? Is he further bolstering his alibi so he can say to the police, if he's a suspect in the homicide, 'We were supposed to have a meeting that night'? 'I never heard from her, so I called her voicemail pager.' "

Thompson said that the evidence suggested that Kevin had led Deepti up to the turnout to give her an unspoken ultimatum: either abort the baby or die.

" 'I don't want to do this, but if I have to, I'm going to do it,' " Thompson said she believed Kevin was thinking. " 'I'm going to let her decide. If she has this child, if she's going to insist on having this child and ruining my life, ruin what I've worked so hard for all these years, if she's going to insist on doing that—I'll kill her.' She would have signed her own death warrant."

It was undisputed that Kevin took no steps to revive Deepti after he'd strangled her.

It was only when he was on the witness stand, Thompson said, that Kevin first said that if he'd had it to do over again, he would have attempted to revive her.

"Where is that coming from?" Thompson asked. "That is a man who is really thinking, 'Darn. If I had to do it all over again, I would have told [the police] that I *had* tried to revive her.'

"Because if this is really the heat of passion and I had just killed her because I was so upset, and I realized, 'Oh my God, what have I done?'—the first thing I would have done is try to revive her. I wouldn't sit here, not even check to see if she was breathing, not even putting my ear to her neck, checking her pulse."

The reason Kevin didn't try to revive her, Thompson said, is that he wanted her dead. "It is very telling, ladies and gentlemen, very telling."

Kevin, she said, actually went through three different stories after crashing his 4Runner while trying to get away. First he said he had "snapped" because the Guptas were threatening to sue him; next he told the detectives that Deepti had threatened his daughter; and finally, on the witness stand, he said that Deepti had threatened both his daughter *and* his wife. Never did he admit that he and Deepti had been lovers until the DNA tests showed that he was the father of her child.

The supposed threats from Deepti were simply made-up stories, she said, concocted by Kevin in an effort to reduce his culpability.

"She may have threatened to tell his wife about the pregnancy, but would she have ever threatened to harm his daughter? You heard *zero* evidence that this woman was capable of violence. That this woman had ever behaved in an irrational fashion. Absolutely none."

Kevin, she said, was clever. "Did you see him on the stand? This man is three steps ahead of the game, being cross-examined. When I'm asking [about] resuscitation, who here believes this man cannot resuscitate or revive an adult? I can't believe he could actually sit there and make that statement. That is so unbelievable."

The jury had to decide whether Kevin's actions were reasonable under the circumstances.

"Ladies and gentlemen, the evidence is overwhelming that this man committed this crime in a cold and calculated fashion. He pursued it with determination and calm. It was the perfect plan. It was the perfect murder, and it would have been. He would have gotten away with it, but for the fact that Mr. La·Riviere drove by Mile Marker Thirty-three at the exact moment in time that the vehicle began going over the cliff. He would have gotten away with it.

"I'm going to ask you to do what is right in this case, which is return a verdict of guilty of murder in the first degree, with the special circumstance of lying in wait. He lured her up to that mountain, ladies and gentlemen, to kill her. This was not an act of sudden impulse. This woman was pregnant with his child, and he had everything to lose."

Thompson sat down.

Now it would be up to Abzug to save Kevin from himself.

46

Thompson's opening summation was both cogent and powerful. Suddenly the lawyer who had flailed about for proper foundations, who had struggled to overcome the objections with hearsay and improper questions, was gone—replaced by a rhetorician of acuity and drama, her points sharpened into razored edges of cause and effect.

Abzug was taken aback by the transformation. He had thought he would only need an hour to make his final argument. Instead he would take almost three. Thompson's summary had brilliantly exposed the flaws in Kevin's defense, and Abzug found himself in the uncomfortable position of having to rely on disparagement and ridicule as his only weapons.

A canard often taught in law school has it: If the facts are against you, argue the law; if the law is against you, argue the facts; if the facts and the law are against you, pound the table harder. Now Abzug was eyeing the table unhappily.

"Three weeks ago," he began, "the prosecutor opened up the case by telling you that Dr. Anderson packed his so-called 'murder kit' into the 4Runner and committed the perfect murder. This attempt to portray this crime in the most colorful and exaggerated way possible is exactly why we have jurors, ladies and gentlemen."

Abzug moved almost immediately to defuse his biggest problem, the 6:27 voicemail page from Kevin to Deepti. Thompson's attempt to suggest that Deepti was already dead by that time, and that this was evidence that Kevin was attempting to manufacture an alibi, was "simply not true."

Thompson's entire point about the voicemail page, Abzug said, depended on the AT&T engineer's testimony that the call was made from Mile Marker 33; but on cross-examination, the engineer had admitted that the antenna that picked up the call had been located in East Los Angeles, because that antenna picked up calls that were made above a certain elevation. That meant the call could have been made from anywhere along Angeles Crest Highway, not just Mile Marker 33.

"To claim that this [cell-site] chart proves that Dr. Anderson was right next to Dr. Gupta when he paged her, it's like trying to use a paint roller to paint the Mona Lisa."

Thompson's accusation that Kevin was trying to manipulate the timeline of the killing was a case of the pot disparaging the kettle, Abzug said.

"The prosecution's talking about the defense pushing and pulling the timeline. Well, hey! They are doing the same thing. They are trying to base their estimates as to when calls were made up and down [to] this Mile Marker Thirty-three, Angeles Crest Highway, by a chart that's vague, and by drawing your attention to people's recollections as to where they were when they made certain calls, that are not certain at all."

Kevin had no "photographic recall" of where he was when he made or received particular calls, Abzug said.

"The same thing is true for Richard Burkhart. He can't remember with photographic certainty where he was when he saw Dr. Anderson at one of the turnouts. And yet the prosecution is accusing the defense of pushing and pulling time lines."

Abzug was trying to slip by the devastating testimony of Burkhart by suggesting that it was vague and insubstantial.

The same thing could be said of Gallatin's testimony that it was his "impression" that Kevin had told him, in the unrecorded portion of the interview, that Kevin had the gasoline with him for "the purpose of" threatening to burn Deepti's car, Abzug said.

Usually the police take notes, Abzug said, of their interviews. "In this case we don't have any notes of what Dr.

Anderson told the police." If they had notes, or if the tape recorder had worked, they wouldn't have to rely on anyone's "impression"–they would know for sure. It wasn't Kevin's fault that the police only had an "impression"; he had agreed to be taped, he had cooperated with the detectives, Abzug said.

These were reasonable doubts, Abzug said, that the killing was planned by Kevin. And for Thompson to use her charts to show that the elements of the crime of first-degree murder had been met was misleading, he added.

"She can stand up here and–with the charts, wherever they went [Thompson had taken the charts with her when she resumed her seat]–for two hours and tell you, this is undisputed and that is undisputed. Believe me, I'm not going to go back through that chart with you. It is up to you to decide, not her. It is up to you to decide what's undisputed in this case, or not.

"Ms. Thompson can get up here and laugh at some of the doctor's testimony. I don't think there is anything funny about this case, ladies and gentlemen. It is up to you to decide whether Dr. Anderson's testimony is credible or believable."

The charts weren't evidence, Abzug said. The chart wouldn't come into the jury room with them.

Thompson had "changed the goal posts" in her opening summation, Abzug said, when she suggested that Kevin had first learned of Deepti's pregnancy on Monday, appealing to the "ladies' maternal instincts, I guess."

The prosecution theory required the jury to believe that Kevin had decided that murder was his only option–"that murder was going to be used as a means of birth control, I guess." That because he was unable to think of any way out, Kevin had "coldly and calculatedly selected that option, and no other option, to kill Dr. Gupta."

Kevin had hardly "lured" Deepti up to Mile Marker 33 because it was isolated, Abzug said. The evidence showed that the highway was well-traveled, and Kevin and Deepti were less than twenty feet from the roadway. And the proof that there was no luring, no planning, no calculation, was that Kevin was almost immediately caught.

The idea that Kevin had planned to kill Deepti was absurd, Abzug said. The very fact that they were up at the turnout for almost two hours showed that.

"The evidence is, these people did nothing but talk. They were talking about the patient lists. They were talking about Dr. Richard. They were talking about the Children's Clinic. They were talking about opening up a practice. They had, as Ms. Thompson conceded, if you want to talk about what is undisputed for a moment, plenty to talk about up there at Mile Marker Thirty-three."

The evidence was inconsistent with the idea that Kevin had taken Deepti to Mile Marker 33 for the purpose of killing her. "He's up there for an hour because he's waiting for an opportune time to strike, and his head is swirling around like Linda Blair in *The Exorcist*, as he's looking at the oncoming traffic—that's not what's going on here, ladies and gentlemen. The bottom line here is, Dr. Anderson did not get caught by some unbelievable, unlikely coincidence." The evidence showed that Mile Marker 33 was a popular spot to enjoy the view, not because it was secluded and perfect for a murder, he said.

And it was entirely logical that Kevin and Deepti would have gone up the mountain to look through the telescope. "Dr. Gupta is genuinely interested in the stars. We had testimony from her Hindu astrologer that she was so interested in the movement of the planets that she was basing her life's strategy on whether Mars was in the proper alignment of Jupiter, or whatever those lunar charts showed."

If Kevin had really wanted to murder Deepti, Abzug continued, he could have picked a far better time and place than Mile Marker 33, not next to a well-traveled roadway in the early evening hours of a national holiday. Common sense should tell the jury that, he said.

The idea that Kevin had picked Mile Marker 33 as the best place to stage an accident—because it had a low dirt berm, making it easier to push the Mercedes over the edge–was similarly ridiculous, Abzug said. Kevin wasn't planning to dump an old refrigerator or a stolen car. It was silly to believe that Kevin wouldn't have realized that that police would know that a killing had taken place when they found Deepti's body–that is, if he had really been thinking, not simply reacting.

If jurors believed Kevin really thought this would work–that it wasn't something he'd just made up on the spur of the moment–they had to believe that Kevin believed the authorities would somehow conclude that Deepti had made a high-speed, ninety-degree turn off Angeles Crest Highway to plunge accidentally into the ravine. "It couldn't have happened that way. The police aren't going to think that this happened."

The jury would have to believe that if this was a plan, Kevin was stupid. The reality was that he wasn't stupid, just panicked, Abzug said.

"The evidence is, he wasn't thinking clearly. He didn't soak the car [with gasoline]. He didn't light the match. He didn't strap her in so she would have been confined to a burning vehicle consumed by the fire. He didn't even close the windows. There was no chance that anybody was going to believe this was an accident."

It was true that Kevin had tried to destroy the evidence of the crime, but not because of any plan, Abzug insisted.

"He did these things because he was scared. He did these things because he was stupid. He did these things because he's a weak man. I don't think he's a buffoon, as Ms. Thompson suggested that I thought he was. I hardly think this man is a buffoon.

"He's a man now, based on his own acts, who is without any dignity. His life is destroyed. I don't think he's a buffoon. But I think he's a human being. I think he's a weak human being. I think he made a mistake."

The fact that Kevin hadn't tried to resuscitate Deepti didn't mean anything, Abzug said, except that Kevin was in a panic.

"I don't think he's an admirable person. I would like to

think, if, God forbid, I was in that situation, or, God forbid, one of you was in that situation, we wouldn't behave that way.

"But it is reasonable. It is within the realm of a reasonable human impulse to do what Dr. Anderson did, not because he's a murderer or a buffoon. He's just—he's scared. He just killed somebody. He's a pediatrician. He'd never done anything wrong. How do you think he's feeling?"

The idea that Kevin first banged Deepti's head against the dashboard, then strangled her, was unproven, Abzug said. It was a "fantasy" on the part of Thompson. Even the medical examiner had said it was possible that the bruise had occurred when the car went over the cliff, Abzug said.

Abzug said it was significant that Kevin had admitted killing Deepti. He was being honest about what had happened when the police asked him. That showed that he was also being honest when he said the act had taken place because he had "snapped."

Abzug said it was significant that Thompson had spent as much time as she did on telling the jury what second-degree murder was—that is, intending to kill, but without planning. "The reason for that is, I suggest to you that the prosecution realizes that their theory of premeditation is falling apart, and now they're hoping this case will get saved by a second-degree murder conviction.

"It is not a second-degree murder case. He didn't 'admit' to a second-degree murder. He admitted to killing in the heat of passion, which is a voluntary manslaughter." The use of the tie to strangle showed nothing about Kevin's intent, Abzug said. "It is a classic weapon of rage."

Abzug turned to the matter of motives.

"Really, if you want to give this case a title, the title is not 'Perfect Murder' or 'Murder Kit' or any of those other titles. The appropriate title is, 'A Case in Search of a Motive.'

"They are throwing motive after motive up on the board and hoping something can stick. They can't figure out why Dr. Anderson killed this woman, unless something horrible and unimaginable happened to this guy to make him act totally out of character."

First, Abzug said, the prosecution had suggested that Kevin had killed Deepti because of a business dispute. "They were kind of angry over these patient lists. Maybe that caused him to murder her. [Then] the prosecution says: 'Well, you know, you should disregard all this, and this doesn't matter.' If it doesn't matter, I don't know what we're doing here for three weeks listening to all this stuff. Half of these exhibits don't even mean anything. They're about business disputes. Why is she introducing them? The business dispute motive is completely—how can I put it?— illogical, ridiculous, stupid.

"The civil courts of this city are crowded with people suing each other over millions of dollars. Vast sums of money are litigated. Millions of dollars in legal fees are accumulated. Years of litigation over business disputes happen, and people don't kill each other. I mean—you don't kill somebody over a business dispute."

There simply wasn't enough money at stake to kill over, Abzug said.

"Was it to avoid the payment of child care?" Abzug asked. "Is this the kind of man who is going to kill somebody to avoid paying child care? That is even more ridiculous than the business dispute argument." The evidence showed, Abzug said, that Kevin had no reason to believe that Deepti was really pregnant; and without a reason to believe it, he would have no motive to avoid paying "child care."

There was no reason, based on Deepti's behavior over the prior few months, for Kevin not to believe she was lying about the pregnancy as part of an effort to get some advantage over him.

Besides all that, even if Kevin had believed that Deepti was pregnant, there was no reason to believe that he feared being held responsible for the child support payments. It wasn't as if Deepti was without resources. "She's not an eighteen-year-old, unwed. This woman is an independent physician with her own source of income. She can support *herself*. She's got $200,000 [actually $100,000] in the bank. Do you really think under these circumstances this man is so worried about child care that he's going to go out and kill somebody?"

Another motive thrown up by the prosecution, Abzug said, was that Kevin was trying to save his reputation. "As if anybody in their right mind would think murder is a way to save your reputation. Just an insane idea."

Likewise, the prosecution suggested that Kevin had killed Deepti to preserve his chance to buy Dr. Richard's clinic. " 'I've got to kill her, otherwise I'll lose the opportunity to buy Dr. Richard's practice.' " It was ridiculous, Abzug said. "Dr. Richard doesn't care if Dr. Anderson is having an extramarital affair. As to whether or not he's going to sell his practice to him . . . there is no evidence that Dr. Anderson would have lost a business opportunity to buy a practice if Dr. Gupta would have spilled the beans and said, 'I'm pregnant by this man.'

"The truth of the matter is, ladies and gentlemen, unfortunately we live in a society where the President of the United States slept with an intern, with an approval rating of sixty-five percent. People don't care about that kind of stuff."

To say that one would commit murder to save one's reputation was "just nonsense," Abzug said.

"Was he worried that Heidi would ruin him? There's a motive they throw up there and hope it will stick," Abzug continued. The prosecution had argued that Heidi would "take him to the cleaners, or ruin him in some way," if she found out about Deepti, Abzug said. But that too was specious. "This woman has got to be the most loyal wife in the Western Hemisphere," he declared. "She knows that he was sleeping with another woman and impregnated her. She knows that he killed somebody, that he lied to her, that he impregnated another woman, and she is sitting right there in the audience."

There was no need to speculate about what Heidi would

have done, Abzug said. "The evidence is right in front of you" in the person of Heidi herself.

Just how was Heidi going to have the ability to ruin Kevin? Abzug asked. She just couldn't do it, even if she wanted to.

Thompson's argument that Kevin had killed Deepti because she was "an inconvenient woman" was simply rhetoric, Abzug said. None of the motives that the prosecution had raised was sufficient to show that Deepti had become "inconvenient" to Kevin.

"It is unreasonable, and inconsistent with his character, inconsistent with the evidence, inconsistent with common sense that, as soon as this man learns that this woman is pregnant, his first instinct—within twenty-four hours—his first instinct is going to be 'Yep, got to kill her.' "

The real question—the real doubt—said Abzug, was "whether, in twenty-four hours, a man of this character is going to pick murder of all the other options that would be available to him, to solve his problems."

Killing Deepti was like using an atomic bomb to get rid of a fly, Abzug said. It certainly wasn't something someone would have done with any sort of planning or premeditation.

"People don't behave like that. They don't—unless they are pushed, pushed, pushed right to the max, and they flip out, and that is the only rational explanation here."

The prosecution had failed to prove that Kevin did anything other than just what he'd said, Abzug said. He'd snapped under pressure. One of the saddest things about the case, Abzug said, was that Kevin himself had no idea of why he'd killed her.

"There is an absolute failure of proof, for the prosecution to show beyond a reasonable doubt. There are a lot of reasons to doubt that this man premeditated this crime. There's overwhelming reason to doubt that he had reason to know beyond a reasonable doubt that she was pregnant.

"I'm not asking, ladies and gentlemen, for your sympathy. I'm not asking for your mercy. I'm just asking for fairness. That's all I'm asking for, for Dr. Anderson.

"This case is not a perfect murder. It is a perfect tragedy. And the only thing that could make it worse is that because of the way this case was tried, you are persuaded to find Dr. Anderson guilty of first-degree murder. He's not."

The proper verdict, Abzug said for one last time, was manslaughter.

47

As the prosecutor, Thompson had the last word. She tried to rebut each of Abzug's points by referring once again to the evidence of the timing of the events, and Kevin's demeanor—especially his proven lies.

She asked each member of the jury to imagine that he or she was Deepti Gupta, having just discovered that she was pregnant by a man she had looked up to. That Deepti—the real Deepti—wanted to know from Kevin what she should do. That Deepti wanted to know that she could count on his support if she had to leave Vijay because of the baby. And when Kevin insisted that she get an abortion, and she refused, the real Kevin had decided to kill her.

The facts showed that it wasn't manslaughter, she said.

"Ladies and gentlemen, it is not manslaughter by any stretch of the imagination. I want you to look at the evidence with a clear eye. I want you to look at the evidence. Just use your common sense . . . there is no question that he planned this murder. He lied about everything that was important.

"You heard him when he testified. He spoke with the utmost calm when he testified. You heard his statement to the police. He spoke with the utmost calm. Then ask yourselves where he lied.

"He lied, ladies and gentlemen, about these things because that was the very motive for murdering her. He believed he had too much at stake to lose, too much at stake. And again, it is a crime that has been committed by many, many, many, many men before.

"I told you when we began this trial not to forget Dr. Gupta. Too often in criminal cases, because the decedent isn't here, she can't talk to you. She can't defend herself in front of you. Accusations can fly all over the place about the victim, and she can't defend herself in front of you. So I ask you to consider her—don't forget her. I'm asking you, again, not to forget Dr. Gupta."

At quarter to six on the night before Thanksgiving, Schwartz gave the case to the jury. She ordered the jurors to report back on Monday morning, November 27, to begin their deliberations. The trial had made her deadline.

The jury deliberated all day on the following Monday. On Tuesday, they asked for a portion of the testimony to be read back. Schwartz was at the judges' conference in San Diego, but happened to call into the courtroom just as the request was made.

The jury wanted the testimony about Kevin's encounter with Deepti in the motel room read back. It seemed clear they were grappling with the issues of premeditation and motive. Had Deepti really threatened to tell Heidi about the affair, that she was pregnant with Kevin's baby? Had Kevin demanded that she get an abortion, as Thompson had argued? Had Kevin promised her he would leave his wife if she got an abortion? Had Kevin lulled Deepti into thinking that things would be all right? All of these questions went to the heart of the planning-for-murder question.

Now there arose a dispute over what to read back to the jury. Abzug wanted only Kevin's testimony read back, not Thompson's questions about what *hadn't* happened—about promises, about a possible abortion. Kevin had denied any of those things had taken place, and Thompson's questions were improper, Abzug said. Thompson said they *were* appropriate. Schwartz, communicating over a speakerphone from San Diego, eventually came down on Abzug's side. The court reporter read back those portions of Kevin's testimony, and the testimony of Lorena Ramirez, and the jury went back to its deliberations.

The deliberations continued through the rest of the week, and began again the following Monday. Thompson wasn't sure what it meant. "Obviously, if they're deliberating this long, there must be a difference of opinion," Thompson told reporter Howard Breuer of the *Pasadena Star-News*. The hometown paper had followed the case intensively since its beginnings.

Then, late the same afternoon, the jury sent word that it had reached a verdict.

Just before 4:30 P.M., the jurors filed back into the courtroom where they had spent more than a month of their lives, to give their decision.

Clerk Robin Barnhart collected the verdict forms from the bailiff, who had collected them from the jury foreman. Schwartz asked Barnhart to read the forms.

" 'We, the jury,' " she read, " 'in the above entitled action, find the defendant, Dr. Kevin Paul Anderson, not guilty of the crime of first-degree murder, against Dr. Deepti Gupta, a human being . . . as charged in Count One of the indictment.' "

There was a moment of stunned silence as the verdict sunk in. Then Barnhart began to read again:

" 'We the jury . . . find the defendant, Dr. Kevin Paul Anderson, guilty of the crime of second-degree murder, a felony . . . who did willfully, unlawfully and with malice aforethought, murder Dr. Deepti Gupta on or about November eleventh, 1999, as charged in Count One of the indictment.

" 'We further find the allegation that the defendant, Dr. Kevin Paul Anderson, with intent to inflict injury and without consent, personally inflicted injury on Deepti Gupta, which defendant knew or should have known was pregnant, and said injury resulted in the termination of said pregnancy . . .' "

Kevin was guilty—not of first-degree murder, as Thompson had insisted that he was, or of manslaughter, as Abzug had insisted, but of second-degree murder: he had intended to kill her, but he hadn't planned it, or so the jury believed.

Some thought this was a Solomonic decision: in the absence of truly "overwhelming evidence" as to the planning or the luring, the jury didn't feel comfortable with branding

Kevin a cold-blooded killer. But the actions at Mile Marker 33 showed this was more than just an impulsive act: when he put his Snoopy tie around Deepti's neck, there was no question he wanted his lover dead.

And there was the karmic kicker: the jury decided that Kevin had in fact believed Deepti was pregnant, and that he had known that by killing her, he would make certain his own son was never born.

Balancing the Karmic Accounts

48

More than three months after the jury's verdict, Kevin Anderson was back before Judge Schwartz, this time to receive his sentence. Over the previous months, as he had come to realize that his old life was gone forever, a powerful depression had set in. There, in his cell at Twin Towers, the county's primary lockup, Kevin tried to make sense out of what he had done to himself. He had lost his license to practice medicine upon his conviction. The luxurious house he had shared with Heidi was in foreclosure. From being one of Pasadena's most respected doctors, he was now a criminal. There would be no more waterskiing trips to Lake Powell, no more amateur stargazing, no more neighborhood Halloween hot dog cookouts. No matter what happened at the sentencing, Kevin had lost everything he had ever held dear.

Abzug tried to think of some way to salvage his client. He remained convinced that the crime was one of passion, not planning. As he put it later, "It was Mars colliding with Jupiter," a confluence of circumstances so unusual that it could never be repeated by anyone, anywhere. He wanted Schwartz to throw out the jury's verdict and substitute her own judgment. He argued that when they had rejected Thompson's contention that Kevin had "lured" Deepti to the top of the mountain for the purpose of murder, the jury was implicitly accepting that the crime could only be manslaughter. The judge, by law, could reduce the verdict if she believed that the jury's finding was "contrary to the law or evidence," he noted. And in making such a reduction, Abzug added, Schwartz was entitled to consider Thompson's "highly prejudicial conduct . . . throughout the trial."

Even if the judge didn't agree, Abzug added, she was permitted to sentence Kevin to probation, rather than prison time. Even a second-degree murderer was entitled by the rules of the court to a probationary sentence under certain circumstances, Abzug said, if, in the judge's view, "the interest of justice would best be served . . ."

"The defense submits that this crime was ignited by the particular combination of the personalities and personal circumstances of the defendant and the victim," Abzug said. "This combination will never occur again."

Finally, Abzug asked that Kevin be released on bail pending his appeal; Kevin intended to ask a higher court to reverse his conviction because of Thompson's conduct, which was alleged to be prejudicial, and because of his claim that he had been prevented from consulting a lawyer before talking to detectives Gallatin and McElderry.

Kevin also wrote to Schwartz.

"As you can imagine," he said, "the entire episode was tragic and life-altering for my family as well as for Dr. Gupta's. Each day I think about and pray for all the unsuspecting victims; including my wife, Dr. Gupta's husband and daughter, my own daughter, and all my former patients, who for so long looked up to and admired me. My actions, and mine alone, caused this terrible chapter in all of our lives to unfold. Crying and asking for forgiveness, while trying to forgive myself, has been an almost daily endeavor."

The enormity of his act weighed heavily on him, Kevin said. "There will be two families whose daughters will be without a parent. Two people whose spouses have been taken away from them. Two households who may have had problems associated with life, now having permanent dark clouds that will shadow them forever."

He wanted to try to atone for what he had done, he said. "While I know that I cannot replay the events of that November evening, although I wish I could, and I can't bring back what I have taken away, I have hope I may be allowed a chance. A chance to help patch a gaping wound that may never totally heal. We are all here on earth together, and we can choose to make an effort to help each other or not."

Kevin asked that he be granted probation or some sort of minimal sentence in return for being allowed to put his talent and experience to work for society, such as on an Indian reservation.

"I can only pray that you see enough redeeming qualities in me to allow mercy to enter into your decision. I do understand the tragedy inflicted on the Gupta family, and I am aware of the tragedy upon my own." But locking him up for most of the rest of his life, he said, would only make things much worse than they already were.

No way, said Vijay Gupta.

As time passed since Deepti's death and the subsequent trial of Kevin Anderson, Vijay's anger only seemed to increase. It was horrible to be told that one's wife had been murdered; it was even worse to learn, after her death, that she'd been having a secret affair, and that she had gotten pregnant as a result; it was almost beyond enduring to hear Kevin's defenders drag Deepti's reputation into the mud, as they tried to portray her as a crazy woman obsessed by her desire for a man who claimed to be driven to the brink by her demands. Now, to find out that Kevin wanted to be set free on probation was simply too much.

The whole idea of leniency was madness, Vijay told Schwartz in a letter to the court.

This so-called aberration has had frightening consequences for my family and has completely devastated our lives forever. He claims he will not kill again and asks for a second chance. My question to him and to those who support his position is, can they give a second chance to Deepti's life? Can they return my daughter's mom, my wife, a sister, or a daughter to her widowed mother? If they cannot, they have absolutely no right to ask for a second chance. Just imagine if all murderers were allowed to get away with one murder on the pretense of a first crime, what kind of chaos will we have around us!

We pray that you will put our and society's faith back in the judicial system by sentencing this ruthless, cowardly and arrogant killer to the maximum possible sentence permitted by law.

Kevin was lucky, Vijay insisted, that he hadn't been convicted of first-degree murder. The suppression of "sexual harassment" complaints against Kevin prevented the jury from hearing about his "vile character," while "the victim's character was savagely assassinated by the defense."

No matter what else he was, Vijay continued, Kevin was self-centered, cowardly and selfish; his attempts to blame Deepti for his crime rankled in the sourest way imaginable.

"Your honor," Vijay continued,

not only the people of the U.S., but people as far away as India are looking to you to do justice by sentencing the murderer who stands before you to the maximum extent possible. We Americans serve as keepers of justice in several countries around the world. Now it is our turn to show the world that we do not tolerate crime at home and that heinous crimes are punished without mercy. My mother-in-law calls me frequently from India to inquire if the death penalty was delivered to Kevin Anderson or not. I find it hard to explain how the justice system in America is pro-defendant. I cannot imagine what I will say if this man walks free while awaiting his appeal.

This crime has soured every aspect of my life, whether personal, professional or social . . . my whole life centered around my wife. Deepti was a wonderful wife, a lively spirit, with a great smile, a sense of responsibility, religious and spiritual beliefs, and above all, with a passion to live life fully . . . she was my true soul mate.

His own life was still filled with waking nightmares, Vijay said. He kept thinking about the night the two deputies came to his house to tell him Deepti was dead.

Seeing her lifeless body and then decorating it like a newlywed before it departed forever from home, seeing pictures and videos of her badly mangled body with her eyes wide open, still puts chills in my body in the middle of the night. I cannot sleep properly . . . over and over, my mind draws horrifying pictures of what she must have felt during those infinitely long minutes of strangulation, how she must have pleaded to this animal Anderson to leave her alone, how much she must have wanted to see her daughter, husband, sister and mother while helplessly feeling her life inch out of her body every second against her wishes.

Your honor, I just cannot get over this. My life is devastated forever . . . yes, your honor, I am no superhuman. When the world rests and everyone including my family members are asleep, I am awake, in my bed, remembering the fond moments with my wife, with tears flowing down my face . . . please, do not rob me of those few hours of sleep I seldom get by sentencing him to anything less than the maximum sentence . . .

On March 8, Judge Schwartz held a hearing in her court on what was to be done with Kevin Anderson. Vijay was there, and so was Heidi. So too were numerous people on both sides—supporters of Kevin who had pleaded for mercy, and supporters of Vijay and Deepti, who said there should be none. The court file was thick with letters from advocates on both sides, including many close friends of both the Andersons and the Guptas.

Schwartz had already denied Kevin's request for bail pending his appeal. That left only Abzug's request to change the verdict to manslaughter, and the issue of immediate probation, before Schwartz delivered the sentence.

As to the request to modify the verdict, Schwartz said she agreed with Thompson that the provocation to Kevin by Deepti was far less than required for such a change: "I am satisfied," Schwartz said, "that the evidence presented in this case amply supports the charge of and conviction of second-degree murder."

Schwartz asked Abzug if he wanted to argue for a probationary sentence. Abzug did. The fact that the jury rejected the notion that the crime had been planned itself made leniency possible, he said.

"I think," he said, "that it is obviously true that Dr. Anderson is fundamentally a very decent person, notwithstanding his conviction in this case. This case was tried on a theory that was demonstrated to be absolutely false, that is, that Dr. Anderson is some kind of sexual predator who lured Dr. Gupta up to the Angeles Crest Highway . . . that theory was resoundingly rejected by the jury.

"The prosecution has mentioned the fact that the defense was reprehensible in describing the relationship between Professor Gupta and Dr. Gupta, putting Dr. Gupta on trial, as it were. That's not something I chose to do. It isn't something that I enjoyed doing. The only reason that it became my painful duty to do, was because of the absolute falsity of the prosecution's theory in this case, that somehow Dr. Gupta was not responsible for the romantic relationship which developed between she and Dr. Anderson. And Dr. Anderson somehow became a latter-day Lothario and took her with his wiles. The court knows that is not true.

"Tragically, this case developed out of a mutual attraction that these two developed for one another, and though neither one of them foresaw it, it ended in Dr. Gupta's death."

Kevin fully realized the damage he had caused—to the Gupta family, to Heidi and to himself, Abzug said. Putting him in prison for an extended period wouldn't make that any clearer to him.

Heidi now rose to plead for probation for Kevin. She

said she felt like a victim, too. She declared that she still stood by Kevin, because she did not believe he had planned to kill Deepti.

One of Kevin's lifelong friends also rose to speak, saying that he still could not believe that Kevin had actually killed anyone. The friend asked that Kevin be put on probation, so that his skills could be used by those who needed them.

Then Kevin also addressed the court. He tried to apologize.

"This has been a terrible, terrible, terrible tragedy for everyone involved," he said. "I can't even begin with words to say how I feel about what has happened in the last year and a half. It's beyond sorry. It's beyond the word that's been used here a lot, 'remorse.' Those are good words, but it just goes so much deeper than that.

"There is no question that it was a wrong thing and it is not something that you can get over for a long time. I think there's been a lot of anger and bad feeling on the part of Mr. Gupta, and I don't blame him for that. Certainly, if the shoe were on the other foot, I think I would feel a lot of what he feels."

Kevin told Schwartz that he hoped to be granted probation. "I certainly would like to be able to have the opportunity to do anything that might help mitigate this tragedy . . . this is going to be a very difficult process for everyone involved to get over. Some of us are never going to get over it."

Now it was Thompson's turn. She said that Vijay had two short videotapes of Deepti before her death, and that he wanted to play them for the judge. She said the defense tactic of portraying Deepti as disturbed wasn't fair, and she wanted the judge to see the whole story.

"Throughout the trial Mr. Abzug cast the victim in this case . . . as a seductress, that she pursued Dr. Anderson . . . that she did not have love and affection for her husband and small child, in fact abandoned them, including the repeated contention that she somehow contributed to her own murder." She wanted Schwartz to see those tapes, and to view drawings by Deepti's daughter to show the depth of loss felt by the Gupta family.

But Schwartz said it wasn't necessary. Vijay's letter, she said, "was compelling.

"I have no doubt in my mind that this tragedy has absolutely devastated you and your entire family and your young daughter." Anything more to demonstrate that wasn't needed, she said. "I am prepared to sentence Dr. Anderson," she said. But, she continued, if Vijay or others wanted to say anything else, she would listen.

At that point, Dr. Nilesh Desai, a Burbank physician and friend of the Gupta family, rose to ask for a minute of silence for Deepti. A long pause ensued. No one said a word as the sixty seconds elapsed.

"That was one full minute, Your Honor," said Desai. "It takes five to six minutes for death by strangulation, and I'm a physician. And during that time, if the victim is struggling, it takes even longer." Desai's point was plain: in order for Kevin to kill Deepti, he had to have been strangling her for a substantial period of time.

There should be no mercy for Kevin, Desai said.

After another Gupta supporter told of the pain Deepti's murder had caused Vijay and his daughter, Vijay himself rose to speak. His anger was palpable. He turned in Heidi's direction and addressed his remarks to Kevin's supporters' side of the courtroom. There was nothing that Deepti had done that made him angry, he said. He didn't blame Deepti at all.

"My anger is not radiating from what my wife did. I believe firmly that she was a victim of sexual harassment of this man over here. She was a very religious woman. She went back to India to get religious solace because of that reason. And she didn't have a chance to figure out what she was going to do.

"He may be a doctor. But after November eleventh, 1999, after that he joined the ranks of murderers. He should be treated no different.

"America is the most educated society, and the world looks to you, Your Honor, today, to do the right thing . . . this man is not showing any remorse.

"Did you ever hear him say, 'I'm sorry I took Deepti away'? This is not a man. He's worse than an animal. He's a disease to society—worse. There is no cure for him. He should be put in jail."

Everyone who pleaded for leniency for Kevin was kidding themselves, Vijay said.

"I challenge all these people who wrote letters—not his family members—one day to come and stand in my daughter's [place], with me in my home . . . [They] will be ashamed of writing these letters [so] this man should go free."

People should think about what Dr. Desai had just demonstrated, Vijay said. Those who wrote letters on Kevin's behalf should imagine what he had done—strangling someone to death, minute after minute, an eternity of time. "This is the same man for whom you are writing letters," a man who consciously waited until another human being was dead.

"Can you all feel that? And the life going out, with her legs shivering? Now come, who will stand up despite all these feelings and come in front of the camera and say, 'I still support this guy to be out on bail or parole'? How many of you can stand up and—"

Vijay was getting carried away by his anger. Schwartz decided to get his attention back.

"Professor Gupta, if you would, please direct your comments to the court." Vijay apologized. He turned back to Schwartz.

The judge, he said, had a job: she could either give Kevin the maximum sentence allowed by law, or, "you're going to just make my life, my daughter's life miserable, [as] for the rest of my life I will be wondering what happened."

Vijay sat down, still furious.

Schwartz said she'd been over the law and the court rules.

"This is a classic murder case," she said. There was nothing unusual about it, at least nothing that would permit Kevin to receive probation or any alternative sentence.

"Even if I were to find such," she continued, "the way this crime was committed, the vulnerability of the victim, the way Dr. Gupta looked up to Dr. Anderson as a mentor, as someone he took under his wing . . . when she was just starting her practice. She had no reason to fear this man. She had every reason in the world to trust this man, and ultimately that led to her untimely and tragic death."

The law was clear, Schwartz said, and she had no choice, even if she wanted one: Kevin had to go to prison for fifteen years to life, the statutory penalty for second-degree murder. And, because he knew or should have known that Deepti was pregnant, he would have to serve five more years for killing the unborn baby.

Afterward, there were those who thought that twenty years to life was too light for what Kevin had done—that, having intentionally taken the life of someone who trusted and admired him, he should have been confined to prison until he died of old age, if not executed. The fact that he had tried to excuse himself by putting much of the blame on his victim was despicable, some thought.

And while Thompson and particularly Vijay thought Kevin "lucky" to have escaped conviction for first degree murder and a possible death sentence, a less partisan view suggests that the jury had it exactly right: there was reasonable doubt that Kevin had planned the crime. That he had intended to kill there could be no doubt: as Thompson had said, putting his tie around Deepti's neck and pulling as hard as he could demonstrated his intentions as nothing else could.

What really happened up at Mile Marker 33? Understanding that was the key to the mystery of why a prominent, successful pediatrician would risk everything to kill someone who, by all accounts had admired, respected and probably even loved him. What could Deepti have said to Kevin that night that would have driven him to such desperate measures? What did Deepti want from him, that he was so averse to providing, that he chose to kill rather than to provide it—to take an action so out of character that afterward, almost no one who had known him could believe it?

The key lay in Kevin's predilection for shading the truth, even outright lying. Kevin had lied his way into the mess with Deepti, by portraying himself as a powerful figure, someone with "connections" who could help to realize all of Deepti's dreams, while at the same time casting himself as the long-suffering victim of a grasping harridan, the image of Heidi that he had sold to Deepti. No wonder Deepti felt antipathy for Heidi: every time she encountered her, she saw only the image of the controlling wife painted by Kevin. She had believed she was helping Kevin in his supposed misery. Deepti believed Kevin's lies, even after most American women would have seen through him.

And why not? Here was a woman who had been raised to honor the truth as an essential part of her life, of her Jain upbringing. To lie about matters of the heart was bad karma. To abuse someone's trust was to invite cosmic retribution.

And although Kevin had lied his way into Deepti's heart, and then tried to lie his way out of taking full responsibility for his actions, probably the truest thing he ever said was when he recounted the portion of conversation at Mile Marker 33, when Deepti had told him again that he had ruined so much, that she could ruin him, too.

Here was a woman who for the first time saw Kevin clearly—not for what he had posed as, but for what he really was. A man who had inveigled his way into her affections by telling tall tales about his "miserable" marriage, who had gotten her pregnant, a fact that now threatened her own marriage; who had made her look petulant and even unethical to other medical professionals; who had led her a merry dance to destruction. Kevin had ruined her, and in bitterness, it was only natural that she would want to ruin him.

What did Deepti tell Kevin that she intended to do? What would anyone do, in such circumstances? She would go to Vijay and make a clean breast of all that had happened. And what would Vijay do? The volatile Vijay would turn his wrath on Kevin. And while Vijay's first instinct would be to annihilate Kevin, he would in the end do what he'd already threatened to do to Kevin—sue him. On that point, it is significant that Kevin's first words after his arrest, when trying to explain his actions, were that Deepti and her husband had threatened to sue him.

And what a lawsuit: sexual harassment, for openers—as Deepti's supervisor at the hospital, Kevin's seduction of Deepti made him liable for damages; it was even possible that the hospital itself might be named as a defendant. Vijay would have a companion action against Kevin for alienating the affection of his wife, and possibly the hospital administration for allowing its relocation grant process to be used as a seduction lure. The pregnancy would stand as Exhibit A.

That sort of lawsuit could ruin Kevin, there is little doubt of that. When Deepti finally saw through Kevin on that night at Mile Marker 33, Kevin realized that his own destruction was at hand. What for Kevin had started as the sort of casual affair he was prone to engage in with American women who were used to this kind of dishonesty, had instead grown out of control—because of his own failure to understand the sort of woman he was dealing with. When he tried to lie again, to assuage her angry feelings, this time Deepti knew better. To save himself, Kevin decided that Deepti must die.

The Western idea of justice is rooted in the notion of atonement—from an eye-for-an-eye to penal punishment, but all in this life. Kevin had taken the life of Deepti Gupta, and the life of their unborn child. American law said he must pay, if not with his own life, at least a significant portion of it, accompanied by a loss of all that he held dear. But in the broader Eastern view—the one held by Deepti Gupta—there were far deeper consequences, manifested in the Law of Karma, and they could be seen everywhere in the tragedy of Mile Marker 33.

Jay La Riviere, for instance—what permutation of his own karma led him to lock his keys inside his rental car, thus delaying him for an hour or so, so that he arrived at George's Gap just in time to see Deepti's SUV go over the side? What about Richard James Burkhart, who happened to get a cup of coffee in time to see Kevin and Deepti pull off the highway for their fateful encounter? What about Vijay, or Heidi, whose own relations with their respective spouses played a role in the tragic events?

What of Deepti herself? Did her fate as the victim of a murderer wipe clean her own transgressions? Was her affair and eventual murder by Kevin retribution for something that had happened in some prior existence? Were she and Kevin caught up in some sort of cosmic web of destruction that neither could foresee? And Kevin: his lies in this life had led directly to his own unhappy fate. If souls really do transmigrate, what will the eternal future hold for him?

From the ancient mists of antiquity, the powerful truth or reaping what one sows echoes throughout this tragic story of the death of a doctor, a tapestry of forces little noticed but seemingly all-pervading: the Law of Karma. And in this final sense, what the Hindus have always said remains true: it's not what you say you believe that really counts, it's what you do.

Author's Note and Acknowledgments

The contents of this book were derived primarily from the official record of the trial of Kevin Paul Anderson, including the daily verbatim transcript, and various other court records, such as docket listings, pleadings, search warrants, affidavits, declarations, grand jury transcripts, and similar legal documents. A number of documents of the Los Angeles County Sheriff's Department were likewise consulted. These public records were supplemented by interviews with a variety of individuals familiar with the case.

The author would like to thank Los Angeles County Deputy District Attorney Marian Thompson for agreeing to a number of interviews over a series of months, and defense lawyer Michael Abzug, for the same; the Honorable Teri Schwartz, Judge of the Superior Court, for her assistance in logistical matters, particularly in the matter of viewing the hundreds of exhibits spawned by the trial; Superior Court Clerk Robin Barnhart, who provided invaluable help in tracking down hundreds of pages of various court filings; court reporter Katie Ingersoll, who provided vital assistance in collecting important parts of the record; Los Angeles lawyer Phil Boesch and his associate Howard Stern, Vijay Gupta's civil counsel; Los Angeles County Sheriff's Sgt. Ken Gallatin for his shared recollections of his investigation; and a number of nurses and administrators at St. Luke Medical Center and Huntington Memorial Hospital, all of whom shared information and perceptions of the events that led to the tragic death of Deepti Gupta.

Two principal witnesses, Professor Vijay Gupta and Heidi Anderson, were not interviewed for this book. Requests made to Ms. Anderson through Kevin Anderson's attorney, Michael Abzug, did not receive a response. Likewise, efforts to contact her through Huntington Memorial Hospital were rebuffed. Professor Gupta indicated a willingness to be interviewed only if the content of the book was placed under his control. As this was not an acceptable condition, no interview was conducted with Professor Gupta by the author.

Thanks are also due to those in the Hindu and Jain communities who provided important if informal background on their respective philosophies, as well as Indian culture and history.

WITHDRAWN